Modern Poetry in
New Series / No.21

GW00361664

Looking Eastward

Edited by Daniel Weissbort

Published by
KING'S COLLEGE LONDON
University of London
Strand, London WC2R 2LS

Modern Poetry in Translation
No. 21, New Series
© Modern Poetry in Translation 2003
ISBN 0-9533824-9-4
ISSN 0969-3572
Typeset by WM Pank
Printed and bound in Great Britain by Short Run Press, Exeter

Editor:
Daniel Weissbort

Manuscripts, with copies of the original texts, should be sent to the Editor
and cannot be returned unless accompanied by a self-addressed and
stamped envelope or by international reply coupons. Wherever possible,
translators should obtain copyright clearance. Submission on 3.5" disk
(preferably Macintosh formatted, in MSWord or RTF) is welcomed.

Advisory Editors:
Michael Hamburger, Tomislav Longinović, Arvind Krishna Mehrotra,
Norma Rinsler, Anthony Rudolf
Managing Editor: Norma Rinsler

Subscription Rates: (two issues, surface mail)
UK and EC   £22.00   post free
Overseas   £26.00 / US$40.00 post free

Sterling or US dollars *payable to King's College London*
Send to:
MPT, The School of Humanities,
King's College London,
Strand,
London WC2R 2LS

Represented in UK by Central Books, 99 Wallis Road, London E9 5LN
Orders: tel +44 (0)2 0845 458 9925, fax +44 (0)2 0845 458 9921.
email magazines@centralbooks.com

Contents

Subcontinent

China

Plus

Featured Translators

Reviews

To The Reader

"Looking Eastward"? In general I prefer magazines which are miscellanies, ragbags, the product of what comes through the post or/ and may be solicited by the editor, depending on his or her mood at the time. The present issue of *MPT* is just such a one, with some emphasis, though, on what East Europeans prefer to call Central Europe and on Asia, at least on the Subcontinent and China. I have indulged myself to the extent also of inviting certain friends whose work I value to contribute and in writing a number of the reviews myself. For the most part these reviews are shorter than I would have wished, but they are perhaps better than nothing. Some of them, as indicated, have been long promised, so here I am trying belatedly to keep at least some of the promises I had made over recent years. I have been optimistic, but then, I suppose, optimism is called for in this business.

On the other hand, it had been my intention – perhaps vague hope is a better way of putting it – to end with an issue devoted to 'Eastern Europe', Eastern Europe Revisited, since *MPT* 1 (1965) was largely devoted to that region or, more precisely, to the first post-War generation of poets, like Zbigniew Herbert, Miroslav Holub, Vasko Popa . . . I was keen to explore the changed world and to interview writers of succeeding generations as well as a few survivors from the Herbert generation, like for instance Tadeusz Rozewicz (more on him in the present issue of *MPT*). But life – at least life as editor of *MPT*, long as it has been – has not been long enough.

Even though its biannual issues now look like books and its aspirations have always been overweening, *MPT* is, I hope, still a 'little' magazine, essentially a serendipitous phenomenon. Tempted though I am to recapitulate the magazine's agitated history, I shall refrain, since I have written of it elsewhere and shall be writing of it again in a book on Ted Hughes and translation. In any case, Ted Hughes himself has described the circumstances that led to the publication of the journal (see his introduction to *Modern Poetry in Translation: An Annual Survey*, Carcanet, 1980). Incidentally, the idea of turning the magazine into an 'annual survey' did not catch on; instead it returned to being a periodical, albeit a biannual affair, the present issue being the last in that series and indeed the last issue to be edited by me of the journal Ted and I founded in 1965. It seemed proper, therefore, to include a tribute to him, in his capacity as translator. Again I shall not write about this at any length, as it would be to anticipate the aforementioned book as well as a *Selected Translations of Ted Hughes* which I'll be editing for Faber. Still, by permission of the Estate of Ted Hughes, we are able here to offer some items from Ted Hughes's quite numerous unpublished translations.

One of these is a long poem by the Hungarian poet Ferenc Juhász, 'The Boy Changed into a Stag Cries out at the Gate of Secrets'. In addition we are printing, for the first time, some versions that Ted Hughes did of poems by Yves Bonnefoy. Anthony Rudolf, as a noted translator and interpreter of Bonnefoy's poetry and a longtime supporter of *MPT*, kindly consented, in consultation with Norma Rinsler, to examine the photocopies of these drafts from Ted Hughes's notebooks in the Hughes archive at Emory University, Atlanta, and has written a brief commentary.

I should like also to draw attention to the section in this issue on the Academy for Gifted and Talented Youth. For some time it has seemed to me that literary translation might well play a part in secondary education. I shall limit myself to remarking that translation, after all, is the most concentrated form of reading; translating from another language or even from within the language – e.g. poetry into prose – obliges one to scrutinize the so-called target language, to test its limits and so forth. I was delighted, then, when asked by David Hart last year to conduct a day-long workshop with students, in the first intake of the Summer School known as the Academy for Gifted and Talented Youth at the University of Warwick. I told the students – as I had told my graduate students in the University of Iowa Translation Workshop – that I hoped to publish some of the results. In Iowa, this promise led to the establishment of *Exchanges* – regrettably this journal ceased publication when I left Iowa, but I hope it may be revived – which published work by people in translation programmes in the US and UK. I am relieved still to be in a position to make good on the promise to the students in the Warwick workshop and hope that similar features may become regular in *MPT* and/or other literary journals.

Another feature, for which we lacked the resources at the time, was to be a series of profiles of prominent contemporary translators of poetry. We managed only four: Michael Bullock (*MPT* 3); Robert Friend (*MPT* 4); James Kirkup (*MPT* 11); Peter Viereck (*MPT* 18). I had long intended to devote one to Michael Hamburger, who has encouraged *MPT*'s activities from the earliest days (*MPT* 2 [New Series], Autumn 1992, does in fact consist wholly of Hamburger's translations of Franz Baermann Steiner, bilingually presented). But there were a number of other translators and poets I would also have liked to feature: e.g. Keith Bosley, Elizabeth Bishop, David Constantine, Jonathan Griffin, Peter Jay, Denise Levertov, Christopher Logue, Richard McKane, Christopher Middleton, Anthony Rudolf, Nathaniel Tarn, Charles Tomlinson . . . In this last solo issue Norma Rinsler and I have taken the opportunity of saluting again Michael Bullock and James Kirkup and we are happy also to be able to include a translation by Michael Hamburger from his revised Hölderlin, to be published by Anvil.

In this unusually celebratory issue, it is a privilege as well to be able to congratulate a great Polish poet, Tadeusz Rózewicz, who is the 2003 joint winner of the Librex Montale Prize. At the time of writing (21 April) I am preparing to go to Milan to attend the prize-giving. I am happy to be able to republish a long poem by Rózewicz about the painter Francis Bacon, translated by another long-time supporter of *MPT*, the distinguished Polish poet and translator of contemporary Polish poetry, Adam Czerniawski (see review of Mr Czerniawski's own poetry in the present issue of *MPT*). Rózewicz's vision of post-war reality finds perhaps its closest parallel in the work of Francis Bacon, like Ted Hughes, one of the few in the West whose work (to quote A Alvarez in his review of *Crow*) 'is adequate to the destructive reality we inhabit'.

Finally I must insist on expressing my gratitude to Professor Norma Rinsler, Managing Editor of *MPT* since summer 1992, when King's College published the first in our New Series, an issue which contains a special feature on Yves Bonnefoy, compiled by Anthony Rudolf. With the support of the School of Humanities, King's College London and, in particular, that of Wendy Pank, School Administrator of the Humanities Research Centres at King's College, Norma Rinsler quite simply made it possible for this now venerable magazine to continue into the new century, at a time when I was mostly in the States and when its demise seemed imminent. I myself and, dare I say, our readers owe her a great debt.

Again I am indulging myself, since it is pleasant to conclude on that note.

Daniel Weissbort

The Editorship of MPT

MPT 22 will be jointly edited by the present editorial team and David and Helen Constantine, who will take over from No 23. The survival of this journal had been in some doubt, but, with the help of our Board and the advice of the Arts Council of England and of Philip Spender of the Stephen Spender Memorial Trust, we have been able to formulate a business plan and are now able to look ahead with confidence. We are delighted that Helen and David Constantine have agreed to take over as editors and believe that *MPT* can now proceed with much greater confidence towards the fulfilment of its numerous plans and projects.

Ted Hughes: Unpublished Translations

Compiled by Daniel Weissbort

Ted Hughes and Translation

In this last *MPT* under my editorship, I am including some uncollected translations by Ted Hughes, who co-founded this journal in 1965.

Since this issue of *MPT* contains also a good deal of material from that part of the world, Eastern and Central Europe, which was so strongly represented in the early issues of the magazine, I am happy to be able, finally, to publish Ted Hughes's re-working – intended for a Hungarian issue that did not materialize – of a long poem by Ferenc Juhász, 'The Boy Changed into a Stag Cries out at the Gate of Secrets', which WH Auden (see his Foreword to *The Plough and The Pen: Writings from Hungary 1930-1956*; 1963) believed to be 'one of the greatest poems written in my time'. Ted Hughes's version is a virtuoso performance and of much interest, not only because it is so powerful a piece of writing, but also, I think, because of the intimations of his much later involvement in the translation of Ovid's *Metamorphoses*.

I have written elsewhere of the origins of the magazine, and *MPT* 14 (Winter 1998-99) includes an editorial written shortly after Ted Hughes's death in 1998, where I tried to represent his views and commented briefly on the evident significance for him of translation. While I have no wish to reiterate what has already been said, or to anticipate what I may wish to say – in a forthcoming book, I shall explore some of Ted Hughes's more important translations – I should like once again to draw attention, in the magazine which was his brain-child, to an important aspect of his work.

The first issue of *MPT* preceded the first Poetry International readings in London (1967), which like the magazine originated in an initiative of Ted Hughes who, with Patrick Garland, was its first director. The Penguin Modern European Poets series, of which A Alvarez was the Advisory Editor, started a little earlier, although it too really gathered steam from around 1967, with the publication of Miroslav Holub. Between then and 1970, the Penguin series published, among others, Zbigniew Herbert, Vasko Popa and Yehuda Amichai, poets featured also in the early issues of *MPT*. Tadeusz Różewicz (see the present issue), who was included in the Penguin series in 1976, was actually represented in English translation considerably earlier (*Faces of Anxiety*, 1969). So, from the mid- to late- Sixties, a good deal of attention was paid to the poetry of the first post-war generation (writers born in the 1920s), especially from Eastern and Central Europe (see also my *The Poetry of*

Survival, Post-war Poets of Central and Eastern Europe, Anvil Press 1991, Penguin 1993).

The poets who read at the first Poetry International, from eight countries (Austria, Chile, France, Germany, Great Britain, Ireland, Israel and the USA), included Yehuda Amichai, W H Auden, Ingeborg Bachmann, Yves Bonnefoy, John Berryman, H M Enzensberger, Allen Ginsberg, Robert Graves, Anthony Hecht, Patrick Kavanagh, Hugh Macdiarmid, and Anne Sexton. The second Poetry International (1969), again directed by Hughes and Garland, included Holub, Popa and Janos Pilinszky; a selection of the latter's poetry was later translated by Ted Hughes, with Janos Csokits (Carcanet and revised edition Anvil, rather than Penguin).

Ted Hughes, regarded as among the most English of English poets, wrote a brief Introduction for this international festival. Here is the complete statement, a portion of which (in bold) has been quoted from time to time. Idealistic and clearly intended as a fanfare for the international poetry reading in London, it is nevertheless indicative of a serious commitment in the first place of course to poetry itself, but even more widely to poetry as a global phenomenon, as well as to translation which begins to make it available world-wide (the highlighted section, in particular, seems to echo what Walter Benjamin, in his famous essay on 'The Task of the Translator' says about an *Ursprache* or original/ elemental language):

'In this Festival, poets from nine [actually eight, as the Soviet authorities did not permit Bella Akhmadulina to attend!] different countries will take part. The idea for such a gathering was suggested by the great and growing public for poetry which is making itself felt in London just as surely as in Moscow and New York. **However rootedly-national in detail it may be, poetry is less and less the prisoner of its own language. It is beginning to represent, as an ambassador, something far greater than itself. Or perhaps it is only now being heard for what, among other things, it is – a Universal language of understanding, coherent behind the many languages in which we can all hope to meet.**
We now give more serious weight to the words of a country's poets than to the words of its politicians – though we know the latter may interfere more drastically with our lives. Religions, ideologies, mercantile competition divide us. The essential solidarity of the very diverse poets of the world, besides being a mysterious fact, is one we can be thankful for, since its terms are exclusively those of love, understanding and patience. It is one of the few spontaneous guarantees of possible unity that mankind can show, and the revival of an appetite for poetry is like a revival of an appetite for all man's saner possibilities, and a revulsion from the materialist cataclysms of recent years and the worse ones which the difference of nations threatens for the years ahead.

The idea of global unity is not new, but the absolute necessity of it has only just arrived, like a sudden radical alteration of the sun, and we shall have to adapt or disappear. If the various nations are ever to make a working synthesis of their ferocious contradictions, the plan of it and the temper of it will be created in spirit before it can be formulated or accepted in political fact. And it is in poetry that we can refresh our hope that such a unity is occupying people's imaginations everywhere, since poetry is the voice of spirit and imagination and all that is potential, as well as of the healing benevolence that used to be the privilege of the gods.

It is in this belief, that a gathering of the inspired poets of nine different countries [see above] is timely and amounts to much more than a great cultural event, that this Festival is planned.' (Ted Hughes, 1967)

Hughes translates Juhász

Ted Hughes had seen the Juhász poem in the anthology mentioned above. While I was visiting him in Devon, presumably to plan the forthcoming (as we thought) *MPT* issue on Hungary, he re-wrote the translation, working with great concentration and at great speed. I carried it off with me, but as the issue for which it was intended ran into difficulties and was indefinitely postponed, I eventually returned it to Ted. I did not photocopy it and Ted had on this occasion not made a carbon copy. The sole copy of the translation fortunately surfaced again, however, when he was going through his papers before they were shipped to Emory University, in Atlanta, where I discovered it.

It may interest readers of *MPT* to compare Ted Hughes's version with versions by Kenneth McRobbie (in the 1963 anthology) and David Wevill (in *Selected Poems of Sándor Weöres and Ferenc Juhász*, Penguin, 1970; Weöres was translated by Edwin Morgan). Here are the opening lines in each:

Kenneth McRobbie

Her own son the mother called
from afar crying
her own son the mother called
from afar crying,
she went before the house, from there calling
her hair's full knot she loosed,
with it the dusk wove a dense quivering
veil, a precious cloak down to her ankles . . .

The mother called to her own son,
cried from far away,
the mother called to her own son,
cried from far away,
went to the front of the house: from there she cried,
unwound her heavy knot of hair
dusk wove to a shimmering bride's veil
that flowed down to her ankles . . .

"What is intriguing", as I wrote in a note on a poem (see my *Letters to Ted*, Anvil 2002), "is that [Ted Hughes] felt able to rewrite the English version without reference to any source text. It is interesting that he is able, in this situation, simply to write his own version, based on someone else's, whereas in other circumstances, i.e. when faced by the poet himself or by the source text in a literal translation, he feels compelled to stay as close as possible to the wording and even syntax of the original." I had in mind, in particular, two major translations by Hughes, his selection of poems by another Hungarian, Janos Pilinszky, which he did under the rigorous guidance of Janos Csokits, and the versions of Yehuda Amichai, which he based on literal versions by the poet himself, who was a close friend and "the tone and cadence" of whose voice, "speaking English", he was above all anxious to preserve.

I have corrected some obvious typos. Where Hughes has written an alternative word in the margin and deleted the original, I have altered the text accordingly. Where he has not deleted the original I have included both words. The lineation appears not to have been finalized and I have left it as it appears in the typescript. I have, however, somewhat regularized the punctuation.

Ferenc Juhász was born into a peasant family, in Western Hungary, in 1928. His earliest collections appeared in 1949 and 1950. In 1954 he published an epic poem, 'Prodigal Land', about Dozsa, the martyr leader of the 1514 peasant rebellion. Juhász is a prolific poet, much of his work originating in a folk-tale peasant tradition.

The Boy Changed Into A Stag Cries Out At The Gate Of Secrets

The mother called after her son
from the far distance
The mother called after her son
from the far distance,
she went out in front of the house, calling

and she loosened her hair's thick knot
which the dusk wove to a dense, stirring veil,
a valuable robe sweeping the earth,
wove to a stiff and heavily-flaring mantle,
a banner for the wind with ten black tassels,
a shroud, the fire-slashed blood-heavy twilight.
She twisted her fingers among the fine tendrils
of the stars, the moon's suds bleached her features,
and she called after her son shrilly
as she called him long ago, a small child,
she went out from the house talking to the wind,
and spoke to the song-birds, her words overtaking
the wild geese going in couples,
to the shivering bullrushes,
to the potato flower in its pallor,
to the clench-balled bulls rooted so deeply,
to the fragrant shadowy sumch, [mulch?]
she spoke to the fish where they leaped playfully,
to the momentary oil-rings, mauve and fleeting.
        You birds and branches, hear me,
listen as I cry,
        listen, you fishes and you flowers,
listen, I cry to be heard,
        listen, you glands of the pumping soils,
        you vibrant fins, you astral-seeding parachutes,
decelerate, you humming motors of the saps,
screw down the whining taps in the depth of the atom,
        all iron-pelvissed virgins,
        sheep alive under cotton,
listen as I cry,
I am crying out to my son.

The mother called out to her son
and her cry climbed in a spiral
within the gyre of the cosmos it ascended,
her limbs glancing in the lightrays
like the skid-scaled flanks of a fish,
or a roadside boil of salt or crystal.
The mother called out to her son,
        Come back, my own son, come back,
            I am calling, your calm harbour,
        Come back my own son, come back,
            I am calling, your pure fountain,
        Come back, my own son, come back,

I am calling, the breast where your memory sucked,
Come back, my own son, come back
    I am calling, your almost sightless lamp.
Come back, my own son, for this world of spiky objects has
    put out my eyes,
my eyes are sealed under yellow-green bruises, my jaw
    contracts,
my thighs and my shins are skinned,
from every side things batter in on me like crazed rams,
the gate, the post, the chair try their horns on me,
doors slam against me like drunken brawlers,
the vicious electricity snaps at me,
my scaling skin leaks blood a bird's beak crushed with a
    rock,
scissors slither off like spider-crabs of nickel,
the matches are sparrowfeet, the pail hacks back at me with
    its handle.

Come back, my own son, come back,
my legs no longer lift me like the young hind
        festering blooms open on my feet,
        gnarled tubers screw into my purpling thighs,
the skin over my toes glazes to bone,
        my fingers harden, already the flaking flesh
shells off like slate from weathered geologic formations,
        every limb has served its time and sickens.

Come back, my own son, come back
        for I am no longer as I was,
        I am a used-up shadow from the inner visions
        that flare through the thickening organs
        like an old cock's crowing, on winter dawns,
from a fence of shirts hanging board-frozen.
I am calling, your own mother,
come back, my own son, come back,
force new order onto the anarchic things,
discipline the savage objects, tame the knife and domesticate
    the comb,
because now I am only two gritty green eyes
glassy and weightless, like the dragonfly,
whose winged nape and mouth, that you know so well, so
    delicately clasp
two crystal apples in the green-illumined skull,
I am two staring eyes without a face,

14 / Hughes

seeing all, and one with the unearthly beings.
Come back, my own son, come back into place,
  with your fresh breath bring everything again to
  order / into place.

  In the remote forest the boy heard.
  He jerked up his head in an instant,
  his spread nostrils testing the air,
  his soft dewlap throbbing, the veined ears pointing
  tautly to that lamenting music
  as to the still tread of the hunter,
  as to hot wisps fronding from the cradle
  of a forest fire, when the skyline trees
  smoke and begin to whimper bluely.
  He turned his head to the old voice,
  and now an agony fastens on him,
  and he sees the shag hair over his buttocks,
  and he sees, on his bony legs,
  the cleft hooves that deal his track,
  sees, where lilies look up in pools,
  low-slung hair-pursed buck-balls.
  He forces his way towards the lake,
  crashing the brittle willow thickets,
  haunches plastered with foam that spatters
  to / on the earth at his every bound,
  his four black hooves rip him a path
  through a slaughter of wild flowers,
  sock a lizard into the mud,
  throat ballooned and tail sheared,
  till he reaches the lake at last,
  and looks in at its lit window
  that holds the moon, moving beech-boughs,
  and a stag staring at him.
  For the first time he sees the bristling pelt
  covering all his lean body,
  hair over knees and thighs, the transverse
  tasselled lips of his male purse,
  his long skull treed with antlers,
  bone boughs bursting to bone leaves,
  his face closely furred to the chin,
  his nostrils slit and slanted in.
  The great antlers knock against trees,
  roped veins lump on his neck,
  he strains fiercely, stamping he tries

to put out an answering cry, but in vain,
it is only a stag's voice belling
in the throat of this mother's son,
and he scatters a son's tears, trampling the shallows
to drive out that lake-horror, scare it
down into the whirlpoool gullet
of the water-dark, where glittering
little fishes flicker their laces,
miniature bubble-eyed jewellery.
The ripples smooth off into the gloom,
but still a stag stands in the foam of the moon.

Now in his turn the boy cries back,
    stretching up his bellowing neck,
Now in his turn the boy cries back
    crying through fog from a stag's throat,
           Mother, my mother
           I cannot come back
           Mother, my mother
           you must not lure me,
           mother, my mother,
           my maker, my nurse,
           mother, my mother
           fresh foaming/bubbling fountain,
           safe arms that held me,
           big breasts that fed me,
           my tent in the frost,
           mother, my mother,
           never seek my coming
           mother, my mother
           my frail silky stem,
           mother, my mother,
           my gold-mouthed bird
           mother, my mother
           you must not lure me.
           If I should return
           my horns would split you,
           from point onto point/fork onto fork
           tossing your body,
           if I should return
           you would fall under me,
           your loose veiny breasts
           shredded by hooves,
           I'd stab with bare tines,

I'd rip with my teeth,
and stamp in your womb, even,
if I should return
I'd hook your lungs from you,
blue flies would be clouding,
stars would gaze
on your spilled flower-vitals,
which once housed me,
they were summer suns over me,
a glistening peace
their warm clasp unbroken
as once the warm cattle
breathed gently to Jesus.
Mother, my mother
do not summon me,
your death would be home
as my shape entered,
as this son approached you.
Every prong of my antlers
is a golden thread,
every branch of my antlers
a winged candelabra,
each spine of my antlers
a catafalque candle,
each leaf of my antlers
a gold-laced altar.
It would be your death
to see my grey antlers
lifting in the sky
like an All Souls
candlelit cemetery,
my head a stone tree
and the leaves flames lengthening.
Mother, my mother,
if I came near you,
I would burn you like tinder grass,
scorch you to charred clay,
you'd explode like resin,
and I would roast you
to black rags of flesh.
Mother my mother
do not summon me,
I would devour you
at my coming,

your bed would be havoc,
your flower garden
ploughed by the thousand
blades of my antlers.
I'd chew through the trees
in the stag-torn coppice,
empty the one well
with one swallowing,
at my coming
your cottage would be blazing,
then I would run
to the ancient graveyard,
with my narrow soft nose
with my four hooves
I'd dig up my father,
my teeth would be wrenching
the cracked coffin lid
to scatter the bones.
Mother O mother
do not lure me,
I cannot come back,
if I come back
I bring your death.

In a stag's voice the boy cried,
And in these words his mother answered:
    Come back, my son, come back,
I call you, your own mother,
    come back, my own son, come back,
I'll cook brown broth and into it you'll slice onion rings.
They'll crunch in your bite like quartz splintering in the
        champ of a giant,
I'll bring you warm milk in a jug
and trickle wine from my last keg into bottles necked like
        the heron,
and I know how to knead bread under my stony knuckles, I know
        how you like it,
bread to bake to soft-bellied buns, the sweet bread for
        feasts,
    come back, my own son, come back.
From the live breasts of screeching geese I have pulled the
        down for your eiderdown,
weeping I plucked my weeping geese, and the bald patches
        whitened angrily on their breasts, like the mouths of the dying,

I have shaken out your mattress in the sun, freshened it for
    your sleeping
the yard is swept for your coming, the table is laid.

    Mother, my mother,
     for me there'll be no homecoming
    do not lay the plaited white bread out for me,
     or the goat's sweet milk foaming in my flowered mug
    do not prepare my soft bed for me,
     or ravage the breasts of the geese for their feathers,
    pour away your wine, let it soak into my father's grave,
     braid the lovely onions in a garland,
    fry up for the little ones the big-bellied frothy-topped
        dough.

    The milk would be vinegar at a touch of my tongue
    and the white bread would be struck to a stone turtle
    your wine filling/spilling like warm blood into my
        tumbler
    the eiderdown dissolving in a silence of blue flame
    and the brittle-beaked mug splintered to swordgrass.

    O mother, O mother, my own good mother,
     my step will never ring out in my father's house,
    I have to live in the thick of the forest,
     your shadowed house has no room for my meshed antlers.
    Your yard has no room for my cemetery antlers
     because my reaching-out horns are a loud world tree,
    their foliage arches to constellations, their green moss
       is the Milky Way,

    Into my mouth comes only sweet-breathed herbs,
    only the first-growth grasses that melt my saliva
    and I can never drink again from the flowered mug you
       bring me,
    only from a clear brook, only from a clear brook.

I do not understand, I do not understand your strange and
        tormented words, my son,
you speak like a stag, a stag's spirit has possessed you my
        unhappy one.
When the turtledove cries, when the turtledove cries, when
     the little bird sings, when the little bird sings, my son,

why in the whole Universe am I the last soul left, the
                  solitary one?
Do you remember, do you remember, your small once-young
                  mother, my son?
I do not understand, I do not understand your sad and
                  tortured words, O my long-lost son.
Do you remember how you came running, running home to me, so
                  happy with your school report,
you dissected a bull-frog, splayed his freckled paddle feet
                  on the fence,
how you pored over books about aircraft and followed me in to
                  help with the washing,
you loved Irene B, your friends were VJ and HS, the wild and
                  orchid-bearded painter,
and do you remember the Saturday nights, when your father
                  came back sober how happy you were?

O mother, my mother, do not speak of my sweetheart of those
                  days, or of my friends,
they flit by like fish in the cold depths, that painter with
                  his chin of vermilion
who knows down what road he has gone shouting, who knows,
                  mother, where my boyhood has gone?
Mother, my mother, do not remember my father, for sorrow has
                  bloomed from his flesh,
sorrow flowers out of the dark earth, do not remember my
                  father, my father,
he'll heave from the earth, gathering about him his
                  yellowing bones,
and stagger from the grave with his nails and his hair new
                  grown.
Oh, Oh, Uncle Wilhelm came, the coffin maker with his puppet
                  mask, he told us to hold your feet and drop you
                        neatly into the coffin,
And I retched because I was frightened. I had come that day
                  from Pest,
you too, my father, went back and forth to Pest, an office
                  messenger, till the rails writhed up,
such rending knives in my belly then, your tight cheeks
                  gashed by the candle's shadows.
Your new son-in-law, Lacy the barber, shaved you with care,
                  while the candle dribbled lke a silent baby,
regurgitating its glistening entrails, its long luminous
                  nerves like vines,

the choral society surrounded you under their purple hats,
              mourning you at the tops of their voices,
with one finger tip I traced the rim of your forehead, your
              hair was so alive,
I heard it growing, I saw the bristles thicken and your chin
blackened by morning, and the next day your throat sunken in
              under spines of new hair like the snake-grass,
curved like a soft-haired cantaloupe, cabbage skin blue under
              the yellow hair of the caterpillar,
Oh and I thought your hair, your beard, would bush the whole
              room full, and would overgrow the yard
and the entire world, that the stars would nestle like cells
              in the living strands.
Ah the ponderous green rain began to fall then, and the team
              of red horses on the hearse whinnied in terror,
one lashing out over your head with a thunderbolt hoof, the
              other relentlessly pissing,
so that his purple parts passed out with it like a hanged
              man's tongue, while the coachman cursed.
The downpour sluiced around the huddled brassbandsmen, and
              then all those old friends blew with a will
blew as they wept, by the chapel wall studded with
              globethistles,
the old friends blew till their lips swelled purple and the
              music spiralled out and up,
the old friends blew till their lips cracked, till their lips
              bled, their eyeballs staring,
blew for the cards and the booze, and the trumped women, the
              bloated and the withered,
blew for the beer-money of their redletter days, the tips
              tossed whirling into space after you,
blew as they sobbed, blew sadly down into sedimentary layers
              of silted sadness,
music poured from the burnished mouths, from rings of brass
              into putrefying nothingness,
out of it streamed the petrified sweethearts, rotten women
              and mouldered grandfathers, out of the music,
with little cottages, cradles and a whole generation of
           silver-bellied watches thick with enamel, rolling like
              onions,
Easter bells and multitudinous Saviours flew out on the wide
              spread wings of the sound,
with railway wheels and infantrymen brass-buttoned at the
              salute, and satchels,

the old friends played on, teeth crimsoning under lips that
        peeled back swelling like blackened liver,
and yourself conducting the choir: well done boys, that's
        grand, don't stop now, keep it up,
all the time your hands folded hard, and those gold spiders
        with their huge wheel-spoke-jointed legs sitting on
        your heart,
and in the cupboard your collapsed boots wait for their
        relatives, the white socks on your curling bread
        crust feet,
the old friends blew for you that day out under the crashing
        rain, valves snapping like adam's apples of steel,
fangs of antediluvian birds, teeth of the Carcharodon,
        cruising for carrion out of the brazen mouths of
        the trumpets,
O mother, my mother, do not recall my father,
let my father lie, lest his eyes erupt from suddenly opening
        earth.

        The mother called after her son
        from the far distance,
        come back, my own son, come back,
        turn from that stone world,
        you stag of the stone forest, the chemical air, the
                electric grids,
        industrial lightning, rivetted bridges, streetcars, lap
                at your blood,
        hourly they attack you a hundred times afresh, yet you
                never hit back,
        I am calling, your own mother,
                come back, my own son, come back.

He stood on the perpetually renewing crags of time,
he stood over the Universe, on the ringed summit,
there the boy stood at the gate of secrets,
his stag's antlers were toying with the stars,
and his stag's voice down the lost paths of the world
        answered to his mother his maker

        Mother, my mother, I cannot come back,
        new gold boils in my hundred wounds,
        every day a hundred bullets blast me off my feet,
        every day I get up a hundred times more whole

every day I die three billion times,
every day I am born three billion times,
every branch of my antlers is a double-based pylon,
every tine of my antlers is a hightension cable
my eyes are ports for sea-going tankers, my veins are
 tarry hawsers, my teeth
are iron bridges, in my heart surge the monster-infested
 seas,
each vertebra is a seething capital, and a barge belching
 black smoke is my spleen,
my every cell is a factory, my every atom a solar system,
and sun and moon swing in my testicles,
and the Milky Way is in my bone marrow,
space's every point is a part of my body,
and my brain's rhythms come in from far out in the
 circling galaxies.

O my lost son, no matter for that,
 your mother's eyes are sleepless, they watch for
 you still.

Only to die shall I come back, only to die shall I come back,
yes, I shall come back to die
and when I have come, but only to die, O my mother,
then you can stretch me out in my father's house,
then with your marble hands you can wash my body,
then you can close my glandulous eyelids with a kiss,
 and then when my flesh falls to pieces
and lies in its stench, yet deep among flowers,
 then I shall feed on your blood and be fruit of your body
then I shall be your own small son once more,
and this shall give pain to you alone, O mother,
to you alone, O my mother.

 [Translated by Ted Hughes]

Hughes translates Bonnefoy
Commentary, transcription and notes by Anthony Rudolf

I was privileged to be a friend of Ted Hughes. We met from time to time and corresponded sporadically for more than thirty years. I know his handwriting quite well. Since I have myself translated whole books of Yves Bonnefoy, I was in a position to make educated guesses concerning illegible words in Ted's manuscript version of 'Théâtre', a complete section of *Du mouvement et de l'immobilité de Douve*. Nonetheless several problems remain unsolved even after I incorporated most of the corrections and additions made by Norma Rinsler to my draft notes.

Among the earliest of my dealings with Ted – the very first had been an exchange of letters about poetry translation in 1966, after I read an announcement concerning a new magazine, *Modern Poetry in Translation* – was a 'negotiation' involving Yves Bonnefoy, and this might give us a clue about the status of the present version – hitherto unpublished – which is patently a first draft, done very quickly.

Ted Hughes was the founder of Poetry International, which first took place in 1967. Yves Bonnefoy was one of the participants invited to that gathering of famous poets. I had already been translating Bonnefoy for about four years. It was my friend Alberto de Lacerda who brought my translations to the attention of Nathaniel Tarn, and it was certainly Tarn who brought them to the attention of Ted Hughes.

I learned that Hughes himself would be one of the readers of translations alongside the original poets. In those far-off days translators, and certainly unknown translators, rarely if ever read their translations in public. That Ted, a poet I admired greatly, would read my translations, suited me fine. He, however, hurt his back and could not be present. I volunteered or was volunteered to read them, and so my first public reading took place in the Queen Elizabeth Hall.

This is the cue for my one and only personally attested WH Auden story: as I was reciting my translations I and many others heard Auden, who was seated behind me on the platform, say in a stage whisper: 'I wish that young man would hurry up, I need a drink'. Later that evening the young man apologised and asked him to sign a copy of a book he had brought with for that purpose. At the same reception I remember having an argument with James Fenton about the quality of Auden's early work relative to his late work.

I am inclined to think that Ted Hughes started translating Bonnefoy for Poetry International, perhaps because he did not know of any other versions and then, doubtless having other priorities, ceded to me when he learned of my translations. But this version or translation of events might be wrong: there are tantalising glimpses of solutions found by myself and / or by Galway Kinnell to problems or difficulties in Bonnefoy's poems and Ted might have incorporated them. Yet this could be coincidence since I don't think any of my *Douve* translations had yet appeared, and Kinnell's complete *Douve* only appeared in 1968. (It was reprinted by Bloodaxe in 1992. My version is still not complete or ready for publication.) Parts of Kinnell's *Douve* were published in *Poetry Chicago* in 1962, but not 'Théâtre'. However, Kinnell's 'Théâtre' was published in Willis Barnstone's anthology, *Modern European Poetry*, in 1966 – early enough for Ted to have read it.

Another possibility, floated by Daniel Weissbort on the phone when discussing this transcription, is that Hughes translated the poems for private reasons, in order to get to know them better. Whichever explanation is the correct one and even allowing for the fact that these versions are a first draft, the hard-line literality of some solutions – see for example my note to poem 8 *line 3* – raises fascinating questions about Hughes's approach to poetry translation. Daniel has reminded me that in an unsigned editorial Hughes had already embarked on his strategy of rough/literal versions in preference to the approach exemplified by Robert Lowell's recently published *Imitations*, a hugely influential book, and one Ted admired as 'Lowell' rather than as translation. Hughes's views can be found in various places, for example his accounts of co-translating Yehuda Amichai.

My own approach over the years, successful or not, has been that of Michael Hamburger, Daniel Weissbort and others: the famous 'third way', between the Scylla of Hughes and the Charybdis of Lowell, attempting to produce the Golden Fleece of a 'faithful' version that is also an English poem. Ted's versions are sometimes too prosaically mimetic for my taste. A *locus classicus* of this whole problematic is Yves Bonnefoy's critique of Joseph Brodsky's views on poetry translation. Brodsky, however, is at right angles to both Hughes and Lowell. A forthcoming book from Chicago University Press of Bonnefoy's essays on translating Shakespeare will shed much light and doubtless some shadow on these great issues, issues that *MPT* has worried about throughout its life. There is an important essay to be written on Hughes, Lowell, Brodsky and Bonnefoy as translators.

A brief comment on the transcription: in all cases except one I have corrected Hughes's punctuation to conform to the original. It is very clear that his changes were insignificant modalities of haste. The one case I have left – Poem 19 *line 3* (not included here) – is indicative of an unsuccessful attempt to interpret the complex syntax of the poem rather than carelessness or haste. I have also replaced his ampersands with 'ands' since they occur randomly.

Even the first draft of a version by one great poet of another will be of abiding interest to readers of *MPT*, not least when the translator poet in question was the co-founder of the magazine and the translated poet has made superb translations of Shakespeare and Yeats. There are brilliant local victories among the failures and mistakes in this first draft, but we will never know, and more's the pity, what Ted Hughes would have ended up with. He and I sometimes discussed Bonnefoy, but he never referred to his own versions. He had either forgotten about them or considered them superseded by Galway Kinnell's. Yves Bonnefoy himself, who met Ted Hughes for the first and only time at that Poetry International, is moved and fascinated by this discovery among Hughes's manuscripts. Its inclusion here happily coincides with the 50th anniversary of the original publication of *Douve*.

Note: italicisation of words in the text refers the reader to a note.

from *Du Mouvement et de l'immobilité de Douve* (1953) by Yves Bonnefoy

Some draft translations by Ted Hughes

Three

It *marked* itself with a wind stronger than our memories,
Stupor of robes and cry of stones – and you passed before the flames
With head quartered and hands riven and all
In quest of death on the exultant drums of your *gestures (heroic deeds)*.

It was day of your breasts
And at last you reigned outside my head (*absent from my head*).

Four

I awake, it is raining. The wind penetrates you, Douve, resinous waste lulled asleep close to me. I am on a terrace, in a hole of death. Great dogs of foliage tremble.

The arm you hold up, suddenly, in a doorway (*gorge*), *blazes the ages alight*. Village of embers, every moment I see you born, Douve,

Every moment die.

Six

What pallor strikes you, underground river, what artery bursts in you, where the echo of your fall resounds?

This arm you heave up suddenly opens, bursts into flame. Your face recoils. What *growing* fog tears your *core* from me? Slow cliff of shadow, frontier of death.

Mute arms gather you, trees of another shore.

Seven

Confused wounded in the leaves,
But carried off by the blood of footprints that lose themselves,
Accomplice of life still.

I have seen you sand-spattered at the end of your struggle
Hesitate at the borders of silence and of water,
And the soiled mouth of the *last* stars
Break with a cry of horror from *aging* in your night.

O raising in the hard air sudden as a rock
A beautiful gesture of coal.

Eight

The ridiculous music begins in the hands, in the knees, then it is the head which crackles, the music affirms itself under the lips. Its certitude penetrates the *versant* (*pouring, overturning*) of the face.

Just now dislocating the facial carpentry. Just now one proceeds to the uprooting of the view.

Twelve

I see Douve stretched out. In the scarlet *village* of the air, where the branches fight on her face, where roots *search* their paths through her body – she radiates a strident joy of insects, a fearful music.

At the black step of the earth, Douve ravaged, exultant, rejoins the knotty lamp of the plateaux.

Fifteen

O endowed with a profile where the earth *fleshes* its frenzy,
I see you vanish.

The naked earth on your lips and the shiver of the silex
Invent your last smile,

Profound science where the ancient
Cerebral bestiary calcines itself.

Seventeen

The gulley penetrates your mouth now,
The five fingers deploy themselves in the *fortunes* of the forest now,
The *first head* flows between the grasses now,
The throat paints itself with snow and wolves now,
The eyes *wind* on what *fleetings* of death and it is us in this wind in this
      water in this cold now.

Notes (Line numbers refer to the transcript not to TH's hand-written draft.)

Poem 3
Line 1: *marked*
This is a guess – completely illegible. Perhaps TH misread 'il s'agissait' as 'il s'agitait'.
Line 4: *gestures (heroic deeds)*
The phrase in parenthesis is TH's alternative version, suggestive of dictionary research
or his own knowledge, but either way it should have been rejected. 'Geste' as in
chanson de geste.
Line 6: *absent from my head*
The phrase in parenthesis is TH's alternative version.

Poem 4
Line 4: *gorge*
The word in parenthesis is TH's alternative version, suggestive of dictionary research,
but in this sense 'porte' is usually plural, which TH has not noticed, and this alternative
should have been rejected; it was clearly suggested by the first paragraph of this poem.
Line 4/5: *blazes the ages alight*
A simple misunderstanding of the French.

Poem 6
Line 4: *growing or crossing*
The word is fairly illegible but 'growing' makes sense of the French word 'croissant'.
'Crossing' would make sense if TH misread the French word as 'croisante', although
the usage would be incorrect.
Line 4: *core*
The word could either be 'core' or 'love' but both are strange and surely un-Hughesian
extrapolations from the meanings of the French word 'regard'. A stretch of the retinal

imagination detects the correct word 'look' in his handwriting. (Without stretching, I have no doubt that 'look' is the correct reading. [NR])

Poem 7
Line 6: *last*
Likeliest reading of illegible word.
Line 7: *aging*
This is a bad mistake: TH confuses 'vieillir' = 'to age' with 'veiller' = 'to watch'.
Line 6/7: TH has misread the syntax: 'break' refers back to 'you' in line 4, not 'mouth'.

Poem 8
Line 3: *versant (pouring, overturning)*
TH's parenthetical proposals suggest that he did not have his dictionary to hand at this point, since the French word 'versant' = 'slope'. And yet, had he not guessed at it – presumably from his knowledge of the meaning of the verb 'verser' – he could have left the archaic English word 'versant' (or slope) as it was, but I suspect he did not know it existed in English, as I didn't until about ten minutes ago when I checked the OED! TH omits an adjective qualifying 'versant', namely 'souterrain' ('underground').

Poem 12
Line 1: *village*
TH has misread 'ville' (city) as 'village'.
Line 2: *Search*
Fairly illegible but this reading (or less likely 'march') makes obvious if wrong sense for 'trouver'.

Poem 15
Line 1: *fleshes*
If this smudged and virtually illegible word is 'fleshes', one wonders how TH arrived at 'fleshes its frenzy'. Perhaps an association with 'charnel'? 'S'acharner' means 'persist'. Kinnell has 'rages' and my old published version reads 'never relents'; circumstantial evidence that TH saw GK's version in Willis Barnstone's anthology.

Poem 17
Line 2: *fastness*
The word is difficult to make out, but could be 'fastness', a clever solution to the difficult problem of the French phase 'en hasards [de forêt]'.
Line 3: *first head*
The French 'tête première' means 'primal head'; 'first head' would have to be 'première tête'.
Line 5: *wind*
This is a Poundian, even Zukofskian, translation of 'ventent'. It should, of course, be 'blow'.
Line 5: *fleetings*
An eccentric use of this archaic word.

Acknowledgments

We are grateful to Carol Hughes, for the Estate of Ted Hughes, for allowing us to use this material. Acknowledgements are also due to Special Collections and Archives, Robert W Woodruff Library, Emory University, where the bulk of Ted Hughes's manuscripts are housed. Special thanks to Anthony Rudolf who examined the Bonnefoy drafts, transcribed all of them and provided us with a commentary. Extracts are included in this tribute.

Vladimir Gandelsman
Russia

Translated by Nika Skandiaka and Yana Djin

Vladimir Gandelsman *was born in 1948 in Leningrad (St Petersburg). He has lived in New York since 1991. Gandelsman has published a number of poetry collections in Russian and a verse novel, as well as translations of Lewis Carroll, Wallace Stevens, Tomas Venclova and others. His poetry, in English translation, is to be found in* Crossing Centuries, The New Generation in Russian Poetry, 2000.

Gandelsman is the founder and director of a project associated with a new non-profit publishing house in New York, Ars-interpres, *dedicated to translation of contemporary English-language poetry into Russian.* Ars-interpres *has published bilingual collections of Eamon Grennan, Louis Glück and Frederick Smock. Announced are collections by Billy Collins, Robert Hass, Jorie Graham, Anthony Hecht, Paul Muldoon, Charles Simic, Mark Strand and many others. The translators are all leading Russian poets and translators resident both in Russia and the Russian diaspora overseas.*

Ars-interpres also announces publication of an international annual journal of poetry and translation, edited by Vladimir Gandelsman and Grigory Starikovsky. More information can be found on the web-site: http://arsintrerpres.narod.ru/all_news.html.

Nika Skandiaka *was born in 1978 in Russia and has lived half her life in the English-speaking world. She translates poetry between the two languages.*

Yana Djin *was born in 1967, in Tblisi. She lived in Moscow and emigrated to America in 1980 where she studied philosophy. She writes poetry and journalism in English. She has published two collections of poetry.*

A tall and narrow bridge looming

A tall and narrow bridge looming
over the engines' whistling, the gears' thunder,
a full bush of lilacs blooming
and a legless beggar under,

a town of sandy streets and heart-cutout shutters,
white in the morning; blue at night; at noon, yellow,
with its own madman and its own haircutter,
and a wooden stand in its market, rank with melon;

God, with the red-headed, freckled life of two twins,
with a flimsy fence as its guardian,
with a pure sound, a future first violinist's
student sound from the garden;

with a lump in the throat
as good as in me,
in what, too, could be me except there's
no me; with a distant girl cousin, so white and skinny
over a dish of biped cherries,

and with a sharp, an incestuous yearning
for her, a caress betraying a recent
childhood, and in the air, like in a learning
institution, a summer recess;

and with an uncle who's always kidding
and waltzing about, and who in ten
years, God, is to forget it all at Your bidding,
and in twenty more, in the final stanza, to rise again.

[NK]

Chess

A lacquered chessboard.
Appetizing din of the strewn pieces.
One flap of the checkered wings –
And the square butterfly descends upon the table.
Two little fists are hiding the first move,
Which you could easily pawn.
Yet, you still end up with the whites.
A meek movement of the outermost pawn.
That's not the way to move. Take a step.
And you do.
You take a step familiar to all.
You recall
" The Opening of the Four Knights",
"The Sicilian Defense" –
thanks to their noble sound –
which lasts as long as the first five moves.
Afterwards, you begin to yawn and look out the window –
Thinking: well, I'm going to lose,

Thinking: hell with it all!
I am going to lose but I will not hold back the tears
And learn to live with my helplessness . . .
(Later, when they manoeuvre to catch you yawning,
you become suspicious and a bit more artful.
A good game requires a nasty disposition,
And only when you get a partner weaker than yourself,
You understand that it is better to be defeated than to see his face.)
Thus, you learn to love the pieces unconditionally –
For their instant beauty, rather than their intention:
The bishop's diagonally wild glare at the rook,
Or the knight's sudden jolt onto the forking path
Which will forever separate the King from his Queen.
In despair,
You attempt to castle – but again –
You make the wrong move.
You feel just like your King crossing the defeated field:
You feel beastly fear, horror, and shame.
What liberates you, however, is the hopelessness of your position.
Now, you can keep losing:
Without looking back,
Without stirring,
Without effort.
Besides, in the endgame, which the naked Emperor
Has reached by some miracle,
There is an abundance of space.
And you can calmly observe how your opponent's pieces
Crowding together in anger and greed
Are asserting their existence.
How they randomly proclaim a checkmate.
You observe calmly –
Without a smile of condescension,
Without giving in,
Yet, with a surprise at seeing
That your opponent,
Inebriated by the array of the alternatives
Is promoting his pawns to the dwellings of the Queen.
You see that you're losing not on account of
Some risky combination but simply because
Of the hysterical onslaught of black pieces across the board.
Neither a noble victor who refrains from looking you in the eye,
Nor a felicitous fool, who offers you to play another game,
Can now stir you from your calm.
You – taking advantage of your right as the loser –

Gandelsman/ 33

Collect the fallen figures. Stripped of the anticipation for a new life.
You collect them into their wooden sarcophagus and think:
Everything turned out to be just.
Everything is as it should be.
Because even if your game was filled with love,
Then, it was love which lies outside of yourself –
Which, indeed is the very place for defeats –
In reality – a cemetery –
Where victors hesitate to linger.

[YD]

Ivan Andreevich Krylov
Russia

Translated by Gordon Pirie

Robert Chandler *writes:* **Ivan Krylov** *(1769-1844) is one of the great tellers of fables. Both his original works and his many adaptations of La Fontaine are remarkable for their wit, musicality and linguistic vitality. Krylov's wit is often, though by no means always, directed against the ruling establishment. The musicality of his verse no doubt owes much to his being a gifted violinist; throughout his life he performed both as a soloist and, alongside the most famous musicians of the day, in quartets. His language remains close to that of folk poetry at the same time as attaining an unusual degree of formal elegance; as Paul Friedrich has pointed out, many of his most famous lines draw equally on the peasant proverb and the salon epigram. With his deep understanding of both the human and the animal worlds, Krylov can also be considered one of the founders of Russian realism.*

Gordon Pirie (1936-84) was for some years head of the English department at Winchester College, where he also taught French and Russian. In the early seventies he left Winchester to live with his family on a smallholding in Wales. There he began to translate poetry from French and Russian.

Most of his translations are of fables: by La Fontaine and the equally great Ivan Krylov. These translations deserve to be known, even to other translators. Pirie's translation of La Fontaine's 'The Ant and the Grasshopper', for example, has more vivid detail and rhythmic vitality even than Richard Wilbur's – and Wilbur is one of the finest of all verse translators. The last stanzas of Pirie's version are memorable:

> 'Tell me, what were you playing at,
>   While summer days were long?'
> 'Why, in the grasses tall I sat,
>   And sang my busy song.'

> 'You sang, you say? How very charming!
>   Well, summer days are fled,
> And since your talents aren't for farming,
>   You'd better dance instead!'

In comparison Wilbur's last lines seem dull:

> 'What did you do all summer, friend?'
> She asked the would-be borrower.
> 'So please your worship,' answered she,

'I sang and sang both night and day.'
'You sang? Indeed, that pleases me.
Then dance the winter-time away.'

The Geese Going To Market

            Geese prize their dignity,
And hate to have it ruffled; so, to be
    Driven along a public road
        To market by a peasant
                Armed with a goad –
                A great long stick
To prod you when your progress isn't quick
    Enough – is really most unpleasant.
    The peasant didn't think of that:
Christmas was coming, and his geese were fat.
With jabs and prods, and now and then a curse,
    He drove them down the road pell-mell,
    Eager to have not birds to sell,
        But money in his purse.
    Now I don't blame the man for this
    (Men do things infinitely worse
    To one another, I'm afraid,
    When there's a profit to be made.)
But those poor geese, they took it much amiss,
    And thus addressed a passer-by
Who seemed to view them with a pitying eye:
        "Sir, did you ever see
        Unhappier geese than we?
    Look how this peasant's treating us!
    But then he's just an ignorant fellow,
        And obviously doesn't know
    That we're no ordinary geese,
    But come of ancient Roman stock,
And trace our ancestry, unbroken, back
        To that illustrious flock
That saved the Eternal City from the sack.'"
                    "I see",
        Replied the passer-by,
    "So you've a longish pedigree . . . "
"Why yes! Our forefathers, you know . . . " "All right!
        All right! I've heard the story
    Of how they raised the alarm at night;

But that can hardly qualify
      A modern goose for glory.
You'll have to find a better claim
To honour, than your forebears' fame.
More to the point, would be to know
What you yourselves have ever done
That's been of use to anyone.
What's that you say?   Nothing to show?
      Well then, you silly geese,
You'd better leave your ancestors in peace!
   They've had whatever fame's their due;
            And as for you,
         In spite of all your boasting,
I'd say you're only fit for roasting!"

      To make the moral plain
Would only irritate the geese again,
            So I'll refrain.

The Fly And The Traveller

   One hot July, about midday,
      While from a burning, cloudless sky
The sun looked down, and with his fiery eye
      Turned fields of cut grass into hay;
         While panting flocks and herds
Took shelter in what little shade
         Was left them, and the birds,
         For all the noise they made,
         Could well have flown away;
Four sturdy horses, pulling with a will,
Had dragged a big coach half way up a hill.
The coach was laden, and the roof piled high
With trunk and hamper, chest, and bag, and poke –
The copious luggage of the gentlefolk
Inside. The wheels – for this was long before
      The days when roads were tarred –
   Sank deep into the summer dust,
   Which made the going doubly hard.
   No wonder that the team of four,
      Sweating and straining fit to burst,
Slowed down, and would have dearly liked to stop
   And rest before they reached the top.

But this was not to be allowed. Down came
The coachman from his seat, and set about
The luckless horses with a wicked knout,
While from the other side a servant did the same.
     In vain – the team could go no faster.
     So out from inside clambered master,
Mistress, son and daughter, governess
     And tutor, chambermaid – the lot!
     With seven passengers the less,
The team would surely quicken to a trot.
       But no – their weight was small
     Compared to their impediments;
And soon the pace had dwindled to a crawl,
     When who should happen to come by,
     But a busy little buzzing fly,
Who thought that Providence had surely sent her
To help those plodding horses climb the hill.
     In any case, she'd try her skill.
So down she comes, and buzzes round their eyes
And ears and noses. They, well used to flies,
     Pay no attention, so she tries
       Some other likely places:
     She settles on the shaft, the traces,
She even gets astride the coachman's nose;
     And when he sneezes, off she goes
To see what all those passengers are at.
     The servants, deep in idle chat,
     She finds are lagging far behind;
     Delighted to be unconfined,
The children gambol with the dog, or chase
     A butterfly; my lady's walking
With governess and tutor, quietly talking;
     Unmindful of his proper place,
The master's wandered off into the shade
To look for mushrooms with the chambermaid –
          All very fine
(And here her tone changed to a plaintive whine),
       But this was not the time
To look for mushrooms, with a hill to climb!
     While thus the insect fussed around,
     The patient horses, flogged and fagged
     Almost beyond endurance, dragged
The coach up to the top, and stood on level ground.
         "There now!" exclaimed the fly,

"We've made it to the crest!
Well, that was quite a strain!
And now you're on the flat again,
                                    I'll say goodbye.
I reckon I've deserved a good long rest!"

A lot of people, like this fly,
Poke fingers into every pie,
And never guess you're not delighted
To see them, though they weren't invited.

The Farmer, His Flock And The Sea

A farmer, by the sea in Wales,
Had land too stony and too steep
For ploughing, so instead of growing crops,
        He kept a flock of sheep
    Who grazed along the bare cliff-tops,
        And didn't mind the gales.
The flock prospered and multiplied, and he,
        Though not exactly wealthy,
    Had outdoor work to keep him healthy,
    And best of all, security.
Now many men would not have wished for more;
        But while his flock was grazing
    Happily along the shore,
Sometimes the farmer stood beside them, gazing
    At passing ships far out to sea,
        And thinking of the tales
        He'd heard, of fortunes made
        By merchant men in trade –
    Men not afraid to risk their all
        In hopes of a good haul.
        He thought, too, of the bales
        Of wool (from his own fleeces?)
And other goods that sometimes, after gales,
    The tide washed up along the beaches.
He thought of coins piled up on counters, or
Heavy in bags – crowns, nobles, angels, pieces
        Of eight, and louis d'or.
And soon, from thinking that he wasn't rich,
He fell to feeling positively poor;
    And life became a constant itch

Until he'd sold both farm and flock,
And ventured all upon a vessel fraught
With rich goods destined for a distant port.
            The vessel struck a rock
                              And sank.
            His hopes sank with it, and,
            With nothing in the bank,
                              Back to the land
He went, and took to shepherding again.
Plain Hodge he was at first, a hireling fain
To do what he was told and earn his keep;
            But worked with such good will
            And unforgotten skill,
That from the herding of another's sheep,
He rose in time to purchasing a few
And now he stood again beside the shore,
            The happy owner of a score
Of ewes. The day was fine, the sea was blue,
And barely ruffled by the breeze. It drew his eye
            To where, meeting the sky,
The two together seemed to close the boundless view.
            He gazed in silence for a while.
Then to the ocean, with a rueful smile,
            "Today," said he, "you're quite the charmer;
            But if you're hoping to beguile
            Some silly fool to sell his sheep
            And risk his fortune on the deep,
            You'd better try another farmer!"

The Pig Under The Oak Tree

A pig, let out to forage in a wood,
Snuffled her way to where an oak tree stood,
                              And found
            An autumn scattering
            Of acorns round it on the ground -
Good food for pigs, tasty and fattening.
            She ate as many as she could,
            Lay down under the tree, and slept;
            Then, waking full of energy,
                  Began to root about,
                              Adept
            At digging with her pointed snout.

"That doesn't do the oak tree any good",
Remarked a crow
Perched on a branch, watching these antics down below.
"If you expose the roots like that,
The summer drought
Will dry them out,
And then the tree will die."
"Who cares?" replied the pig. "Not I!
Maybe you birds think differently,
But I don't fly,
So this old tree's no use to me,
And might as well be lying flat
As poking up there in the sky.
Now acorns – they're another matter.
They're good to eat, and make me fatter!"
At that, the oak
Rustled and spoke:
"Ungrateful creature! Why,
You've only got to lift your snout, to see
Those acorns you're so fond of, growing on me!"

Demyan Kudryavtsev
Russia

Translated by Daniel Weissbort

Born in Leningrad in 1971, **Demyan Kudryavtsev** *studied at Leningrad and Jerusalem Universities. From 1990, he lived in Israel for some years. He is the publisher of the journal* Obitaemy Ostrov, *and editor of the Internet journal* Eye, *among the first literary publications of the Russian Internet. His first poetry collection appeared in 1991. Since 2001 Kudryavtsev has lived in London where he has been working on his first novel. His most recent poetry collection,* The Practice of Russian Verse, *was published in Moscow in 2002. The translations below are taken from this collection.*

from Memories of a Bay

3.

If to us rivers returned
like the last water to Jerusalem
where we lived
burned by noon
the one
hitherto
not known
I call anna
Anna!
And she
won't pass by
from the window
we'll see a sea
and where a wall was
the wall of the heavens
indistinguishable
and a seascape
where was a scape of plain.

I
inhabitant of the future ocean depths
watch one ignite
and fade
and the last wave

overtop
Jerusalem's battlement.

Hadj-1

1.

And the darker the water was
centuries back

in the magic land a child's sob
was nothing more – just that

and mills hustled the water
to its sources

and
to where disaster originated

the rooster's clamour was
not to be outdone

2.

And the grass greenness mounted
towards the pennants, surmounting them

and what's my number in the ranks
and as for me, what sort of groom

they fought not disturbing your rest
so sound you slept

an eagle outflying itself
above it a dragon swept.

3.

Let the chronicler place a sign
a cross in my margins

magic land
so longed for

and the house full of children and mutts
and of women from those kids

and not a sound except for the wall clock
awaiting guests.

    4.
In the magic land there's weeding
to last for ever

centuries behind us
you and I were there in the never-never Mecca

and at that time water was the colour of water
and the walls, speaking of towns,

were
stone walls

and we were still awaiting the horde
like a fleeting shadow.

    [1996]

Pushkin
Russia

Translated by Robert Chandler

Robert Chandler *has been a regular contributor to* MPT *for some years. His own poems have appeared in the* TLS *and* Metre. *His translations of Sappho and Apollinaire have been published in the series 'Everyman's Poetry', and his translations of prose works by Vasily Grossman and Andrey Platonov are available from Harvill. The most recent of these is Andrey Platonov's short novel,* Soul *(Harvill, April 2003). His translation of Pushkin's unfinished* Dubrovsky *will be published by Hesperus in July 2003; the book will also contain* The Egyptian Nights, *from which the following excerpts have been taken.*

Robert Chandler writes: The Egyptian Nights is among the finest, if most fragmentary, of all Pushkin's works. The prose sections were probably written in autumn 1835; the first passage of verse incorporates lines from a poem written in 1832, *Yezersky*; the second passage of verse is an expansion of a poem about Cleopatra written in 1828. Like the poet evoked by his mysterious Italian *improvisatore*, Pushkin moves quickly and gracefully between a variety of subjects and tones of voice. The witty description of the audience's behaviour before the *improvisatore*'s performance allows us a vivid glimpse of high-society Petersburg. Pushkin's portrayal of Charsky, and of his awkward relationship to his calling, is fascinating – all the more so since Pushkin has clearly endowed Charsky with at least some traits of his own character. There is subtle discussion, in both verse and prose, of the poet's responsibilities to his art and his place in society. Another central theme is the interdependency of poise and awkwardness. Pushkin contrasts the plain awkward girl with the majestic beauty, and both Charsky and the *improvisatore* move between extremes of fluency and embarrassment. The work ends with a passage of narrative verse that is impassioned yet deftly controlled. The idea that men might be ready to accept execution in exchange for a night with Cleopatra appears at first to be the height of Romanticism; with a slight shock, however, we discover that Flavius, at least, is moved not by passion for Cleopatra but by fury at her arrogance. *The Egyptian Nights* is full of delicate paradoxes, contrasts and parallels. The topic assigned to the Italian for his first improvisation is that no poet should be assigned topics; the Italian then demonstrates, through his fluency, the opposite of what his words assert. The audience that gathers to hear his second improvisation is initially unresponsive – just as the audience described in this improvisation is initially unresponsive to Cleopatra.

Like the Italian *improvisatore*, Cleopatra's lovers must surrender their own selves; like any great artist, Cleopatra can divine a man's hidden wishes. Almost everything in *The Egyptian Nights* is surprising. The work's only flaw is that it ends so soon; like Shakespeare's Cleopatra, Pushkin 'makes hungry where most (he) satisfies'.

Egyptian Nights

> – Quel est cet homme?
> – Ha! C'est un bien grand talent, il fait de sa voix tout ce qu'il veut.
> – Il devrait bien, madame, s'en faire une culotte.[1]

Charsky was a native citizen of Petersburg. He was not yet thirty; he was unmarried; his work in the Civil Service was not burdensome. His late uncle, a vice-governor during prosperous times, had left him a decent estate. His life could have been most pleasant; but he had the misfortune to write and publish poetry. In journals he was called a poet; in servants' quarters a scribbler.

In spite of the great advantages enjoyed by versifiers (it has to be said: apart from the right to use the accusative case instead of the genitive and a few other examples of so-called poetic licence, we know of no particular advantages enjoyed by Russian versifiers) – be that as it may, in spite of all their possible advantages, these people are also subject to great disadvantages and unpleasantnesses. The versifier's bitterest, most unbearable affliction is his title, his sobriquet, with which he is branded and from which he can never escape. The public look on him as their property; in their opinion, he is born for their benefit and pleasure. Should he return from the country, the first person he meets will greet him with: 'Haven't you brought anything new for us?' Should he be deep in thought about the disorder of his affairs, or about the illness of someone close to him, a trite smile will at once accompany the trite exclamation: 'No doubt you're composing something?' Should he fall in love, his beautiful one will buy herself an album from the English Shop and be waiting for elegies. If he goes to visit someone he hardly knows, to talk about an important matter, the man will summon his son and make him read *this gentleman*'s poems aloud – and the little boy will treat the versifier to the versifier's own mangled poems. And if these are the laurels of the craft, then imagine its pains! The greetings, requests, albums and little boys were so irritating, Charsky confessed, that he had to be constantly on his guard lest he let slip some offensive remark.

Charsky made every possible effort to escape the insufferable sobriquet. He avoided his fellow men of letters, preferring the company of even the most vacuous members of high society. His conversation was exceedingly banal and never touched on literature. In his dress he always followed the latest fashion with the diffidence and superstition of a young Muscovite visiting Petersburg for the very first time. His study, furnished like a lady's bedroom, did not in any respect call to mind that of a writer; no books were piled on or under the tables; the sofa was not stained with ink; there was none of the disorder which reveals the presence of the Muse and the absence of dustpan and brush. Charsky despaired if one of his society friends discovered him pen in hand. It is hard to believe that a man endowed with talent and a soul could stoop to such petty dissimulation. He would pretend to be a passionate lover of horses, a desperate gambler or the most discriminating of gourmets – even though he could not tell a mountain pony from an Arab steed, could never remember trumps and secretly preferred baked potatoes to every possible invention of French cuisine. He led the most distracted of lives; he was there at every ball, he ate too much at every diplomatic dinner, and at every reception he was as inevitable as Rezanov's ice-cream.

But he was a poet, and his passion was not to be overcome: when he sensed the approach of that 'nonsense' (his word for inspiration), Charsky would lock himself in his study and write from morning till late at night. Only then, he would confess to his closest friends, did he know true happiness. The rest of the time he went out and about, put on airs, dissembled and listened again and again to the famous question: 'Haven't you written anything new?'

One morning Charsky was in that state of grace when fancies outline themselves clearly before you and you discover vivid, unexpected words to embody your visions, when verses flow readily from your pen and resonant rhymes come forward to meet orderly thoughts. His soul was deep in sweet forgetfulness – and society, society's opinions and his own foibles no longer existed for him. He was writing poetry.

Suddenly there was a creak and a head came round his study door. Charsky started and frowned.

'Who's that?' he asked in annoyance, mentally cursing his servants for always leaving his vestibule unattended.

The stranger entered.

He was tall and lean, and he looked about thirty. The features of his dark face were distinctive: a pale, high forehead shaded by dark locks, gleaming black eyes, an aquiline nose, and a thick beard framing sunken, bronzed cheeks – all these made it clear he was a foreigner. He was wearing a black frock coat, turning white along the seams, and summer trousers (even though it was now well into autumn), and on his yellowish shirt front, beneath a worn black cravat, shone a false diamond; his fraying hat had clearly seen both sun and rain. Meeting this man in a forest, you'd take him for a brigand; in society – for a political conspirator; in your vestibule – for a charlatan peddling elixirs and arsenic.

'What do you want?' Charsky asked him, in French.

'Signor,' the foreigner answered with low bows, 'Lei voglia perdonarmi se . . .'[2]

Charsky did not offer him a chair but stood up himself. The conversation continued in Italian.

'I am a Neapolitan artist,' said the stranger. 'Circumstances have obliged me to leave my homeland. Trusting in my talent, I have come to Russia.'

Charsky thought the Neapolitan intended to give some cello recitals and was selling tickets from door to door. He was about to hand the man his twenty-five roubles, to get rid of him quickly, but the stranger went on:

'I hope, Signor, that you will be able to assist a fellow artist and introduce me to the houses where you yourself are received.'

No blow to Charsky's vanity could have been sharper. He looked haughtily at the man who called himself his fellow artist.

'Allow me to ask who I am speaking to and who you take me to be,' he said, struggling to hold back his indignation.

The Neapolitan sensed Charsky's annoyance.

'Signor,' he stammered, 'ho creduto . . . ho sentito . . . la vostra Eccelenza mi perdonera . . .'[3]

'What do you want?' Charsky asked drily.

'I have heard a great deal about your astonishing talent; I am certain that gentlemen here consider it an honour to offer their patronage in every possible way to so outstanding a poet,' the Italian replied, 'and I have therefore taken the liberty of presenting myself to you . . .'

'You are mistaken, Signor,' Charsky interrupted. 'The title of poet does not exist here. Our poets do not enjoy the patronage of gentlemen; our poets are themselves gentlemen, and if our Maecenases (the devil take them!) don't know this, then so much the worse for them. Here we have no tattered abbés whom a composer might take off the street to write a libretto. Our poets don't go on foot from door to door, soliciting donations.[4] And whoever told you I am a great versifier must have been jesting. I admit I did once write a few poor epigrams, but, thank God, I neither have nor wish to have anything to do with gentlemen versifiers.'

The poor Italian was in confusion. He glanced round the room. The paintings, the marble statues and bronze busts, the expensive gewgaws displayed on Gothic étagères, astonished him. He understood that there was nothing in common between himself, a poor wandering artiste in a worn cravat and an old frock coat, and this haughty dandy standing before him in a tufted brocade skullcap and a gold-embroidered Chinese gown with a Turkish shawl for a belt. He uttered some incoherent excuses, bowed, and was about to leave. His pathetic look moved Charsky who, for all his affectations, had a kind and noble heart. He felt ashamed of the touchiness of his vanity.

'Where are you going?' he said to the Italian. 'Wait. I had to decline an undeserved title and confess to you that I am no poet. Now let us talk about your affairs. I am ready to be of service to you in any way that I can. You are a musician?'

'No, Eccelenza!' the Italian answered. 'I am a poor *improvisatore*.'

'An *improvisatore*!' exclaimed Charsky, sensing all the cruelty of his behaviour. 'Why didn't you say at once that you're an *improvisatore*?' And Charsky pressed the Italian's hand with a sense of genuine remorse.

His friendly air was reassuring. Straightforwardly, the Italian began to deliver himself of his proposal. His outward appearance was not deceptive. He needed money; he was hoping, here in Russia, to get his personal affairs onto a sounder footing. Charsky listened to him attentively.

'I hope,' he said to the poor artist, 'that you will enjoy success; society here has never heard an *improvisatore* before. Curiosity will be aroused. Italian, I admit, is not spoken here, so you will not be understood; but that doesn't matter; what matters is that you should be in vogue.'

'But if no one here understands Italian,' said the improvisatore after a little thought, 'who will come and listen to me?'

'They will come, don't worry; some out of curiosity, some for a way of passing the evening, and others to show they understand Italian. All that matters, I repeat, is that you should be in vogue – and you will be in vogue, you have my word for it.'

After noting his address, Charsky parted affectionately with the *improvisatore*, and that very evening he began making arrangements on his behalf.

Chapter Two

> 'I'm Tsar and slave, I'm worm and God.'

The following day Charsky was walking down a dark, dirty tavern corridor in search of room 35. He stopped at the door and knocked. Yesterday's Italian opened it.

'Victory!' said Charsky. 'Everything's as good as done. The Princess —— is lending you her hall; at a reception last night I managed to recruit half of Petersburg; you must print your tickets and announcements. I guarantee you, if not a triumph, at least some profit.'

'That's what matters most!' exclaimed the Italian, showing his joy through the lively gestures of a man from the South. 'I knew you would help me. *Corpo di Bacco*! You're a poet, just as I am; and say what you like, poets are splendid fellows! How can I express my gratitude? Wait . . . would you like to hear an improvisation?'

'An improvisation! But surely you need an audience, and music, and the thunder of applause?'

'Nonsense, nonsense! Where can I find a better audience? You are a poet, you will understand me better than anyone, and your quiet encouragement means more to me than a whole storm of applause . . . Find somewhere to sit and give me a theme.'

Charsky sat down on a trunk (one of the two chairs in the cramped little kennel was broken, the other covered by a heap of papers and linen). The *improvisatore* took a guitar from the table – and stood facing Charsky, plucking the strings with bony fingers and waiting for his command.

'Here's a theme for you,' said Charsky. *'A poet chooses the matter of his songs himself; the crowd has no right to direct his inspiration.'*

The Italian's eyes gleamed; he played a few chords, proudly flung back his head – and impassioned stanzas, the expression of immediate feeling, flew harmoniously from his lips. Here they are, transcribed freely by a friend of ours from the words preserved in Charsky's memory.

> Here comes the poet – he can see
> No one, and yet he's open-eyed.
> Then someone's pulling at his sleeve
> And he must listen while they chide:
> 'No sooner have you climbed to heaven
> Than back to earth you cast your eyes;
> By what strange power are you driven
> To wander down such aimless ways?
> A fruitless fever grips your soul;
> Your vision's blurred, your view's obscured;
> It seems you can't escape the hold
> Of matters pointless and absurd.
> A genius soars above the earthy;
> True poets sense an obligation
> Only to sing what's truly worthy
> The Muses and their inspiration . . .'
> '. . . What makes a wind sweep down ravines
> And whirl dry leaves through dusty air,
> While ships becalmed on silent seas
> Wait for its kiss in numb despair?
> What makes an eagle leave his height
> And, flying past towers, choose to alight
> On some old stump? The eagle knows.
> And Desdemona's heart is closed
> To all but black Othello, whom
> She loves just as the moon adores
> The blackest night. Hearts know no laws;
> Eagles and winds are free to roam.
> A poet too is like the wind;
> He too escapes all ties that bind.

And like the eagle, he flies far;
Like Desdemona, he must love
Whatever idol charms his heart,
And not care who may disapprove.'

The Italian fell silent. Charsky said nothing, amazed and moved.

'Well?' asked the *improvisatore*.

Charsky took his hand and pressed it firmly.

'Well?' asked the *improvisatore*. 'What do you think?'

'Astonishing!' said the poet. 'How can this be? Another person's thought has barely reached your ears – and at once you make it your own, as if you've been nursing it, cherishing it, tirelessly developing it. For you, then, there exists neither labour, nor dejection, nor the anxiety that precedes inspiration. Astonishing, quite astonishing!'

The *improvisatore* answered, 'Every talent is inexplicable. How is it that a sculptor, seeing a slab of Carrara marble, can glimpse a hidden Jupiter and bring him out into the light, splitting the stone casing with hammer and chisel?[5] Why does a thought leave a poet's head already equipped with four rhymes and divided into feet that are harmonious and of equal length? Similarly, no one but the *improvisatore* himself can understand this quickness of impressions, this intimate link between his own inspiration and the will of a stranger. Even my own attempts to explain this would be in vain. However . . . it's time to think about my first evening. What do you suggest? How should tickets be priced so as neither to burden the public nor leave me out of pocket? La signora Catalani, they say, charged twenty-five roubles. That's not a bad price.'

Charsky found it unpleasant to be brought down so suddenly from the heights of poetry into the bookkeeper's office; but he well understood the imperatives of everyday need, and, together with the Italian, he plunged into matters pecuniary. The Italian then revealed such unbridled greed, such an unabashed love of profit, that Charsky felt disgusted by him and hastened to leave, so as not to lose entirely the sense of wonder aroused in him by the brilliant *improvisatore*. The preoccupied Italian did not notice this change; he accompanied Charsky along the corridor and down the staircase, seeing him off with deep bows and assurances of eternal gratitude.

Chapter Three

> Tickets are ten roubles each; the
> performance begins at 7.0 p.m.
>
> *A poster.*

Princess ——'s reception hall had been placed at the *improvisatore*'s disposal. A stage had been erected, and chairs had been set out in twelve rows; on the appointed day, at seven o'clock, the hall was lit up and an old long-nosed woman, wearing a grey hat with broken feathers and with rings on all her fingers, sat at a little table by the door, checking and selling tickets. Gendarmes stood by the main entrance. The audience began to gather. Charsky was among the first to arrive. He was very concerned that the performance should be a success, and he wanted to see the *improvisatore* and find out if he was satisfied with everything. He found the Italian in a little side room, glancing impatiently at his watch. The Italian was dressed theatrically: he was in black from head to toe; the lace collar of his shirt was turned back, the strange whiteness of his bare neck stood out sharply against his thick black beard, and locks of hair hung down over his forehead and eyebrows. Charsky greatly disliked all this, finding it unpleasant to see a poet in the costume of a travelling player. After a brief conversation, he returned to the hall, which was filling up steadily.

Soon the chairs were all occupied by dazzling ladies; tightly framing the ladies, the men stood in front of the stage, along the walls and behind the last row of chairs. The musicians and their music stands took up both sides of the stage. On a table in the middle stood a porcelain vase. There were a lot of people. Everyone was waiting impatiently. At half past seven the musicians finally bestirred themselves; they raised their bows and began the overture to *Tancredi*.[6] The last notes of the overture thundered out; everything went still and silent. And the *improvisatore*, greeted by deafening applause from all sides, advanced with low bows to the very edge of the stage.

Charsky had been feeling anxious, wondering what impression the first minute would make, but he noticed that the Italian's costume, which to him had seemed so unfortunate, appeared otherwise to the audience. Charsky himself found nothing absurd in the man when he saw him on stage, his pallid face brightly lit by a multitude of candles and lamps. The applause died away; conversation ceased. The Italian, expressing himself in broken French, asked the ladies and gentlemen present to propose some themes, writing them down on separate bits of paper. At this unanticipated invitation, the audience all began looking at one another in silence; not one of them responded. The Italian waited a little, then repeated his request in a timid and deferential voice. Charsky was standing right by the stage; he was seized with anxiety; he sensed that nothing would happen without him and that he would have to write down a theme himself. Several women's heads had indeed turned towards him and begun to call out his name, at first softly, then louder and louder. Hearing this, the *improvisatore* looked round for Charsky, saw him there at his feet, and, with a friendly smile, handed him pencil and paper. Charsky found it most unpleasant to have to play a role in this comedy, but he had no choice: he took the pencil and paper from the Italian's hands and wrote a few words; the Italian took the vase from the table, stepped down from the stage, and held the vase out to Charsky, who dropped in his piece of paper. This set an effective example: two journalists considered it their duty as men of letters to write down a theme each; the secretary of the Neapolitan embassy and some young man, only recently returned from his travels and still raving about Florence, placed their folded papers in the urn; lastly, at her mother's bidding, a plain young girl with tears in her eyes wrote a few lines in Italian and, blushing to her ears, handed them to the *improvisatore*; the ladies watched in silence, with faint smiles of mockery. Returning to his stage, the *improvisatore* put the urn back on the table and began, one by one, to take out the pieces of paper, reading each out aloud:

The Cenci family (La famiglia dei Cenci).
L'ultimo giorno di Pompeia.
Cleopatra e i suoi amanti.
La primavera veduta da una prigione.
Il trionfo di Tasso.[7]

'What is the wish of the esteemed company?' asked the deferential Italian. 'Will you yourselves select one of the proposed themes, or will you let the matter be decided by lot?'

'By lot!' said a voice from the crowd.

'By lot, by lot!' the audience repeated.

The *improvisatore* stepped down again from the stage, holding the urn in his hands, and asked, 'Who will be so kind as to draw a theme?' The *improvisatore* looked entreatingly up and down the front rows. Not one of the dazzling ladies moved a finger. The *improvisatore*, unaccustomed to Northern indifference, seemed agitated. Then, over to one side, he noticed a raised hand, in a small white glove; he quickly turned round and walked up to a majestic young beauty sitting at the end of the second row. She stood up without any embarrassment and, with the utmost simplicity, put her small aristocratic hand into the urn and drew out a folded slip of paper.

'Be so kind as to unfold the paper and read it out,' said the *improvisatore*. The beauty unfolded the paper and read out aloud: 'Cleopatra e i suoi amanti.'[8]

These words were pronounced quietly but such was the silence reigning over the hall that everyone heard them. The *improvisatore* bowed, with an air of deep gratitude, to the beautiful lady and returned to his stage.

'Ladies and gentlemen,' he said, turning to the audience, 'I am directed to improvise on the theme of Cleopatra and her lovers. I humbly ask whoever proposed this theme to clarify their thought: which lovers did they have in mind, *perche la grande regina n'aveva molto?*[9]

At these words many of the men burst into loud laughter. The *improvisatore* appeared somewhat confused.

'I should like to know,' he went on, 'what historical moment was in the mind of the person who proposed this theme . . . I shall be most grateful if they can clarify this.'

No one hurried to answer. Several ladies glanced at the plain young girl who had written down a theme at her mother's bidding. The poor girl noticed this unkind attention and was in such confusion that tears appeared on her eyelashes. Charsky could not bear this and, turning to the *improvisatore*, he said to him in Italian, 'It was I who suggested the theme. I had in mind the testimony of Victor Aurelius, who maintains that Cleopatra proposed death as the price of her love and that there were admirers neither frightened nor repelled by this condition. I think, however, that the subject is a little difficult. Perhaps you would prefer to choose another?'

But the *improvisatore* could already sense the approach of the God. He signalled to the musicians to play. His face went terribly pale and he began to tremble as if from fever; his eyes gleamed with a strange fire; he smoothed back his black hair with one hand, wiped beads of sweat from his high forehead with a handkerchief, and suddenly strode forward, folding his arms across his chest. The music died away. The improvisation began.

The palace shines. Sweet melodies,
Accompanied by flute and lyre,
And her sweet voice, and her bright eyes,
Make light of dark, make night expire.
All hearts bow down towards her throne;
She is the Queen whom all must court –
But then her own fair head sinks down
Towards her golden cup in thought.

Flutes, lyres and voices – all goes dead.
A deepening silence fills the hall.
But when once more she lifts her head,
Her words both frighten and enthrall:
'My love holds bliss, so I keep hearing.
If there is truth in what you claim,
Blessed is he whose love has daring
Enough to pay the price I name.
My contract binds all equally:
He who would claim me as his wife,
He who desires one night with me,
Must for that night lay down his life.

'Once I lie on the bed of pleasure –
I swear by all the gods above –
I'll bring delight beyond all measure
Yet be the humblest slave of love.
Hear me, O splendid Aphrodite,
And you, dread God who reigns below,
And you above, great Zeus almighty –
I swear: until the dawn's first glow
Brightens the sky, I shall divine
Each hidden wish of my lord's heart;
I'll set on fire, then soothe with wine;
I'll bare the mysteries of love's art.
But when the Eastern sky turns red,
When my lord feels the morning's breath,
Soldiers will lead him from my bed
To meet the lasting kiss of death.'

All hearts rebel, and yet they all
Remain enslaved by beauty's charm.
Uncertain murmurs fill the hall;
She listens with untroubled calm
And looks around with haughty pride,

Thinking her suitors spurn her offer.
Then one emerges from the crowd;
Two others follow quickly after.
Their steps are bold, their eyes are bright;
She rises to her feet to meet them.
The bargain's struck; each buys one night,
And when it's over, death will greet them.

The lovers' lots are blessed by priests
And dropped inside the fateful urn.
Then, watched in silence by the guests,
A lot is drawn. First comes the turn,
The gods decree, of gallant Flavius,
Flavius whose courage never wavers.
Such scorn in a mere woman's eyes
Is more than Flavius can endure;
Amazed by Cleopatra's gall,
This grey-haired veteran of war
Now leaps to answer pleasure's call
As once he answered battle cries.
Criton comes next, a youthful sage
Born in the groves of Epicure,
Whose graceful verses sing the rage
Induced by Venus and Amor.
The third is like a glowing rose
Whose petals dawn has coaxed apart,
A joy to both the eye and heart,
A youth whose name the centuries
Have lost. The softest shadow lies
Over his cheeks; love fills his eyes.
The passions raging in his breast
Are like a still-closed book to him
And Cleopatra looks at him
With eyes surprised by tenderness.

Notes

1   'Who is that man?' 'Oh, he's someone very talented. He can make his voice do anything.' 'He'd do well, Madam, to make himself a new pair of trousers with it.'

2   Signor . . . please excuse me if . . .

3   I believed . . . I thought . . . your excellency will forgive me . . .

4   No doubt because of the censorship, Pushkin deleted the original continuation of this sentence: 'and all they ask from Maecenases (the devil take them) is that they should not secretly denounce them (and not even this wish is granted).'

5   The thought in this sentence is borrowed from a sonnet by Michelangelo.

6   An opera by Rossini, written in 1813.

7   The last day of Pompei. Cleopatra and her lovers. Spring seen from a prison. The
triumph of Tasso.

8   Cleopatra and her lovers.

9   since the great queen had many of them.

Boris Slutsky
Russia

Translated by Gerald Smith

Boris Slutsky *(1919-1986) was one of Russia's great 20th century poets. See the present issue of MPT for a short review of* Boris Slutsky: Things That Happened, *1998, edited, translated, and with an introduction and commentaries by Gerald Smith.*

Gerald Smith *is Professor of Russian in the University of Oxford and Fellow of New College, Oxford. He has translated much contemporary Russian poetry and has written extensively on Russian versification, for example Joseph Brodsky's prosody. Clarendon Press published Gerald Smith's and Marina Tarlinskaja's translation of ML Gasparov's classic text,* A History of European Versification, *1996. Since Professor Smith told Valentina Polukhina that he regretted not having included the poem printed below in his Slutsky collection, I invited him to send it to MPT. It is with much pleasure that we publish this characteristic and perfectly aimed piece (*Nachinaetsya novoe vremia*), which speaks to and for many, including the present editor of MPT, at a certain staqe in their careers.*

A new piece of time is beginning

A new piece of time is beginning:
the epoch after my own.
It comes to us all, that's a given,
but it's been much harder for some.
Lots and lots of honest tryers,
who stayed honest for many a year,
have been cancelled without any prior,
like the buses we have round here.
Lots and lots of very fine fellows
in return for the good they did
have been dumped like leaky old wellies
in a foul-smelling garbage pit.
I'm paid off with best suit and pension,
I can pat my own back today;
I sing as I make my exit,
I'm walking, not running away.
I will quietly live, nice and snugly,
I will warm up my tea on the stove.
Like that dog through the port of the sputnik

I'll gaze down at the faraway globe.
With my old prose rhythm and metre,
I'll translate the odd poem for fun,
and like a raw youth, through a peephole
spy on things that can never be mine.
I will contemplate duty and conscience,
cherish friendship and cherish love.
And wait for new news to astonish
the old but unused news I own.

Marina Tsvetaeva (1892-1941)
Russia

Translated by Angela Livingstone

Angela Livingstone *read Russian and German at Cambridge; taught in the Department of Literature, University of Essex, 1966-1995 and is still there now as Research Professor.* She has published one book in the field of German literature and thought: Lou Andreas-Salomé, Her Life And Writings, *London, 1984; and several in that of Russian:* Pasternak *(with Donald Davie),* Modern Judgments, *London, 1969;* Pasternak On Art And Creativity, *Cambridge, 1985;* Pasternak, Doctor Zhivago, *Cambridge, 1989;* Art In The Light Of Conscience, Eight Essays On Poetry By Marina Tsvetaeva *(translation with commentary), Bristol, 1992;* The Ratcatcher *(verse-translation of Tsvetaeva's epic poem, with introduction and notes), London, 1999;* Andrei Platonov, The Return And Other Stories *(with R and E Chandler; translation with commentaries), London, 1999. Her translations of nine poems by Pasternak appeared in MPT 18. Now mainly working on Platonov, she recently edited the two volumes,* A Hundred Years of Andrei Platonov, Essays in Poetics, *nos 26 and 27, Keele University Press, 2001 and 2002. Meanwhile she is continuing to translate Russian poetry.*

Poem of the Air
[1927]

I

So here is a couplet
To start with. A nail, the first.
The door had gone silent
Like one that conceals a guest.   4
He stood there like pine wreaths
At porches – oh, widows know,
And full of sereneness,
A guest who possessed the cue,   8
The call, from the master:
A waited-for guest. In fine:
All full of steadfástness,
Like one who possessed the sign   12
– Pitch-dark from the hostess! –
Flashed over a servant's back!
Alive or a ghost, he's
A guest who's possessed the knock   16

(Unceasing, past bearing
By any: we die from these!)
Of the hostess's raring
Heartbeats: the fell of trees.   20
(Prised open, Pandora's
Casket, that trouble-box!)
In-comers are numerous,
But who is it waits, not knocks?   24
No doubt of a hearing
Or timeliness. Leaningly –
No doubt of an answering
Ear. (You've no doubts in me.)   28
A sureness of entrance.
That sweet (when we just pretend
To fear!) special instance
Of lingering – with key in hand.   32
Despiser of feelings,
High up above husbands, wives –
That monastery, Optin,
Renouncing its very chimes.   36
A soul with no strata
Of feelings, and fellah-bare.
The door – yet alerter.
And what of the pricking ears?   40
They stood up like 'Squadron:
Fire!' Like a faun's horns.
A tiny bit more and –
The door would unhinge, be torn   44
By force of the presence
Of something behind its back.
Thus sinews at moments
By deathbeds will almost crack,   48
Being stretched beyond limit.
Yet *no* knocking came. The floor –
Afloat. To my hand – the door.
The darkness – a jot retreated.   52

   II
Absolute – this naturalness.
Stillness. Sense of right.
Ordinary staircases,
Normal hour (of night).   56
Flat along the wall a spread
Shadowy somebody,

Done with gardens, letting me
Walk a step ahead –   60
Into night's full godliness.
Absolute the sky's
Height (like foam that laps beside
Bridges, larches' sighs . . .)   64
Into total witlessness
Of the hour and place.

Into total sightlessness
Even in sightless shade.   68
(Not just black as pitch – by far
Blackest-pitchiest!
Carmine, red of cinnabar,
Stain our irises –   72
Now my retina has sieved
World – to 'this' and 'yours' –
Never soil my eyeball with
Beauty, any more!)   76
Dream? But dream's at best a mere
Word. And what's inside?
Seemings? Let me try to hear:
We – yet a single stride!   80
Not the paired or marital

Double-orphan step:
But a lonely – everyman's –
Step, enfleshed as yet: 84
Mine. (It's not the holes that shame,
It's the need to patch!)
Levels should be made the same:
Either you – to match   88
Me – by just an inch descend
To the all-thinkers' world!
Or – and I'm already heard:
I no longer sound.   92

III

Absolute and perfect rhyme.
Rhythm – at last my own!
Like Columbus once, now I'm
Greeting an earth unknown: 96
Air. Forget pedestrian
Truths! This ground has great

Power of rébound, like the wan
Breast of woman laid   100
Under a much-tramped soldier-boot.
(Or a mother's breast
Underneath her baby's foot
Softly trampling . . .) Step   104
Into tautness. Sheer against
Any thought of air's
Path as easy. – 'Through the sphere's
Tight resistance' means   108
Hike through Russian rye, or rice
Old as the Chinese!
Thus against (but, for 'against'
Read 'with zest') the seas   112
Went a shoulderous throng. I hence
Fight like Hercules!
Emanation of the earth.
The first air – is dense.   116
You're my dream? Or maybe I'm
Yours? Absurd! A theme
Fit for profs. Now let me feel:
We – yet a single sigh.   120
Not the paired and unitary
Twin-asthmatic sigh –
But the sigh of solitary
Prison: 'is it high,   124
Yet, the Dnepr?' That Jewish sob,
Zithering: 'Art Thou deaf?'
Levels should be evened off:
Either you – by a breath's   128
Length – give in, by all who here
Live (I ask in fear) –
Or – and I'm already freed:
I no longer breathe.   132

     IV
What a time of siege that was –
Moscow typhus-days!
Over now. All suffering done
Down the stony lung –   136
Sack! Go on, investigate
Mucus! Air's gate –
Lifted, gone. The settled Pale –
All its walls fail.   140

V

Mother! – as you hoped, the air's
Fighter lives! But why
Offer him apparatus? He's
Nothing else but sky!   144
Firmament, be spread below
(Fragile!) the light boat . . .
Yet he's lung-light through and through:
Why the loop, the inert   148
Noose? And look – with all the purl,
Plash and flow of height –
Don't lament the pilot's fall.
That – *is* his flight.   152

Don't disguise his bits of bone
In shroud and grave-stone.
Death's a course in how to float.
Air-natation. No   156
Trace of deadness in it. (Crazed
Search – propeller? screw?)

Listen, air-Achilleses
All of you, and *you*:   160
Don't breathe fame, the atmosphere
Breathed by grounded folk.
Death's a course in how to float –
All things shall appear   164
New . . .

VI

Glory to thee who let gaps be wide open.
I'm no longer weighing.
Glory to thee who let roof-tops be broken.   168
No longer hearing.
Solar-initiate, I'm no longer peering:
Spirit – unbreathing.
Body that's solid is body that's mortal.   172

Conquered the downpull.

VII

Lighter, no skiff lighter
Lying on littoral mica.
O how light the air is: 176

Rare and ever rarer . . .
Slide of ludic fishes –
Tail-of-trout elusive . . .
O the air is streamy,
Streamier than speeding 180
Hounds through oat-fields – slippery!
Soft the – air so wafty! –
Hair of crawling infants – 184
Watering-cans aren't streamier!
More: it's streamier even
Than a lime-bark lining
Freshly stripped, or onion. 188
Through bamboo and beaded
Melodied pagodas,
Through pagoda-veilings . . .
Splash! We'd move for ever . . . 192
Why should Hermes wear wings?
Fins would be more floating-
Fitting! Lo, a downpour!
Iridescent! Iris! 196
Isn't this your shower of
Silk, Shemákhan . . . ?
　　　　　　　Upward
Dance! Like paths from hospitals:
First no pulling dust-ward, 200
Then no take of footfalls.
Fathomless, yet firm as
Ice! The law of all the
Absences: earth's surface 204
First won't hold you, then de-
weights you. Nymph? Or naiad?
Some old peasant-daughter!
Age-old loss of body 208
When it enters water.
(Water-turbulation's
Splash. A sandy slide.)
Earthly liberation. 212
The third air is void.

VIII
Greige, like greyness streaking
Granddad's sweepnet, striping
Grandma's plait. And sparely! 216
Sparse, more sparse than drought-struck

Millet. (Shaven, naked,
Spikes of it all grain-shed.)
O how sharp the air is,   220
Sharp, more sharp than jagged
Combs for raking dog-locks;
Happy-coppiced woodlands'
Space; in starts of waking   224
(Nodding off, *we*'d call it) –

Crisscrossings' delirious
Scantness – links are vanished.
O how sharp the air is,   228
Sharp, sharper than scissors,
Nay, than chisels. Lances
Into pain – it's waning.
Sparsely, as when fingers   232
Fence the heart, or – straining –
Teeth are reason-sifters
Onto lips' creed-murmur.
O the air's all filters: 236
Creativity's sieves are
Not more filtery (silt is
Wet, but dry – infinity).
Filt'rier than Goethe's   240
Eye or Rilke's hearing . . .
(God but *whispers*, fearing
His own mightiness . . .) It's
Not more filterous solely –   244
Surely – than the hour of
Judgment . . .
                Ache of backbone,
Reaping: why give birth, then?
Tread the whole no-harvest,   248
Whole no-yield, of height. Best
Furrows need no oxen,
Need no ploughs . . .   From earth an
Excommunication.   252
And the fifth air: sound.

        IX
Thundering lungs of pigeons –
They are here-begotten!
O the air is droning,   256
Drony, droninger than

New Year tunes, or axe-drone
Hewing into oak-roots.
How the air is drony,   260
Droning, droninger than

New-fall'n sorrow, monarchs'
Thank-yous, more than sonorous
Hail on tin, more droning   264
Still than roll of stone or
Trove in national folksong,
Big-mouthed, unforgotten.
Surging warbler-gullets'   268
Thunder – here-begotten!
Lachreous, cupreous, clangorous.
Move through this, melodious:
Snowstorm-Theologian-   272
John's intoning drone. A
Palate's vault? Or turtle-
Shell of lyre lap-rounded?
Drone – strong as the warring   276
Don, more strong than scaffolds'
Mowing. Over curvings
Frighteninger than mountains':
Curves of sound – like glebes in   280
Thebes the no-man-founded.
Seven – the layers and ripples!
Seven – heilige Sieben!
Seven, ground of the lyre,   284
Seven, ground of all being.

Since the lyre's foundation's
Seven, the world's foundation's
Lyric. Thus the Theban   288
Glebes could glide to lyre-string
Tones. O yet in body's
Cauldron – "light as feathers!"
Age-old loss of body   292
Through the ear. Whoever
Turns to ear will be sheer
Spirit. Leave the letters
To the secular. Do we   296
Move through sound, or sheerest
Hearing? Dream's pre-tuning.
Ecstasy's pre-fever.

Drumming, more than mainsail's   300
Equinoctial headwind,
More than crack of cranium
Epileptic, famine
Ventral. Not more humming   304
Solely than the paschal
Sepulchre . . .

      X
             Droningly, more and more –
Lulls of power, intermittences,
Mobiler even than motion these   308
Lulls and pauses and breathing-gaps
– Grain-locomotives that pause to gasp.
Alternation of all the best
Lurings as though from deities: 312
Air alternates with more-than-air!
And – not to call them sensuous –
Lulls: transferrals, like changing trains,
Leaving the slow for the interspace –   316
Lulls, little halts along the ways,
Halts of the heart when the lung gives off
'Okh!' in half-stoppages of breath,
Kin to a fish's sufferings: 320
Lulls – interrupting, cutting off
Current, or vapour abruptly thinned,
Lulls and hiatuses, sundering
Pulse – but is this intelligible?   324
Lulls are a lie, there's a spasm of – see –
Breath . . . It's the chasm unfathomable:

Lung, caught off guard by eternity,
Lung in the endless. Not all would say   328
That. There are some who call it 'death'.
Separation – from the earth.
Air is finished. Firmament.

      XI
Music straining like a rack!   332
Sighs, forever vain!
Over. All the suffering's done,
In the gaseous sack
That's the air. Now, compass-free,   336
Into heights! A child

Like (and into) father. Trice
When heredity
Really – truly – tells. A firm   340
Road of brakeless heads!
How they're severed: fully torn
Sinciput from shed
Shoulders. Ground of groundless beings!   344
Hermes, ours indeed!
Here's the full and accurate
Feeling of a head
Borne on wings. There's no two ways –   348
Only one – and straight.
Sucked up into space, the spire
Drops its church – to days.
Not in one day – slowlier! –   352
God – through the obscure
Trash of feeling. Like a shot
Into heights. To – not
Realms of souls, but full-enthroned   356
Brow. The limit? Learn:
In that hour when Gothic tower
Catches up its own
Spire, and – having counted all   360
Numbers – hosts of them! –
In that hour when Gothic spire
Catches up its own
Meaning . . .   364

The Metres

My translation reflects Tsvetaeva's metres wherever possible (rhyme is
included more randomly). Thus: Part I alternates lines of two
amphibrachs with lines of two amphibrachs plus a single stress
[./. ./. - ./. ./. /]; Parts II, III, IV and V alternate trochaic tetrameters
with the same minus final unstressed syllable [/ . / . / . . - / . / . /];
Part VI alternates lines of three dactyls plus one trochee with lines of one
dactyl plus one trochee [/ . . / . . / . . / . - / . . / .]; Parts VII, VIII and
IX are in trochaic trimeters [/ . / . / .]; Part X is in variable lines of,
mainly, dactyl plus trochee plus dactyl [/ . . / . / . .] ; Part XI alternates
lines of two trochees plus a dactyl with lines of two trochees plus a single
stress [/ . / . / . . - / . / . /].

Summary of the poem

In the following summary of the bare narrative of the poem, or 'poema', 'she' is its speaker; in brackets are my occasional comments.

The Poem narrates a spiritual journey, from the heaviness of the body and the earth, up through seven levels of air – which become ever lighter and sparser – through a shedding of all weight and, finally, even of breath, to an ecstatic ultimate condition beyond breathing. Although the poet acknowledges that others may call this 'death', for her it is something else: an experience of infinity and power.

I

She senses someone silently waiting for her, a passionately desired guest* at the door (like a lover, but who is to be her otherworldly guide). Like a hostess flashing a glance across the servants' heads, she has sent him her welcoming sign. But commonplace emotions have no place in this scene of intensely, almost mortally, mounting desire for a union between other-world and this-world. Somehow the door does open and . . .

II

. . . it feels absolutely right to be outside in the dark with the shadowy guest. Emotions were renounced, now colours and the pleasures of ordinary perception are renounced. (She is moving into a dimension where the spiritual and mental are more powerful and more absorbing than emotional or perceptual experience.) Though at first she begs her spectral companion to come down a little and be joined with her, it is she who slightly rises up, to him; her footsteps now become silent.

III

Again the change feels right and natural: perfect, in fact, like fully achieved rhyme or rhythm. She is in the new element, air, which turns out to be difficult to move in, offering resistance and a challenge which she is glad to meet. This 'first air'* is 'dense'. Again, she asks her invisible conductor to yield a little, this time by very slightly breathing, but again he does not and she, instead, gives up breathing. (After this, the companion is not mentioned – his task as initial guide presumably fulfilled.)

IV

The untrammelled climb in air is compared to the removal of quarantine from Moscow when a typhus epidemic is over, and to the breakdown of the Pale of Settlement.

V

Addressing the mother of a pilot (perhaps of Lindbergh),* she asks why, being himself already air, he should need any apparatus in order to fly. A course in flying is death / Death is a course in flying – and is a new kind of flight.

VI
Praise for the one (a god?) who made holes in the world for us to go up through. She is victorious, has risen up.

VII
In this part (which Mikhail Gasparov* calls the 'brightest'), she describes the wonderful sensation of the air now attained, and of rising upwards through it: it is light, rare, slippery, watery and – like water – reductive of weight. (Gasparov notes verticality in many images.) She ascends not like some fabulous naiad, but truly physically, like a peasant woman who slides into a pool; and according to laws as real as Archimedes'. This leads to the 'third air' which is 'empty' –

VII
– it is sparse and painfully sharp, full of well-placed gaps, and resembling a sieve, as do great creative minds (i.e. they filter out all that is irrelevant to the subtlest of messages?); only the Last Judgment would separate things out more finely. This thought leads to speculation on the futility of human labour. Renounce earthly things altogether, she concludes.

IX
The 'fifth air' is sheer 'sound' and is compared to bird-song and birds' heartbeats, to forest felling, kingly speeches, hail-falls, folk-music, the Book of Revelation, an ancient lyre, scaffolds (the swish of the axe?), mountains (the wind there?), and the building of the city of Thebes; the mystical number seven is celebrated. Now the stage reached is the one preceding the supreme ecstasy and its sound is like that of sailing at the equinox or of the cracking head before an epileptic fit. Only Christ's tomb would be more resonant.

X
Now the air is largely not-air – it is all lulls, gaps and pauses. Finally giving up all breathing, she attains what others might call 'death': the end of air.

XI
Breathing and its products, such as music, are over, and she is free – to speed upward (for ever?), unhindered. Here the condition is that of winged heads which have shed their bodies, and of spires which have

shed their churches. The 'brow' (intellect?) predominates. Still to come is the moment when 'the spire catches up with its own meaning'; the Poem ends with a row of dots.

Notes to the Summary

I: Although it is not stated, critics and readers generally assume that the otherworldly guest is Rilke, who died at the very end of 1926 and with whom Tsvetaeva had been corresponding during that year, hoping to meet him.

III: Below is a note on the numbered levels of air.

V: On May 21 and 22 1927, Charles Augustus Lindbergh became the first person to cross the Atlantic in a solo, uninterrupted flight. At the end of the manuscript of 'Poem of the Air', Tsvetaeva noted: 'Meudon. In the days of Lindbergh'.

VII: Mikhail Gasparov's article explicating 'Poema vozdukha' is published in his *Izbrannye stat'i*, Moscow, 1995, pp. 259-74.

Numbered levels of air.

There are seven airs, or levels of air. Tsvetaeva mentions the 'first', the 'third' and the 'fifth', and she celebrates the 'number seven'. Part III of the Poem describes the first (dense) air. Part VII may be about the unnamed second (watery) air. The opening part of VIII describes the third (empty, sharp) air. The second part of VIII perhaps describes the fourth (sieve-like) air. IX evokes the fifth air, which is 'sound'. X – the unnamed sixth air, which is full of gaps. According to Gasparov, the seventh air is reached at the end of (what I call) Part X. Then, in XI, what is reached is, it seems, a final (though not static) stage of 'no air'. [In Russian the words Tsvetaeva uses to describe the three airs which she mentions all have the same vowel and all are monosyllabic: the first is ГУСТ (gust): thick, dense; the third is ПУСТ (pust): empty; the fifth is ЗВУК (zvuk): sound (noun).]

Stages of the spiritual journey.

Gasparov entitles the Poem's parts as follows, identifying them differently from how I do, and numbering them 1-8; for ease of reference, I here use my own numbering (Tsvetaeva did not number the Parts of her Poem):

1	'Prologue: Earth'	Part I – 'Door'
2	'Leaving the Earth'	Part II – 'Footstep'
		Part III – 'Breath'
		Parts IV, V, VI – 'Flight'
3	'Overcoming the Air'	Part VII – 'The Wet'
		Part VIII – 'The Dry'
		Parts IX, X – 'The Sounding'
4	'Epilogue: Sky'	Part XI – 'Infinity'

Diana Burgin writes that 'the literal contents of *Poema vozdukha* trace a poet's creative odyssey, or spiritual progress, from inside her earthly dwelling to realization of her infinite creative self. She is accompanied on her journey (flight) by her Poet-Other, who has recently died, and whose spirit, she believes, has come back for her. The poet's flight proceeds in ten stages, and at the end of each she has attained a new, spiritually and creatively higher location . . . ' (See note to line 378 below.)

Notes

To line 2 The first nail hammered into some artistic construction, or into a coffin?

8 I have added 'cue'.

20 In the original: 'of a birch tree'.

23 Many enter my house, but the one important one does not enter.

24 All commentators take the guest to be Rilke (see above, note to summary of part I).

35 Optina pustyn' is a well-known monastery, to which many (including Dostoevsky) made pilgrimages; here a symbol of renunciation of pleasure.

38 fellah – a poor peasant, in Egypt.

48 One edition has 'strastei' (passions), another 'smertei' (deaths); I am following the latter.

50 'Pol plyl': the floor floated. 'Pol' is a homonym, also meaning 'sex'; Gasparov thinks Tsvetaeva intends both meanings.

80 She is walking with him but, as he is a ghost, his footstep makes no sound; only hers can be heard. This single audible step is not that of two people (married, or in some other – e.g. conventionally romantic – pairing), i.e. not a step so well synchronised that it *sounds* like only one step – it really *is* that of only one person and thus betrays the existential loneliness of every one of us so long as we are 'enfleshed'. She longs for the disparity between her step and his to be removed, and hopes to remove it by getting him to 'descend by just an inch', coming closer to the living – at least just down to the highest level of their world, that of the thinkers. Instead, presumably by virtue of her strong desire, it is she who goes up a level and their steps are equalised not by his step sounding but by hers becoming silent.

85-6 The bracketed piece is obscure. A possible reading is: holes, in shoes or clothes, are not shameful, what is shameful is the need we feel to patch them. This could be taken as a declaration of simplicity and unconventionality.

91 'i uslyshana' – could mean 'even if I'm heard', but the alternative ('and I'm heard') makes more sense, especially in its echoing form in line 131.

97 'Khodiachie / Istiny . . .' : pedestrian truths. Rather like the English, this means 'commonplace, hackneyed truths', but the root 'khod-' is more obviously the word for 'walk' than is 'ped-' in 'pedestrian'. Leave the world where people walk, enter the one where you fly.

107-8 No quotation marks here in the original.

113 'hence' is added by me.

115 'Emanation . . .' – see note to line 212.

124-5 and **126** No quotation marks here in the original.

125 Is the river Dnieper swollen, i.e. is the ice about to break: is my release about to take place? (I have left the Russian form of 'Dnieper', *viz*. 'Dnepr', in order to have a monosyllable here.)

125-6 Both Gasparov and Burgin connect this with David the Psalmist singing in the wilderness, wanting God to hear him.

129-30 'by all who here / Live' (na vsesushchie / Vse) – I think this means: 'the phrase "by (as much as) the length of a breath" is equivalent (in this unutterably strange context) to: "by as much as the existence of everyone in the world"; i.e. if a ghost were to take even *one* breath of air this would be equivalent to a change in the entire make-up of human existence.

141 The mother of any pilot? Or, probably, of Lindbergh, who in 1927 (the year of the writing of *Poem of the Air*) was famous for having flown across the Atlantic alone and non-stop?

141-2 vozdukhobor (air's fighter) must suggest 'dukhobor' (spirit's fighter), member of a morally strict religious movement which arose in the eighteenth century in Russia and which was strongly against the ritual and dogma of the Orthodox Church.

147 The Russian for 'lung', legkoe, is also the adjective 'light'. In translating this word I have put side by side both meanings – he is lung and he is light.

148-9 Here too I have sought to offer the two meanings of a single Russian phrase: mertvaia petlia means both a 'dead noose' and the 'loop' in 'looping the loop'.

155 'Kurs vozdukhoplavaniia – smert'' – could conceivably be translated the other way round, i.e. 'A course in air-floating is /leads to?/ death'.

160 'and *you*' – perhaps Lindbergh.

172 'mortal' – I have used this word for the sake of euphony; the original has 'dead' (mertvyi).

193 Hermes: Greek god of, among other things, trade, messages and travel.

196 Iris: Greek goddess of the rainbow.

198 'Shemákhan' calls to mind the beautiful maiden in Pushkin's 'Golden Cockerel' who appears to Tsar Dadon at the peak of his quest and seduces and ruins him; 'silk' – Tsvetaeva writes 'kashemir', which is used in Russian for any fine cloth.

200 'perst'' – an old and rare word for 'dust'.

200-201 Like 'first . . . de / weights you . . . ' three lines later, what is being described is a progressive increase in weightlessness.

207 I have added 'daughter'; the Russian has 'baba' (peasant woman) – and so had to leave out 'vegetable garden'.

208-9 Gasparov suggests that the reference to the law of Archimedes is here related both to healing through the movement of water (as in St John 5: 2-4) and to suicide by drowning (op. cit. 269).

212 'Liberation from the earth' (Zemleotpushchenie); see also 'Emanation of the earth' (Zemleizluchenie), line 115; at the end of part VIII, the idea of excommunication from the earth (Zemleotluchenie); and, at end of part 10, that of severance from the earth (Zemleotsechenie).

214 'greige': grey colour; cp. French 'grège', like which it is to be pronounced.

225 What non-poets call waking up, poets call falling asleep, because to them sleep or semi-sleep is full of poetic insights. Gasparov writes that to fall asleep means, for Tsvetaeva, to wake up to post-mortal life (op. cit. 269).

226-7 The abrupt and disconnected quality of dreaming or half-dreaming may also describe *Poem of the Air* itself. According to Burgin, the Poem is 'made of air' (being full of significant gaps).

233-5 The list of examples of creative or exhilarating sparseness ends with the spaces between teeth when they narrowly allow rational argument to filter through onto the statement of faith uttered by the lips (not enough to disturb it?).

239-40 Mud or earth cannot be sieved but the infinite is 'sieved', being dry.

242 'God creates at half-power, fearing himself' (Gasparov, op. cit. 270).

255 Birdsong (says Tsvetaeva) originates in the upper air.

265 I have put 'stone' instead of 'clod' (glyba) for the sake of its vowel.

266-7 Alexandra Smith writes (in 'Surpassing Acmeism? The Lost Key to Cvetaeva's "Poem of the Air"', in *Russian Literature* / North Holland / XLV, 1999, pages 209-22) of 'the overpowering sound of a people's choir which is presented as multi-mouthed national memory' (p. 217).

272 '. . . And James the Son of Zebedee, and John the brother of James; and he surnamed them Boanerges, which is, the sons of thunder' (St Mark 3:17). Tsvetaeva writes, however, 'v'iugo-Bogoslova', i.e. 'blizzard (or snowstorm)-theologian', thus insisting on snow rather than thunder and suggesting the author of the Book of Revelation.

276-7 'warring / Don . . .' – this recalls both Grand Duke Dmitri's defeat of Mamai of the Golden Horde, in the battle of Kulikovo on the upper Don in 1380 (the first important victory over the Mongols who occupied Russia for two centuries), and battles between Red and White armies in the Civil War which followed the October 1917 Revolution..

278 'mowing' (v zhatvu) may echo 'Zhnut golovy kak kolos'ia' (they mow heads like ears of corn) in the 12th-century 'Tale of Prince Igor'.

283 'heilige Sieben' [holy seven] – seven is a magical number in many myths, and was Tsvetaeva's favourite number. Since she makes so much of the image of a sieve, it is relevant that 'Sieb' (with dative plural Sieben) is the German for 'sieve'.

284 Hermes made the first seven-stringed lyre, from the shell of a tortoise.

289 'Theban / Glebes' – The ancient city of Thebes was partly built by Amphion and Zethus, sons of Zeus, Amphion's stones moving gently into place in response to the sound of his lyre.

297 'move through' – both meanings of 'through' ('penetrating' and 'because of') are required here.

301 Winds are especially strong at the two equinoxes.

310 'grain-locomotives' – trains on which speculators from the towns ('known as 'meshochniki' [bagmen]) travelled into the countryside at great risk to their lives, to exchange urban objects for flour, during the period of War Communism (1918-1921).

313 The alternation of air with no-air (the absence of air). She is gradually moving out of the air.

332 Music is something produced in – or by – air, with effort and not with that absolute naturalness towards which this spiritual journey is leading.

337-8 'Ditia v ottsa' means: 'the child takes after (is like) the father', but the context suggests also the literal meaning of these words: 'child *into* father' (i.e. she moves upward into, as it were, God).

340 The original reads: 'skaz – y – va – iet – sia', thus dividing a single word into its five syllables.

357 'Brow' – Thought, or intellect, goes beyond flesh *and* spirit.

361 'numbers', or ciphers – Diana Burgin's interpretation of *Poem of the Air* in her essay 'On Magics, Airs and Kaballas, of Tarot Cards and Tsars' (in her forthcoming book *'Ottiagotela': russkie zhenshchiny vne obydennoi zhizni*, Inapress, St Petersburg, 2002) makes substantial reference to the theory and magic of numbers.

Text

The text from which this translation was made is that published in ML Gasparov, *Izbrannye stat'i*, 'Novoe literaturnoe obozrenie', Moscow, 1995, pages 259-262; i.e. the text published in *Volia Rossii*, 1930, No. 1, pages 16-26 (the only publication of the *Poema* in Tsvetaeva's lifetime).

Acknowledgments

I am grateful to Mikhail Gasparov for his attentive commentary on this translation, which led to my being able to make numerous improvements, and for his help with several of my Explanatory Notes.

I also thank Diana Burgin for sharing with me her ideas about this Poem; and I thank Irma Kudrova, Alexandra Smith, Daniel Weissbort and David Wolfe for their encouragement – much needed in the task of translating something as hard and as strange as 'Poem of the Air'!

Climbing The Air

> *[a respectful abbreviation of Marina Tsvetaeva's
> 'Poem of the Air']*

I

Who is that waiting
outside, silent?
(First nail hammered
in, by a couplet.)
Behind the alerted
door, like a pine-wreath,

the guest, certain
of welcome (my signal
flashed like red lightning
over the shadows of

visitors, servants,
to him: 'Come in!')

My heart is pounding
like birch-trees falling –
axed, crashing;
like the evils flapping
their bird-wings out of
Pandora's casket.

He'll never come in
(though he's got the key!)
– he won't even knock.
He listens: I'm listening.
Ah, is he a ghost?
But feelings aren't needed.

Unemotional
sinews yearn,
the floor – floats,
the door – leaps
into my hand, the
dark recedes.

II

And now it's becoming unutterably natural
to be out here in the dark with somebody
garden-surpassing, invisible, ghostly,
full of forbearance, walking behind me
under the high sky with its sound of
foam lapping at night-time bridges;
natural to give up longing for colours
for ever: my retina's finished its sifting
of this world (beauty) from your world – henceforth
the sole desired one. We're two, and yet only
my step is heard. Come down, please, be audible!
No. I go up, by an inch, to be soundless.

III

Perfection of rhyme and of rhythm, Columbus'
view of a new earth: Air! – It's as bouncy
as woman's bosom to torturer or infant.
Taut and elastic this air, resistant –

I'm fighting through it, from now on fearless
as Hercules. This is the first air, thick.
But you – come down if only a breath's length,
please, give in to the living a little!
No. Instead I go up by an inch,
no longer breathing.

IV
Breathing was torment,
lung – a stone cauldron.
Air's gates have opened,
all its walls fallen.

V
Airmen don't need apparatus – the sky is their body!
Pilots don't need any aeroplanes – look, they're already
made up of lightness, height and the boundless!
Fame brings their grounding, alas! But in unfamed
flight they're achillean, groundless.

VI
Now to give thanks – for the rifts in the stiff world
which let us escape it.
Thanks – to the holes in the roof where we hurl down
ballast. Unweighted . . .

VII
Light, rare, ludic, slippery, streamy
air like fleet elusive fishes,
air like speeding hounds through oat-fields,
not to be caught nor held, it slides
like sliced onion, like lime-bark lining,
like bamboo curtains that veil pagodas
(Hermes ought to wear fins, not winglets),
showers all shimmery, paths releasing
dance – like entering water: weightless.
No more earth: the third air's empty.

VIII
Grey, grey, grey. A sweepnet
streaked with shapes, an aged hair-plait
striped with greige.

Spare, sparse, like spikes of millet
shaved by drought. Sharp as a comb's teeth

raking dog hair, spaced as coppiced

copses, scant as
linklessness when you're waking up
('falling asleep' is what I'd call it).

This air is sharper than scissors, chisels,
lances, scalpels – it's fiercer, sharper
than teeth clenched against chant of credos.

This air is a sieve, a filter, fine as
Goethe's eye or Rilke's hearing,
able to just-catch God's thin whisper.

Why have harvests? Choose the no-harvest!
Why have the ache of reaping? Why have
furrows, oxen, ploughing – give

all of it up! Prefer the no-ox,
no-plough. Finish with earth and the earthly.
Here's the fifth air: pure sound.

IX
As axes drone,
so this air drones,
as monarchs drone
their fine monotones,
or as hail drones
on tin, or the folk
drone their poems,
or John the Divine
drones, intones . . .

like sounds of scaffolds,
sounds of mountains,
glebes of Thebes
inspired by lyre-sounds . . .
Entering hearing's
like entering water:
absolute weight-loss.
The seventh air
is the herald of rapture.

X
And now there are only the gaps, intermittences,

increase of space
between movements of power,
and now there's the alternating and weaving
of something-better-than-air with air,
ecstatic stoppings of breath like a caught fish,
like cuts to electric current, hiatuses,
sunderings of pulse, and at last an end
to lung-work. Why do you call it 'death'?
It's separation, discovery,
firmament.

XI

An end to the pains
of music, of breathing.
Wing-borne heads,
ripped from futile
shoulders, dash
along, unbraked.
The Gothic spire
has dropped its church.
And – beyond?
That's the hour
when meaning's
over-
taken
by

Note: I wrote the above verses immediately after completing the first draft of my
translation of 'Poem of the Air'. They are meant neither as an alternative
translation nor as an independent poem. I offer them as a possible help to
reading Tsvetaeva's rather difficult work and as the sigh of relief that they
were to me upon finishing the translation.

Aleksandr Vvedensky

Russia

Translated by Eugene Ostashevsky

Eugene Ostashevsky *is preparing an anthology of OBERIU writings in translation. His own poetry chapbook* The Off-Centaur *was recently published in New York and California by the editors of* The Germ.

Eugene Ostashevsky writes: Aleksandr Vvedensky was born in 1904 in St Petersburg. In the mid-twenties he worked as a researcher of trans-sense language (*zaum*) with some of the more radical Futurists at the State Institute of Artistic Culture (GINHOOK), headed by Kazimir Malevich. It was then that he and the poet Daniil Kharms put together their own literary group, which, incorporating the poet Nikolai Zabolotsky, became known as the Union of Real Art, or OBERIU. The group also had theatrical and film-making sections; most of its members made a living as children's writers. On January 24, 1928, OBERIU carried out its most ambitious performance, 'Three Left-Wing Hours', in which poetry reading alternated with circus acts, a found-footage film and Kharms's absurdist play *Elizaveta Bam*. Soviet reviewers met the *oberiuty* with increasing hostility that culminated in accusations of aesthetic sabotage. In late 1931 Kharms and Vvedensky were arrested as part of a case against anti-Soviet trends in children's literature.

When they returned to Leningrad a year later, OBERIU as an organization was finished. What survived, albeit in total obscurity, was the informal philosophical circle composed of Kharms, Vvedensky, Zabolotsky (initially), the poet Nikolai Oleinikov and the philosophers Leonid Lipavsky and Iakov Druskin. The intensity of their creative exchange is attested by shared themes, concepts and even terminology. The political and intellectual climate of the thirties made their work unpublishable: members of the circle were among the first to write, as Russian has it, "for the drawer". Then the circle fell apart. In 1936 Vvedensky moved to Kharkov. Oleinikov was executed by firing squad in the Great Purge of 1937. Zabolotsky, by then estranged from the group, was imprisoned in 1938. Lipavsky fell in the first days of the war. Later in 1941, Vvedensky and Kharms, rendered politically unreliable by their previous arrest, were arrested again. Kharms died in a prison asylum during the blockade of Leningrad; Vvedensky died in a prison train headed east.

Most of the writings that we have by Kharms and Vvedensky are those saved by Iakov Druskin, the group's sole survivor. Certain by the

1960s that his friends were not coming back, Druskin started circulating their work in *samizdat*. In 1980, the underground Leningrad scholar Mikhail Meilakh published a Russian-language edition of Vvedensky's works in the States. In the poet's homeland, however, his writings first saw print only during *perestroika*, with an updated version of Meilakh's edition appearing in 1993, over fifty years after Vvedensky's death.

*

Vvedensky came out of Futurism but a Futurism that had found out it had no future. His work inverts Futurist attitudes: it is antimetaphorical and not metaphorical; it is private and not public; it breaks things up but doesn't rebuild them; its lyrical I is abstract, not vatic. "In poetry," Vvedensky said, "I am only a harbinger." Allowed a spasm of impressionistic criticism, one may say that his art, in its emphasis on reduction, looks forward to Celan as much as it does back to its antecedents.[1] In a late piece, Vvedensky asks us to "respect the poverty of language". In a period remarkable for its aural lushness, he cuts down the range of his rhymes, metres and other sound structures. Accounts of his readings invite contrast with the more histrionic scansion style we hear in the recordings of his contemporaries. He shirks the sensuousness of expression common to the best poetry of those days.

At the same time, his is very much a poetry of and about language. Refusing to distinguish between the "real world" and the words that describe it, Vvedensky posits a single plane where words are one with what they stand for, and where such word-thing-processes tend to obey linguistic rather than natural laws. His lines have grammatical rather than paradigmatic correctness. A striking "description" from his *Elegy* of 1940 proclaims: "The divine birds fly, / Their braids wave, / Their bathrobes glint like knitting needles." Birds don't have braids or bathrobes, nor do bathrobes glint, but, on the level of grammar in the broad sense of the term, the "description" is perfectly intelligible:

object x does x_1
its attribute y does y_1
its attribute z is like z_1.

Or, to give another example, one of the drowned men in 'The Meaning of the Sea', "on dull seaweed / hung his muscle to be laundered": it is clothing, not muscle, that gets laundered; clothes are hung not as they are washed but afterwards (although one *can* wash clothing by securing it in the surf); finally, nothing can be hung on seaweed. And yet still the grammar of the image is there: we are dealing with nonsense sentences of the type "the magenta dog wrote on the yellow squirrel" and not "dog the wrote squirrel magenta on yellow."

What did Vvedensky think he was doing by means of such propositions? He was, as he himself once said, performing "a poetic critique of reason", casting doubt on the ontological classifications and hierarchies of everyday life. "I doubted that, for instance, house, cottage and tower come together under the concept of building. Perhaps the shoulder must be linked to the number four. I did it practically, in my poems, as a kind of proof."[2] The poet's substitution of words within grammatical structures was, at the same time, a critique of language: in demonstrating that language, as a grid through which we formulate the world, allows "nonrealistic" combinations that are somehow as convincing as the "realistic" ones, it undermined the apparent veracity of the latter. In the Soviet Union of the 1930s such a critique of linguistic reference had not only a metaphysical but also a political dimension. "What I write isn't *zaum*," Vvedensky once said, staring at a newspaper; "this article is *zaum*."

The relationship between Vvedensky's "poetic critique of reason" and Kant is extremely complicated. While much of modernism strives to re-apprehend things-in-themselves by somehow breaking through to the other side of our perceptual schemata – this I think is the philosophical meaning of its emphasis on intuition – Vvedensky directs intuition at language in order to render the world of things-in-themselves as again ungraspable. "I convinced myself that the old relations are false, but I don't know what the new ones must be like. I don't even know whether they should form one system or many. And so my basic sensation is that of disjointedness of time and fragmentation of space. Since this contradicts reason, it means that reason does not understand the world." While Vvedensky's critique introduces a chasm between us and the world, his key concept of not understanding bridges that chasm. Rather than just a state of epistemological privation, Vvedensky's not understanding can serve as an instrument for a perception of sorts. In this, it is quite similar to the *docta ignorantia* of Nicholas of Cusa. To summarize the poet's argument in *The Gray Notebook*, only by abandoning understanding can one begin to "understand", and yet this secondary understanding is not so much an understanding of things as it is a "broad not-understanding" of them – an understanding of them as not understandable. "Any person who has not understood time a little bit – and only one who has not understood it has understood it somewhat – must cease to understand everything that exists . . . Woe to us who are pondering time. But when this not-understanding expands, it will become clear to you and me that there is no woe, nor us, nor pondering, nor time."[3]

Despite Vvedensky's emphasis on not-understanding, despite the fact that his syntactic substitution erects "non-realistic" combinations of objects and processes, his poetry cannot be called meaningless or even chaotic. This poetry erects a world that is complicated metaphysically and mythologically: a world peopled by human beings, animals, spirits and abstract concepts. It is an unfixed world, a world in search of an *event*, a world that longs for it. It is a world whose essence is conversation, or rather conversation with oneself: in effect, consciousness. As in consciousness, nothing in this world is quite complete. Its entities are – in an image Vvedensky himself employed – waves, less things than processes. The discontinuous character of such processes refutes the normative understanding of time and, with it, of self-identity, giving the lie to what was once called the metaphysics of presence. Perhaps this is why Vvedensky's poetry is so tragic.

*

The two translations being published here are 'The Meaning of the Sea' and 'The Witness and the Rat'. The companion piece to the former, entitled 'The Demise of the Sea', has appeared in my translation in *Fence* (Fall/Winter 2002; 4:2: 161-66), and is available online at www.fencemag.com. The first and last lines of 'The Demise of the Sea' proclaim that the sea means nothing.

The futurist Velimir Khlebnikov, whom the OBERIU saw as a close ancestor, called time the measure of the world (*vremia mera mira*). Sea in Russian is *more*, and when, in 'The Meaning of the Sea', Vvedensky says that time, sea and the dream are one, he is implicitly equating the world with all three. One of the many eschatological motifs in this poem is that of time flowing backwards. A classic problem in the psychology of dreaming is how the dream narrative can lead up to and incorporate the dream's external interruption. I am dreaming, for instance, that I am taken out to be shot, the soldiers lower their rifles, the officer cries "fire" and – I am jarred awake as the front door slams. For the Russian philosopher Pavel Florensky (1882-1937), this phenomenon attests to the backward flow of dreamtime: I awaken because I hear the door slam, but in the brief moment of my awakening I dream a dream that equips the sound with a sequence of events seeming to precede it. For Florensky, the backwards flow of dreamtime is also why we sometimes know what will happen in a dream "before" it happens.[4] Thus the eschatological "time backwards" motif in 'The Meaning of the Sea' may be linked with the foreknowledge of murder in 'The Witness and the Rat'.

In his obsession with nineteenth-century Russian literature, Vvedensky is very much a St Petersburg poet. The perceptive scholar Anna Gerasimova, in an article dedicated to Vvedensky's relationship with Pushkin, likens the former's composition technique to automatic writing. Since Vvedensky, like all Russian intelligentsia, absorbed Pushkin's poetry in early childhood, the unrestricted character of his composition process brings Pushkinian motifs and vocabulary to the surface, albeit in a scrambled manner.[5] No Pushkinian piece is as central to Petersburg literature and, in particular, to Vvedensky's oeuvre, as 'The Bronze Horseman'.[6] Eugene, the protagonist of this poem, goes mad as the result of the 1824 flood, and imagines himself pursued by the equestrian statue of Peter the Great on Senate Square. Vvedensky's sea, as an eschatological principle, is the direct descendant of Pushkin's flood, a flood, incidentally, that starts with the river flowing backward. 'The Witness and the Rat', on the other hand, throws another major nineteenth-century poet into the equation, and this is Goethe. The form of the dramatic poem as developed by Vvedensky – with its metaphysical concerns, a large, often occasional cast, quick changes of scenes – seems to hark back to *Faust*. The name Margarita in 'The Witness and the Rat' lends credence to this suspicion.

Notes

1   A 1958 statement by Paul Celan offers a striking parallel to Vvedensky's poetic axioms: "Poetry can no longer speak the language which many a willing ear still seems to expect from it. Its language has become more austere and factual; it distrusts the beautiful, and it attempts to be true. It is thus [. . .] a "grayer" language." Celan's program confronts the Holocaust whereas Vvedensky's, needless to say, does not. Still, both are also reacting to high modernism and in a not dissimilar manner. Celan's opposition of beauty and truth as criteria for aesthetic judgment, for instance, appears also in Vvedensky, who held that "one shouldn't speak of poems as beautiful or not beautiful, but as true or false." Druskin finds a parallel statement in Schoenberg. (Celan, "Reply to an Inquiry held by the Librairie Flinker, Paris." Quoted and translated by Leonard Olschener, "Anamnesis: Paul Celan's Translations of Poetry," in *Translating Tradition: Paul Celan in France*, ed. Benjamin Hollander, ACTS 1988; 8-9: 70).

2   This and subsequent statements by Vvedensky about his poetics: Leonid Lipavsky, "Razgovory"; Druskin, "Zvezda bessmyslitsy," "Stadii ponimania," in "'Sborische druzei, ostavlennykh sudboiu': 'Chinari' v tekstakh, dokumentakh i issledovaniakh" (S. l., 1998), 1: 174-253, 549-651. Excerpts from Druskin in my translation are forthcoming in *The Germ* (2003), 7.

3   "The Gray Notebook", as translated by Matvei Yankelevich in *New American Writing*, 20: 139-43, but with minor changes.

4   The Russian titles are *Znachenie moria* and *Ochevidets i krysa*.

5   Florensky, "Ikonostas" in *Sochinenia v 4-kh tomakh* (Moscow: Mysl, 1996), 2: 419-526. Boris Uspensky, *Etiudy o russkoi istorii* (St Petersburg: Azbuka, 2002), 9-76.

6   "*Bednyi vsadnik, ili Pushkin bez golovy.*" Available online at www.umka.ru/liter/950221.html.

The Meaning of the Sea

to make everything clear
live backwards
take walks in the woods
tearing hair
when you recognize fire
in a lamp a stove
say wherefore you yearn
fire ruler of the candle
what do you mean or not
where's the cabinet the pot
demons spiral like flies
over a piece of cake
these spirits displayed
legs arms and horns
juicy beasts war
lamps contort in sleep
babes in silence blow the trumpet
women cry on a pine-tree
the universal God stands
in the cemetery of the skies
the ideal horse walks
finally the forest comes
we look on in fear
we think it's fog
the forest growls and waves its arms
it feels discomfort boredom
it weakly whispers I'm a phantom
maybe later I'll be
fields stand near a hillock
holding fear on a platter
people montenegrins beasts
joyfully feast
impetuous the music plays
finns have fun
shepherds shepherdesses bark
barks are rowed across tables
here and there in the barks
mark the minutes' haloes
we are in the presence of fun
I said this right away
either the birth of a canyon

or the nuptials of cliffs
we will witness this feast
from this bench this trumpet
as the tambourines clatter
and flutter, spinning like the earth
skies will come and a battle
or we will come to be ourselves
goblets moved among moustaches
in the goblets flowers rose
and our thoughts were soaring
among curled plants
our thoughts our boats
our gods our aunts
our souls our breath
our goblets in them death
but we said, and yet
this rain is meaningless
we beg, pass the sign
the sign plays on water
the wise hills throw
into the stream all those who feasted
glasses flourish in the water
water homeland of the skies
after thinking we like corpses
showed to heaven our arses
sea time sleep are one
we will mutter sinking down
we packed our instruments
souls powders feet
stationed our monuments
lighted our pots
on the floor of the deep
we the host of drowned men
in debate with the number fifteen
will shadow-box and burn up
and yet years passed
fog passed and nonsense
some of us sank on the floor
like the board of a ship
another languishes
gnashes his wisdom teeth
another on dull seaweed
hung the laundry of his muscle
and blinks like the moon

when the wave swings
another said my foot
is the same as the floor
in sum all are discontented
left the water in a huff
the waves hummed in back
starting to work
ships hopped around
horses galloped in the fields
shots were evident and tears
sleep and death in the clouds
all the drowned men came out
scratched themselves before the sunset
and rode off on a carriage beam
some were rich some not
I said I see right away
the end will come anyway
a big vase is brought this way
with a flower and a cymbal
here's a vase that's clever
here's a candle snow
salt and mousetrap
for fun and pleasure
hello universal god
here I stand a bit sullied
glory be to heavens washed away
my oar memory and will

[1930]

The Witness and the Rat

HE.
Margarita open
the window for me quick.
Margarita speak
of fish and of beasts.
The shadow of the night descended,
light went out in the world.
Margarita the day is done,
the wind blows, the rooster sleeps.
Sleeps the eagle in the skies,
sleep the legumes in the woods,

the future coffins sleep,
the pine-trees, the firs, the oaks.
The warrior walks out towards disgrace,
the beaver walks out to rob and pillage,
and peering at tall stars
the hedgehog starts the count of nights.
Fish run up and down the river,
fish loiter in the seas,
and the starling softly holds
the dead temple in its hand.
And the blackbirds slightly sing
and the mournful lion roars.
God chases from afar
clouds onto our city
and the mournful lion roars.

HE.
We don't believe that we're asleep.
We don't believe that we are here.
We don't believe that we are sad.
We don't believe that we exist.

HE.
The cold illuminates the mountains,
the snowy pall of the great mountains,
and the horse beneath carpets
dives in the snow like a loon.
A co-ed rides on the carpets,
she is obscured by the moon.
A she-wolf glares at the horse,
saliva leaves her maw like drool.
The poor horseman, lazybones,
rides in the troika like a lackey,
enters a dark palisade
clutching a bone in his fist.
He hands his whip to the co-ed,
he hands his cane to the old lady.
Greeting each hour with a toast,
he caresses the bold bone.
And the co-ed stands all dusty
like a carriage.
She does not move her visage
from the unknown portrait. She glints.

He.
I was examining my thoughts.
I saw they had other forms.
I was measuring my emotions.
I found their close borders.
I was testing my body movements.
I determined their simple significance.
I was losing my benevolence.
I have no more concentration.
Those who guess will guess.
I have nothing left to guess.

He.
I will speak now.

As he speaks, a small room appears. Everything is cut apart into pieces. Where are you our world. You do not exist. And we do not exist. Upon the plates sit Petr Ivanovich Ivanovich Ivanovich, the co-ed, Grudetsky the steward, Stepanov-Peskov and four hundred and thirty-three Spaniards.

Enter Lisa or Margarita.

One or the other.
What do I see.
What is this, an infernal conclave.
It smells of fire and brimstone here.
Your necks are as if it were gunpowdery,
ears arms legs noses
and eyes. You're all so cataleptic.
For hours already it's been winter,
has murder happened here by any chance.

Grudetsky the Steward.
Margarita or Lisa
would you like some tea or a clock.

She (one or the other):
You're a brownnose, Grudetsky.
From the days of Czar on
you're Simon.
I ask you: has a murder taken place.

And after this music sounded for three hours.

Various waltzes and chorales.

In the meanwhile Kirillov managed to get married. But still he just wasn't content.

STEPANOV-PESKOV.
Murder. Don't speak so much of murder.
We still have not understood murder.
We still have not understood this word.
We still have not understood this deed.
We still have not understood this knife.

KOSTOMAROV, HISTORIAN.
Thirteen years.
Twelve years.
Fifteen years.
Sixteen years.
Everything around us is shrubbery.

GRIBOEDOV, WRITER.
What's there to talk about here,
he is a thief, that's clear.
Steep magic visions
visit my soul.
They promise me
unspoken sickly pleasures.
My head is spinning and I feel
as if I were a hamster in a wheel.
O otherworldly creatures get you hence,
I'm off to Georgia today like everyone else.

Four hundred and thirty-three Spaniards, pale and seated upon a plate, cried out inimicably and unanimously:

Let the murther begin.

And there the darkness of darkness happened. And Grudetsky murdered Stepanov-Peskov. But what's there to speak of, anyway.

They all ran into the civilian room and saw the following picture. Across the third table stood the following picture. Imagine a table and the following picture upon it.

> *Staring at the picture,*
> *Grudetsky grasped*
> *in his hand like a picture*
> *the bloody cutlass.*

Blood dripped in drops
and fell flat on the earth,
the earth revolved
and the planets rotated.
Stepanov-Peskov
lay flat on the floor
resembling an eagle
without socks or boots.
He lay barefoot
like wild rose confectionery.
This functionary
was stung by a bumblebee.
　Thereupon Lisa enters again and screams:

Aha, aha, didn't I say there was going to be a murder.

They all cried hush at her and urged her to shut up.

Quiet, Lisa. Lisa, quiet, quiet, you're one or the other.

Then He again started to speak.

We saw the unfortunate body,
it lay without motion and force.
Life in it grew scanter and scanter
due to the wild blow of the cutlass.
Its eyes closed shut like nutshells.
What do we humans know of death.
We can be neither beasts nor mountains,
nor fish nor birds nor clouds.
Maybe the country or sofas,
maybe clocks and phenomena,
volcanoes, the deep of the sea
have some inkling of it.
Beetles and mournful birds
that spiral under the firmament
in their modest shirts
for them death is a familiar event.

HE.
What is the hour.
The hours run. They run.

HE.
I noticed death.
I noticed time.

HE.
They run. They run.

HE.
Again the co-ed reappeared
like a noodle
and the student stooped over her
like a soul.
And the co-ed like a flower
achieved rest.
The swift troika sped away
to the east.

HE.
What is the hour.

HE.
The foliage stands in the forest like thunder.

HE.
Now I will speak.
The tired candle now
is tired of burning like a shoulder.
And yet the co-ed still commanded
o kiss me stephan over and over,
why don't you kiss my thighs,
why don't you give my gut a kiss.
Stephan now felt bereft of force,
and terribly he clamoured,
I cannot kiss you any longer,
I'm off to the university right now
to learn the discipline of science,
how to extract copper from metal,
how to fix electricity when broke,
how to spell bear,
and he declined then like a shoulder
without force upon the darling bed.

Then Kozlov came for his cure. He held loganberry in his hands and made faces. Future words rose before him which pronounced right then and there. But none of this was important. There was nothing important in any of this. What could have been important in this. Nothing.

Then Stepanov-Terskoy came. He was entirely feral. But he was not Stepanov-Peskov. Stepanov-Peskov got murdered. Let us not forget that. We must not forget that. Why should we forget that anyway.

A SCENE ON THE SIXTH FLOOR

FONTANOV.
For five years we've been together,
you and I, you and I,
like a barn owl and an owl,
like the river and the shore,
like the valley like the mountain.
You are co-ed as before,
your hair turns gray,
your female cheeks turn sallow
in all this time you haven't,
why should I lie, filled out.
Your scalp is showing through,
your sweetness is decrepit.
I used to think about the world,
about the glimmer of the spheres,
about waves and clouds
and now I'm old and weak.
I now direct my thought
at radishes and pork.
Was it a co-ed that I married
or an independent clothing designer.

MARGARITA OR LISA (NOW BECOME KATYA):
How do I live? My soul flies off
from a cloddy mouth. Fontanov,
you're pitiful and crude.
Your manhood, where is it?
I'll stand beside the open window.
Look at the massive undulation of the air.
Look we can see the neighbours' house.
Look, look, look, look all around us.
Look I clamber onto the windowsill,
I stand a branch on the windowsill.

FONTANOV.
Co-ed, wait for me.

SHE.
I stand a cup on the windowsill.

FONTANOV.
Co-ed, what's with you.

SHE.
I stand a candle on the windowsill.

FONTANOV.
Co-ed, you've lost your mind.

SHE.
I arrive.

It doesn't say anywhere here that she jumped out of the window, but she jumped out of the window. She fell down on rocks. And she died. Oh, it's so scary.

FONTANOV.
I will not hesitate
but follow her,
smash all the plates,
rip up the calendar.
I'll light lamps everywhere,
call for the steward
and take a portrait of Grudetsky
with me forever for the road.

Then music sounded for three hours.

HE.
Margarita quick
open the door,
the door to poetry is open,
Margarita speak
of sounds.
We hear the sounds of objects,
we chew music like fat.
Margarita for the sake of science

we don't believe that we're asleep,
we don't believe that we breathe,
we don't believe that we write,
we don't believe that we hear,
we don't believe that we are silent.

HE.
Night was rising in the sky.
The dull crescent like a soul
soared above the earth,
rustling in the thick reeds
fish ran up and down in the river
and the mournful lion roared.
Towns stood upright,
the beaver raced after prey.

HE.
I was losing my benevolence.

HE.
The inevitable years
came at us like herds.
Around us green shrubbery
undulated sleepily.
It was not much to look at.

HE.
We have nothing more to think with.

His head falls off.

[1931-1934]

Ludvík Kundera
Czech

Translated by Ian Hilton

Ludvík Kundera, *born in 1920 in Brno, is a poet, dramatist and translator of Brecht, Huchel, Arp, Kubin, Celan, Weiss, Trakl, Eluard, Apollinaire, etc. His editing and translating of works of Halas and Nezval helped to bring those Czech writers to a wider readership. Serious ill-health had allowed him an early return to Brno in 1944 from a forced-labour camp in Berlin-Spandau. After the war, his predilection for Dadaist and Surrealist avant-garde art and literature (he was a founding member of the neo-surrealist group Ra) attracted the attention of the cultural functionaries and the Seventies in particular proved a difficult period. The Velvet Revolution allowed Kundera the literary recognition long denied him and a collected edition of his works in seventeen volumes has been appearing since 1994 under the imprint of Atlantis, Brno. Versions of Kundera's verse have appeared in* MPT 5 & 35 *in the original series.*

Ian Hilton, *born in 1935, is a one-time editor of* Modern Languages *and author of* Peter Weiss: A Search for Affinities *(1970),* Peter Huchel: Plough a Lonely Furrow *(1986) and* Peter Weiss: Marat/Sade *(1990). He has written widely on contemporary German literature. His book on Kundera is due to be published later this year. His translations of poems by Heinz Czechowski appeared in* MPT 16.

Hruden*

Seven times in nineteen years
the pagan Slavs
tried to fit in
between December and January
mostly around the winter solstice
the thirteenth month
which they called *hruden*

An extra month
residual supernumerary additional
a time of bare frozen clumps of earth
A time for levelling
the inequalities of time
human
terrestrial
cosmic

As a final instalment
on this accumulated time
we are wishfully paying off debts
even today
to people and to time
not to mention the cosmos
ungrudgingly:
Harsh *hruden*!

* The thirteenth month in the lunar year of Slav mythology. In the Druid calendar
too there was a thirteenth month, R (Ruis for elder, the tree which holds its fruit
into what we know as December).

In memoriam

This summer
mother unexpectedly said:
"No, don't wish me to stay another winter,
I've been here already too, too long a time,
look…"
Shyly she looked
at father's photograph on the wall
and silently began to cross off
the names of those departed
in her address book.

Autumn
arched then in the blue sky
for its leave-taking.
Only now do we comprehend the happiness
of those bitter sweet
long years.

Three juicy pears

espied in the small hours
on the bare table on which
only the abstract moon shines:
still-life memory
of happy times
in your first pregnancy

when suddenly the world was wonderfully round
as if it had shed
all the usual thorns

Between continents

Tricky waters!
We have sailed out of the storms which
lasted the whole age,
have sought all kinds of sheltered spots
islets and spurs
and forever changing course
in accord with shifts of wind

Now the air is fresh and clear, and not so much
as a breeze ripples the Bering Straits, already
steadily northwards
continuous pieces of drift-ice
glide

From the spot where I'm standing, I can see
from continent to continent.
I call the third:
Farewell!

(which means: *Nazdar*.)

Ewa Lipska
Polish

Translated by Ryszard Reisner

Ewa Lipska *is one of Poland's leading poets, her debut associated with the 'New Wave' period of the late 60s. Her work is distinctive for its insight into personal relationships, the individual's philosophical place. Its distinct poetics obliges the reader to deconstruct the world about him.*

    Ryszard Reisner *is a translator of Polish literature who returned to Poland after spending many years in Australia. At present he lectures at the School of Translation, at the Adam Mickiewicz University, Poznan.*

2001

2001, dear Mrs Schubert, this isn't just the start
    of a new century, but also the size my
    imagination takes.
As you know, for some time now my fiction
has thought ill of me that I court reality,
allying myself with non-useful time.
Thus I am informing you now nears the dead
season which, as always, I spend on
the short-term list of those missing.

Children from My Poems

Children from my poems:
a small girl peeping at the nation
a six-year-old little boy
cheeks of wild strawberries
are all by now about forty.

Art's magic is not enough for them
so as to safely sail through a dream.
Battling bathroom scales. Tripping up on faith.

Best of all they'd go for group holidays.
Outside it is safer. Trainers are standing by.
Nurses. Psychotherapists. Priests.
Vaccinated in case of utopia.

But unexpectedly spring surfaces. Like an anagram.
Carte du jour day deepens. Flowering of roses.
And finally that commonplace we long for.
Garden-fresh lips.

During the Holidays

During the holidays it's possible at last
to unplug the phone.
If God comes to be born
Jadwiga next door will pop in.

I'm watching *Casablanca*
with the same as always
appetite for digression.

I'm having fun with loneliness.
With this, hot milk with honey.
My sixth finger on my hand
types out the symbols.

I won't write a thing any more.
The next part of the evening
is untouchable.

Shops with Pets

Shops with pets.
Camp for the interned
out of my childhood.

Guinea Pigs. Parrots. Canaries.
The sickly smell of captivity.
Scraps of events.

At home I spat depression out.
Antigone's she-cat didn't appear again.
Mousetraps at Verdun
and then the next part right up to
Auschwitz.

Didn't know how this would finish
when I reported for life.
As a volunteer.

The Point Is

The point is
to know if
from out our lips still labour
words words words
or only a stoney fountain
out of which slips a leaf.

Halina Poświatowska
Poland

Translated by Sarah Luczaj

Halina Poświatowska *was born in Poland in 1935. She suffered from a heart condition from childhood. She married a fellow sufferer and was widowed at the age of 26. In 1956 her first collection,* Idol Worship, *came out. In 1958 she travelled to the US for a life-saving operation, and stayed on against all odds to study philosophy at Smith. On her return she taught philosophy at The Jagiellonian University in Krakow, and published* Present Day *in 1963 and* Ode to Hands *in 1966. In 1967 she died during a heart operation in Warsaw.* One More Memory *was published in 1968.*

    Sarah Luczaj *is a British poet, born in 1970. Her work has appeared in many journals, including the* New Statesman, American Poetry Review *and* Cream City Review. *She has been living in Poland for the last five years where she works as a therapist and teacher. Her translations of Poświatowska have been widely published, and she is seeking a publisher for the collection* I carry my heart. *She has translated a haiku collection by Robert Naczas, and published a collection in English and Polish of her own work and that of Cecilia Woloch and Waclaw Turek,* This Line on the Map.

Venus

she was beautiful as stone
alabaster
with green veins
that throbbed with sleeping blood

half a hundred gods
on a cloud
clapped
as she walked
swaying her hips

and not even her head
no
and not even her mouth
a swollen tropical fruit
but her breasts – oh yes
she had such breasts
that you had to stand
and howl to the sky with delight

they were like brother moons
stolen from Saturn's sky
oval – raised
and Hephaestus who shod horses at the smithy
complained that she cheated on him.
Fool.

All My Deaths

how many times can you die of love
the first time it was the bitter taste of earth
bitter taste
tart flower
red carnation burning

second time – only the taste of space
white taste
cool wind
echo of wheels

third time fourth time fifth
I died routinely less exalted
the four walls of the room
and your sharp profile above me

the fire calls for food

the fire calls for food
for life-giving food
it needs to feed – on a body

so I bring it a heart
my hot heart
fire swallows it eagerly

then gambols round the town
but the town is all golden
it's not a town it's a star

Tadeusz Rózewicz

Poland

Translated by Adam Czerniawski

Tadeusz Rózewicz, *born in 1921 in Poland, is one of the most important poets of the twentieth century. His poetry, like that of his peers in the first post-World War Two generation (notably, Zbigniew Herbert, Miroslav Holub, Vasko Popa, Yehuda Amichai), has appeared quite frequently in magazines and in anthologies and is by now familiar to most readers of contemporary poetry.*

To mark the award to Rózewicz of the 2003 Premio Librex Montale in Milan, MPT *is recycling Adam Czerniawski's translation of 'Francis Bacon', taken from a selection,* Recycling *(translated by Tony Howard & Barbara Plebanek, introduced by Adam Czerniawski), also reviewed in the present issue of* MPT. *The Montale Prize citation includes the following: 'Rózewicz is a 'teacher without a school', whose 'naked poetry' epitomizes lyric writing for many post-War poets. Through his profound understanding and concern for the individual, he has created a poetry that speaks directly to the reader.'*

Adam Czerniawski *(see the present issue of* MPT *for a review of his Selected Poems) is our leading translator of Polish poetry. A frequent contributor to* MPT, *he has in addition published short stories, essays on poetry and philosophy, and more recently, his autobiography. Czerniawski, who taught philosophy in London and who has served as Translator in Residence at the British Centre for Literary Translation at the University of East Anglia, lives in Wales. His publications of Rózewicz's poetry date from 1969,* faces of anxiety *(Rapp & Whiting), since when he has published* Conversation with the Prince and Other Poems *(Anvil, 1982) and* They Came to See a Poet: Selected Poems of Tadeusz Rózewicz *(Anvil, 1991). He has also published translations of Rózewicz's plays (e.g.* the card index & other plays, *Calder & Boyars, 1969).*

Francis Bacon or Diego Velázquez in a Dentist's Chair

thirty years ago
I began treading on Bacon's toes

I searched for him in pubs galleries
butcher's shops
in newspaper albums photographs

I met him in the Kunsthistorisches Museum
in Vienna he was standing before the portrait

Infanta Margarita
Infantin Margarita Teresa in blauem Kleid[1]
Diego Rodriguez de Silva y Velázquez

I've got him I thought
but it wasn't him

after his death
after the departure of Francis Bacon
I placed him under a glass-jar
I wished to inspect the painter
from every side

taking into account
his natural tendency
to flee to vanish
to drink
to a shuffle
in time and space
from pub to pub
in the shape of a baroque *putto*
who's lost his hat
and a red sock
I had
to immobilise him

I spent several weeks
visiting the Tate Gallery
shutting myself in with him
consuming him with my eyes
I digested his terrible
meat-art copulating carcasses
shut in myself
I continued my dialogue
with Saturn absorbed in
eating his own children
the way of killing men and beasts is the same
I've seen it:
truckfuls of chopped-up men
who will not be saved
I wrote in 1945

under the influence of alcohol
Bacon became warm sociable

generous hospitable
stood champagne caviar
turned into an angel
with a wing dipped
in a beer-mug

most of my paintings – he would say –
are the work of a man
in a state of Anxiety

while painting a certain triptych
I helped myself to a drink
it only helped once
he mumbled
while painting
Lager Beer Lager Beer on glass
in 1962 I painted
a crucifixion
blind drunk at times
I hardly knew what I was doing
but this time it helped

Bacon achieved a transformation
of a crucified being
into hanging dead meat
got up from the table and said softly
yes of course we are meat
we are potentially carrion
whenever I am at a butcher's
I always think it astonishing
it's not me hanging on the hook
must be pure chance
Rembrandt Velázquez
well yes they believed in the resurrection
of bodies they prayed before painting sessions
while we play
modern art is a game
from Picasso onwards we all play
better or worse

have you seen Dürer's drawing
hands set in prayer
naturally they drank ate murdered
raped and tortured

but did believe in the resurrection of bodies
in life eternal

pity that . . . we . . .
he stopped and left no one knew
where
years passed
in my hunt for Bacon
I had help from Adam
poet translator who owns a *krótkopis*[2]
lives in London
and Norwich
(and hides in Delft)
on 12 June 1985
he wrote to me:
Dear Tadeusz
today I went to a huge Bacon exhibition
and thought you'd find it very
satisfying. I went reluctantly,
but have no regrets because these early chewed-up heads
are very effective
in their composition and pigmentation.
But the newer paintings
failed to convince me. As I've already told you
I'll be coming to Wroclaw (. . .)
(on the back a reproduction of Head IV 1948-1949)
But Adam
I can't tell
Bacon
He doesn't know Polish
I have no English
tell him my first book in 1947
was called *Anxiety*

I wrote: *hacked*
pink ideals
hang in slaughter-houses (. . .)

In 1956 I wrote:

the breathing meat
filled with blood
is still the food
for these perfect forms

they press so close around their spoil
that even silence does not penetrate
outside (. . .)

jeszcze oddychajace mieso
wypelnione krwia
jest pozywieniem
tych form doskonalych

we have both travelled
through a *Waste Land*

Bacon said he liked
looking at his paintings through glass

he even likes Rembrandt
behind glass
and is not bothered by chance viewers
reflected in the glass
who blur the image
and pass
I
hate pictures behind glass
I see myself there I remember once
noticing some Japanese
imposed on Mona Lisa's smile
they were very animated
Gioconda became fixed
in a glass coffin
after that encounter
I've never been to the Louvre
Gioconda smiled into her moustache
Bacon locked
Pope Innocent VI in a cage
then Innocent X
and Pius XII
The Infanta Margarita in a sky-blue dress
also a trial judge
all these personages started screaming

in 1994
on 14th February
St Valentine's Day
Francis Bacon appeared to me

on a glass screen
a round head an oval face
crumpled suit
I listen to Bacon
observe the portrait
the red face of Pope Innocent VI
I observe the Infanta's gentle little mouth

I tried to show
the landscape of the mouth cavity
but failed
Bacon was saying
in the mouth cavity I find
all the beautiful colours
in Diego Velázquez's paintings

glass muffles cries
I thought
Bacon was performing his operations
without anaesthetics
in the manner
of 18th-century dentists
Zahnextraktion[3]
they also cut boils ulcers carbuncles
it's not painful he would tell the Infanta
please open your mouth
unfortunately I have no anaesthetics
this will hurt
The Infanta in a gynaecological chair
Pope Innocent VI in an electric chair
Pope Pius XII in a waiting-room
Diego Velázquez
in a dentist's chair
friend 'George Dyer
in front of a mirror '– 1968
or on a lavatory seat . . .

I painted open mouths
Poussin's cry at Chantilly
and Eisenstein's cry on the steps
I painted
on a newspaper canvas
on reproductions of reproductions
in the corner of my studio

I had a pile of newsprint and photos
when I was young
I bought myself in Paris
a book on mouth-cavity diseases
Bacon was in conversation with David Sylvester
and paid no attention to me

I tried to provoke him
so asked whether he'd heard
about Sigmund Freud's rotting mouth cavity
towards the end of his life even the faithful
dog would run away from his master
couldn't stand the stench
why didn't you paint
a mouth roof eaten by a beautiful cancer
Bacon pretended not to hear

these models of yours rip
like flayed clouds
again you've placed Pope
Innocent whatever his number
in an oven
again you want to administer
"die Applizierung des Klistiers"[4]
to this dreamy well-mannered and well-painted
Infanta

again I thought of asking Adam
for help but Adam
smiled
ate a tuna sandwich
and drank Heineken[5]

Adam tell him
tell him
in English

that for me closed lips
are the most beautiful landscape

the lips of
The Unknown Florentine Woman
Ritratto d'Ignota
by Andrea della Robbia

and tell him also
that Franz Kafka feared open
mouths and teeth full of meat and gold crowns
this is in my play *The Trap*
which was performed in Norwich
pity Bacon didn't paint
a portrait of Eliot suffering
from the inflammation of the periosteum
his face wrapped in a check
shawl

now Adam was eating a smoked salmon
sandwich
Tadeusz! this is your third pint
I did warn you Guinness
is strong
ask Mr Bacon
whether he knows what Wondratschek said
about mouths and teeth
Adam put away his *krótkopis*

Wondratschek said
Der Mund ist plötzlich
der Zähne überdrüssig[6]

Bacon addressed the beer-mug
I never managed
to paint a smile
I always hoped
I would be able to paint lips
the way Monet painted
sunsets

but I painted
mouths full of cries and teeth

crucifixion? I repeat again
it's the only painting
I painted drunk
but neither drink nor drugs
helps you to paint
you just become more talkative
even garrulous

goodbye Francis Bacon
I have written a poem about you
I won't be searching for you any more
end fullstop
wait! there's still the poem's title
Francis Bacon
or
Diego Velázquez
in a dentist's chair
not bad eh
none of the Irish
or English critics
or poets
had thought up
such a title
perhaps I shouldn't have
added such a long long poem
to the title
but one gets talkative
even garrulous
over a pint

[*February 1994 –March 1995*]

Notes by AC:

1   The infant Margarita Teresa in a blue dress

2   *Krótkopis* (short-writer) is a neologism created by the translator, by analogy with *dlugopia* ('long-writer', meaning 'biro' or 'felt-pen'), as the title of his journal which was being serialised in a Warsaw monthly at the time.

3   tooth extraction

4   "the application of the enema"

5   Only because there was no better lager available.

6   The mouth is suddenly / tired of the teeth

Jan Twardowski
Polish

Translated by Ryzsard Reisner

Jan Twardowski *is a priest who lives in Warsaw and enjoys enormous popularity across three generations of readers. His output stretches back to* Anderson's Return *in 1937 but it was not until 1959 that his first book of poems after WWII came out for reasons of humility and lack of publication support. Another quarter of a century passed before Twardowski became a familiar name to the public with his simple formulations of the individual's fate in a world lost for love.*

nothing more

He wrote *My God* but crossed it out, for after all he had
as much *my* in mind, as I am a selfish piglet
he wrote *Humanity's God* but bit his tongue for he still
recalled angels and stones similar in snow to rabbits
finally he wrote simply *God*. Nothing more.
Still he wrote too much.

similarities

Love is similar only to love
truth similar only to truth
happiness similar to happiness
death similar to death
heart similar to heart
to a boy with a smile from ear to ear
similar to the one I once was

stop finally making fools of yourselves
after all even a God similar to God does not exist

so very small

Don't set out to be a great poet
don't set out to be a great painter

don't set out to be a great nobody
in a world too big
in a time too short
God is not ashamed of being so very small

Orsolya Karafiath
Hungary

Translated by David A Hill with Ildikó Juhász

Orsolya Karafiath *was born in Budapest in 1976. She has published one collection* (Lotte Lenya Titkos Eneke; *Noran 1999) from which these four poems are taken, and is a highly regarded member of the younger generation of poets.*

David A Hill *has published three collections of poetry:* The Eagles and The Sun *(1986)*, The Judas Tree *(1993) and* Singing to Seals *(1999). He has translated poetry from Italian (notably Bertolucci), French, Serbian (notably Kostic and Vukadinovic), and more recently from Hungarian, with his wife Ildikó Juhász. As a free-lance English teaching consultant based in Budapest since 1998, he has lectured throughout Europe and beyond on literature in general and poetry in particular, and teaches creative writing whenever the chance arises.*

Ildikó Juhász, *born 1968, is a free-lance English-Hungarian consultant. She has worked as an English language teacher in a famous grammar school in Budapest city centre, and as a translator of tv documentaries for a major local channel.*

Who gives the other one?

So this is what a woman's soul needs: to know
where my place is, who is the master of the house.
My love holds a power-demonstration,
God save the porcelain crockery.

Don't do it – I would whisper gently to him,
but I feel it's better if I'm silent now.
My chief virtue is quick adaptation,
I easily become the ideal subject of suffering.

Behold, here I stand. Neither drama, nor poetry.
My love calls me a frigid cunt,
my solid value-system seems to be crumbling.

(Sweet little pillar of salt – I think of myself,
while I stare at the slammed door.
Behold, here I stand. I lean my head against the wall.)

Note: The title of this poem comes from the Hungarian saying *Akkora pofont kapsz, hogy a fal adja a másikat!* which can be translated as "I'll give you such a big slap that the wall will give you the other one!", implying that the receiver's head will be turned round so much by the force of the slap, that their other cheek will be hit in the same way by the adjacent wall.

Dark colours

I face the sad fact:
sir, you have rejected me. In vain, then,
the tight skirt, the flirty décolleté –
your thoughts no longer roam my mountain-valleys.

Why would I list what you lose . . .
the sensual eating of delicacies, in which you can
no longer take part, an intellectual companion,
a kitchen-fairy, a good mother for your troubles?!

It is already certain that another man will be
the father of my children, my support in old age.
For us there is no happy, certain future.

Just face the sad fact:
emptied, barren days await you,
a dirty bachelor-flat without warmth . . .

Pot-shards

The gossip was spreading like wild fire:
there was word of screwing in the store-room,
they talked of a child, a crying wife.
They blamed the breaker of these sacred
and strong ties, me. Even in a good light
my characterisation started with stinking whore,
I learnt from late-night phone-calls
what a disgusting cow I am.

Not with a florist again, never.
For such a union there is no potting-soil.
Nobody should call me rose, dahlia,
May my love sprout in another's heart after this.

Why did the many flowery words have such an effect on me?!
My good reputation, if I had one, has now gone to pot.

Lotte Lenya's secret song

My voice is always different again:
new cues, new leading roles,
even if I spoke, it's just whispering,
the crossed-out part of a bad script.

Now a diva, now a harlot,
now a teenage girl, the sweetheart John got bored with.
Chanting, easy chansons:
whatever the occasion requires.

Even if I spoke, it's just a mute song,
which replies to a hidden song.

I look at the Moon. The grey Moon
which paints the arena of our days.
Even if I spoke, it's just a mask, make-up,
success for the imagined stage.

This is not the limelight. A spotlight
turned on and broken into shadows.
Behind my eyes is the way
to a shabby, old dressing-room.

Even if I spoke, it's just a mute song –
whose refrain has woven me into silence again.

I fall silent, and this is different again:
bewitching, false – why would you be disappointed?
The threadbare magic remained:
champagne, wild hits, wigs . . .

Note: Lotte Lenya was the singer wife of Kurt Weill, and the original performer of many of the songs he wrote with Bertholt Brecht.

Sandor Marai

Hungary

Versions by Martin Bennett

Sandor Marai *was born in Hungary in 1900. A novelist as well as a poet, he rose to literary prominence in the Thirties. In the 1960s he emigrated to the United States. Although largely forgotten, he continued to write in Hungarian up to his suicide in 1989.*

Martin Bennett *lives and works in Rome. His translations of Blaise Cendrars, Pasolini, Pavese, Quasimodo and others have appeared in previous issues of* MPT. *A book of his own poems,* Loose Watches, *was published by University of Salzburg Press. The two poems printed below were actually translated via an Italian translation of them, published in* Il Messaggero. *Martin Bennett 'Englished them, albeit with a few adaptations, versions in this case rather than translation being the operative word'.*

Casanova

Read between the lines of those his tales –
their disguises physical and spiritual –
and behind the ribbons, masks and frills
we run up against this harsh reality:
that long life so rich in adventures
was filled with second or third rate women
whose favours he paid through the nose for.
His 'Grandi Avventuri' mostly begin
from the fact that he gave his ladies
(or their husbands) rings, carriage-rides, cash,
acquiring thereby fifty to sixty kilos
of flesh, smiles and kisses thrown in.
The funding he needed for such exploits
he got, more often than not, from cards,
his expertise at bending the rules.
Love had nothing to do with it. Athlete,
all-in wrestler, tightrope-walker, magician –
these were what he was, a laureate
in trickery, cold-blooded acrobat
cool and collected even amidst the blaze
he himself had provoked, inside his pocket
a stiletto, some jokers, a rope ladder.
Someone who at the end of the day

has betrayed and derided everything,
adventure itself . . . His long life jam-packed
with women, jail sentences, doses of clap,
unhappiness and delight, he got nothing
free, rather he paid above the going price.
The peasant belle who offered herself gratis
to some Tuscan shepherd: our hero
conquered her to the clink of ducats,
coach trips, an ocean of lies. He was
the softest touch ever, a squanderer
sans pareil. He died with his mouth full
of bitters, the gout, with ink-stained fingers
plus a goose-quill tucked behind his ears,
numb from cold, now stripped of everything . . .

Loss

In the street sometimes I pull up short,
slip my hand in my pocket with the thought
that I have lost something. I hurry home,
open drawers, riffle through old suits,
re-read letters. On other occasions
I find myself giving this or that person
a call, firing off questions, wandering
off the subject. Yes, I have lost something.
I wake up round 3 am, and all at once
it's clear. I've lost the dream. Not your run-
of-the-night version, sleep's detritus,
sweet murky dullness, its videotic mush
of secret long range desires mixed with bits
of yesterday. Not that. This is different,
an oneiric inkling that behind reality
lurks a reason that cannot be expressed
in words. That dream, what was it? How come
it afflicts me even in absence?
Why do I still seek it? Was it youth? Who knows . . .
The one certainty is that I've been fleeced.

Miklós Radnóti
Hungary

Translated by Stephen Capus

Miklós Radnóti (1909-1944) *was born into a Budapest Jewish family, but converted to Catholicism in his youth. One of the most talented young poets in 30s Hungary, Radnóti was also a translator of note, publishing versions of Blake, Keats, Éluard, Rilke, among others. Despite his conversion, Radnóti fell victim to the racial laws of Nazi-controlled Hungary, his last period of forced labour being in a slave camp in northern Serbia. It was here that he wrote his final poems, later found on his body when it was exhumed from a ditch after the war. Radnóti's camp notebook has recently been published in the Arc 'Visible Poets' series, translated by Francis Jones (see short review of this and other volumes in the series in the present issue of* MPT).

Stephen Capus, *whose translations from the Russian appeared in* MPT *20, studied Russian literature at the Universities of Birmingham and London. He has published poems and translations in various magazines, including* Acumen *and* Thumbscrew. *He works as an administrator at University College, London.*

from **'Cartes Postales'**

Jardin du Luxembourg

The children's fingers still sift the fresh
Warm sand with pleasure; but once again
The anxious voices of women enmeshed
In skeins of knitting are calling their names.

Place de Notre Dame

Throw away your paper with its horrors and pay
Attention to the soft white cloud that plays
Among the spires of the church; relax, sit down,
Don't think about anything – just look around.
Because tomorrow the light will dissolve above the square
Of Notre Dame as usual – but you won't be there.

October Forest

A wet confusion glistens on shrubs
And bushes, beneath the naked trees
The mouldering gold of autumn leaves
Has rotted and turned to rich brown mud
Mingled with beetles, worms and seeds.

To look for meaning here is an error,
All of nature is steeped in terror,
– Including that frightened squirrel who,
Dropping his miniscule store of food,
Screams and then scampers away from you.

Learn from him then and don't neglect
Your welfare, winter won't protect
Your interests, angels won't save you either,
A pearl-grey light in the sky quivers
And those who love you die one after another.

And Will I Wonder . . .

I lived, but I lived without guile or dexterity and
I knew all along that they'll bury me in this land,
That year will pile upon year, stone upon stone,
That my body will rot below, that my naked bones
Will freeze in the wormy darkness where they rest;
That up in the world time will put to the test
My work, while deep in the earth my corpse will subside.
All that I knew. But say: has the work survived?

Sándor Rákos

Hungary

Translated by David Hill

Sándor Rákos (1921-1999) *was a member of a group of young writers (with Ágnes Nemes Nagy, Balázs Lengyel, Géza Ottlik, János Pilinszky, Iván Mándy et al) who started an important literary journal after the war and stood for the autonomy and depoliticization of literature. The journal* Újhold *(New Moon) was, however, soon banned by the Communists after severe attacks on its policies by György Lukács, the philosopher. For years these writers were not allowed to publish. During this period Rákos translated the Sumerian epic* Gilgamesh, *which became a great success and made him famous. With the mellowing of the dictatorship he returned to the scene and published more than a dozen volumes of poetry, and for many years headed the Translators' Section of the Hungarian Writers' Association. In its obituary* The Independent *of London wrote of him: 'Rákos's poetry is completely the opposite of what was expected of Hungarian poets in the early 1950s – it is apolitical, introverted and rather pessimistic. It is concerned with the eternal questions of human life and the poet addresses his verse to Homo sapiens, not the person of a definite historical period, in this he is not unlike Sándor Weöres, perhaps the best Hungarian post-war poet.'*

David Hill *has published two poetry collections,* Angels and Astronauts *and* Bald Ambition. *His free quarterly leaflet 'Lyriklife' (www.lyriklife.com) features examples of his published work, including translations from German, Hungarian, Romanian and Russian. He is an enthusiastic poetry performer. Born in 1971, he lives in Budapest.*

Standing-cell

in this cavity that your
body's shrunk to god's shut out
your self creates for yourself
out of yourself a cell-god
which will learn to god around
even in a narrow space
learn to shepherd over you
in the suffocating dark
walled-in duplicate-yourself installed by you
(anti-Adam) as the faeces-lined
standing-cell's inhabitant your creation

Untitled

no   none of them   not one of them
none of these deaths that are gathering
standing in front of me hovering
sniffing up sneaking away again

no   none among them is mine yet
it comes for someone else not for me
with a specially trained nose for the
odour the code of that other one

don't start beating more loudly heart
when in silence it sniffles around
from your throbbing it would suspect

you're lawbreaking stepping out of bounds
to mark me out lead me apart
it doesn't need express instruction

The death of the poem

they say
the polar circle's shifting southward
and the world in its deep-frozen whirling
will screech more and more
moss will overgrow our gardens tomorrow
and with a tinkle the songbird will fall
from the frozen sky to the stone-hard leaf-litter
this more-or-less globe-shaped planet will become
different though also perversely still the same
another glow (or flicker) coming from its sun-moon
saw-teethed shadows of pines will sharpen
against rocky earth's grindstone
and ghost sounds will keen after sounds
and barking like corridors under the ground
roars will echo across icy wastes
yes
maybe we will turn to ice
among evening hills in a high snowdrift
losing our traces on untravelled tracks
fumbling for footprints while silently
feather-fluff envelops us to the neck

snow
deathly snow
however laughable the crown-antlered sun-disk
this spring-playing autumn this writing's
meteorological present-time
may find the vision
the grim wintry presentiment . . .
anybody who's been lost in freezing dark
but kept in their secret innermost pocket
two or three matchsticks deeply concealed
knows very well that even the prospect
of light illumines and that of warmth warms
and that of home conjures home
here is the poem
it is inflammable
its floating-wick or its flaming bonfire
lights up the faces of the people
when it flickers out
even existence bursts
poem-lack strikes like icy lightning
and the snake of freezing
creeps onto the heart of creation

Istvan Szarka
Hungary

Translated by David A Hill and Ildikó Juhász

Istvan Szarka *was born in 1941, in Devavanya in eastern Hungary. He graduated in general medicine from the Budapest University Medical Faculty in 1966, and in 1974 completed his specialisation in dentistry. Since then he has worked as a dentist. He has published many collections of verse, the most recent being* Minden Versem (1957-1996) *(All My Poems, 1999)*, Szender a holdudvarban *(Hawk Moth in Moon's Halo, 2001), and* Husveti Kert *(Easter Garden, 2003).*

Beneath the Aspens

For Mozart

The aspen pollen is already floating away;
matter in its light-state, namely music:
in hard azure fanfaring gold and the sun beyond it
looming from the direction of the boy-trees.
Now the breath-pause silk flares up into a shriek,
and the aspen-girls giggle in the already whispering,
cool flute-foliage, warm snowflakes drift:
billions of little downy seeds
in the resonant stringed light,
in germinative hope,
towards wind-sheltered
tiny seed-bed – behold the sky is all besmeared
with living-scented resin-light, torment glitters
joyfully all around – what can man do
with such great love!:
lightanthem-odes, veiled elegies,
balladshadows, sway-prowl through
the bright gladness of the song, this nothing
rises to the soul
from the spirited matter of the musical instrument
from the crimson of the larynx.
My tree? Just stands
in its ten-chord majesty, like that Salzburg summer –
or that Rhine one, where an acumen
comparable to yours
seized your image

of humankind thus:
A BEING OF UNIVERSAL ABILITY
creates, moulds, contemplates his work,
and he, just like this work,
IS FREEDOM BY NATURE.

Ottó Tolnai
Hungary

Translated by David Hill

Ottó Tolnai *was born in 1940. He belonged to the ethnic Hungarian minority in the former Yugoslavia, where artists and intellectuals enjoyed more freedom of expression that was allowed their counterparts in Hungary. When in 1965 the avant-gardist review* Új Symposion *was founded, Tolnai was among its first contributors and later became its editor-in-chief. In 1967 Tolnai's second book was awarded the Hid Prize, Yugoslavia's highest honour for the literature of its Hungarian community. Post-Communist Hungary honoured him with the Attila József Prize in 1991. Tolnai is an essayist and playwright as well as a poet.*

The wire brush is beautiful

I stole the wire brush
the new copper wire brush
the wire brush is beautiful
only blind tibike's
wedding dance was more beautiful
only tibike's blind blithe
wedding dance with the flamingo
without legs how can i dance
wili wanted to gobble up the flamingo
although he only gobbled up fanny's negligee
I stole the wire brush
the new copper wire brush
the wire brush is beautiful
beautiful like the flamingo
like sunset in
wili's shit-smeared soldier's mirror
fanny's crotch mirrored in the permanganate
basin
the wire brush is beautiful
beautiful like the flamingo
the shit-smeared soldier's mirror
fanny's crotch mirrored in permanganate
i stole the wire brush
the new copper wire brush
if they catch me no dirt ringworm leprosy will remain

no rust will remain on me
the wire brush is beautiful
I too will shine blindingly
like the plowshare after deep plowing
like blind tibike vigh doing his wedding dance
doing his wedding dance with the flamingo
the wire brush
the new copper wire brush

Tin Ujevic
Croatia

Translated by Richard Burns and Daša Marić

Tin Ujevic *was one of the great lyric poets of former Yugoslavia. His work has hardly been translated at all into English. He was a writer of voluminous intellect, whose language and sensibility are similar in some ways to Verlaine's.* His Collected Works *number sixteen volumes, and he is greatly loved throughout the country. Always poor, he lived simply and was a frequenter of bars and cafés. Ujevic wrote in the Croatian variant of the language, with a strong Dalmatian influence. He lived for many years in Zagreb.*

Richard Burns *lived in the former Yugoslavia from 1987 to 1991. His recent collections of poetry include* Book with no Back Cover *(2003),* The Manager *(2001),* Against Perfection *(1999) and* Croft Woods *(1999). He now lives in Cambridge.*

Daša Marić *is a translator who lives in Split.*

Deep in that heart . . .

Deep in that heart, black wounds he dare not show;
He's weary, cursed, a being in distress,
That sparkle in the eyes, that starry brow –
You're dead, Tin. All your paths are emptiness.

Death is your love, in every step you take,
Death, in your belly and in every breath,
Death is your drink and daily bread you break,
In expectation and attainment, death.

What use blind love or hope without a goal,
What use desire's wild dash, when there's no cure
Through breathing lungs or heartbeats, for the soul,

And though your loves are beautiful and pure
Like faded perfume in a broken bowl,
None of your babbling larksong can endure?

Marko Vešović

Bosnia

Translated by Chris Agee

Marko Vešović *was born in 1945 in Northern Montenegro. In 1963 he came to Sarajevo and has resided there ever since. He studied at the University of Sarajevo, where he now teaches literature. Of Orthodox background, he is one of Bosnia's most respected writers. His first collection of poems,* Nedjelja (Sunday) *won the former Yugoslavia's two most prestigious literary accolades, the Trebinje Prize and the Branko Award. He has published three more volumes of poetry, two collections of essays, and a novel. He is also celebrated as a translator of poetry, having published volumes of Baudelaire and Emily Dickinson, as well as selections of Joseph Brodsky, Anna Akhmatova, Marina Tsvetayeva and Pushkin. During the three-and-a-half-year siege of Sarajevo, Vešović remained in the city and wrote numerous essays for* Oslobodenje ("Liberation"), Danni ("Days") and Slobodna Bosna ("Free Bosnia"). *These writings, which exemplify the multi-ethnic defence of the Bosnian capital, were of immense importance to the morale of the city's besieged inhabitants. In 1994, Vešović's wartime essays were collected into a single volume,* Death is a Master from Serbia *(the title echoing the famous 'Death Fugue' of Paul Celan). This was subsequently published in Italy, in an abridged version, as* Excuse Me for Speaking of Sarajevo.

Chris Agee *was born in 1956 in San Francisco but grew up on the East Coast. At Harvard he studied with the poet and translator Robert Fitzgerald. Since 1979 he has lived in Ireland. A first collection of poems,* In the New Hampshire Woods, *was published by Dedalus Press, Dublin, in 1992; a second,* First Light, *was short-listed for the 2000 National Poetry Series in the US. A former editor of* Poetry Ireland Review *and* Metre, *he edited a special double issue on Contemporary Irish Poetry for* Poetry *(Chicago, Oct-Nov 1995). He now edits the magazine* Irish Pages. Scar on the Stone: Contemporary Poetry from Bosnia *was published by Bloodaxe in 1998 and a collection of Balkan essays,* Journey to Bosnia, *appeared in 2002. A selection of his own poetry is included in* The Book of Irish American Poetry, *edited by Daniel Tobin. He teaches at the Open University in Ireland and at The Queen's University of Belfast. He is a frequent visitor to Croatia, where he has a house.*

Summa Summarum

The leaves of the ilex by the graveyard
Whisper prophetically

And barley-corn ripens
Like those actors who
In the same role for the hundredth time
Stand forth before the audience.

Yet do not extol,
To the skies, your native land.
It ought to extol you.

Seen from this cloud
These meadows and fields
Are a stamp album;

And to the ant a smoke ring
Twirling from your cigarette
Is a whole new landscape!

And stop threatening for once
To return next time
To this handful of land without history
Only in the shape of a rider in bronze.

And before you leave
Stroke the bark of these trees
Which all the while have given you
Free lessons in standing tall!

Essential Fire

Rye, broken on the sideboard, unleavened, steaming.
Cupboard glasses chattering to the clatter over the worn
Stoop of the threshold. An ox's wet snout, arrowing
Steam like a teapot, lashes the brow of the ploughman.

Mother's sacral ache, as always, before the rain;
And a scent off the lindens as in the time of Agamemnon.

Pigeons, under the eaves – billowing white sails.
A stallion on his mare secreting the black sex of the male.
Listen hard to how the wheat matures,
Listen hard to how the earth is – *whole*.

Mother's sacral ache, as always, before the rain;
And a scent off the lindens as in the time of Agamemnon.

Purer than milk, or blueness, wild beast wail.
All names preserved the imprint of the Lord.
Goat-udders swinging, gravid and speckled,
Like a bell on a little chapel.

Adolf Endler
Germany

Translated by Stefan Tobler

Born in Dusseldorf in 1930, **Adolf Endler** *moved to the newly-formed East Germany in 1955. However, as his poetry became more sceptical and ironic, he found himself increasingly sidelined. In 1979 he was expelled from the Writers Union. His poetry was then re-discovered through the publication of* Apocalypse Pudding *(Suhrkamp, 1999), which comprises his selected poems.*

Stefan Tobler *translates from German and Portuguese. His poetry translations have appeared in various magazines such as* Ambit, Poetry Wales *and* International Poetry Review *(US). Translated stories and a libretto have also been published. He lives in Wycombe, for his sins, and can be contacted at:* stefan_tobler@hotmail.com

Lice Hunt

I stretch my tongue to get my fingers wetted.
You bow your head, towards the brightest light.
I put my hand into your plait, remove your slide.
The light unfurls your hair and makes it shine bright red.

I'm looking for your lice, stroking from cheek to jaw,
Then up your parting's line above your shell-like ear,
I catch them, crack them, pull them out, the hordes, with fervour,
And sodden fingernails, these two a single claw.

How lovely, what a heart-attack – I'm hunting lice!
You show your holy throat for your decapitation,
Reprieved as I, the slayer, lost my concentration,
I'm catching all your lice like raisins from mum's pies.

I count to thirteen, twenty-two, then thirty-seven,
You too are counting, flushed, and ask: Another one?
I count the louse, the louse's eggs, the louse's son,
This counting frenzy makes me cruel and diligent.

I'm looking for your lice, but oh, where is that swine,
The last, most cunning of the louse's kith and kin?
Your hair's as shiny red as drops of haemoglobin,
Yes, I have caught your lice, now you can look for mine.

After an Illness

In the rosy light, not too late,
I saw
children clamber aboard
the boat, little weights,
each fortifies the water.

I came swimming out of reeds and sand
Water-man, Water-man.
Who was it that took my hand
as the boat pondered its way to the bank?

On my back, I let the water pull
me into the wash of laughter, I bobbed
and they lay slices of apple
on my burst-open gob

Sometimes I wish I was small enough again
To be your captain

Instruction

"When we go out on the green,
There's sometimes a bird there,
You've seen one of them quite often –
What does the little bird's song mean?"

"Caahh!"

"It's from Africa!"

This Summer

1
The roses with their averted lizard-stare.

2
The old hand, lost in thoughts, listening to it.

Antonio Machado
Spanish

Translated by David Curzon

David Curzon *writes: The poems of* **Antonio Machado** *are accessible and wise, and all who are preoccupied with poetry know of him. And yet, considering how great a poet he is, he seems barely present in the general literary awareness of English-speaking readers who know of Lorca and Neruda and Borges.*

Attempting to translate overtones and the weight of simple words expressing clear thoughts, with poetry in its purest form, **David Curzon** *has published two anthologies of twentieth-century poetry based on biblical texts,* Modern Poems on the Bible *(The Jewish Publication Society of America, 1994) and* The Gospels in our Image *(Harcourt Brace, 1995). The majority of poems in these anthologies are in translation. He has also published (with the late Katharine Washburn) a translation of Euripides's play,* The Madness of Hercules *(University of Pennsylvania Press, 1999) and, most recently,* Eustache Deschamps: Selected Poems *(translations in collaboration with Jeffrey Fiskin; Routledge, 2003). Other translations have appeared in literary anthologies and journals, including several issues of* MPT.

from **Parables**

Know how to hope, wait for the tide to flow;
Like a beached boat, depart without unease.
That victory is theirs, all who wait will know,
For life is long, and art is just a sport.
And if life is short
And your galleon is not reached by the seas,
Then wait, and always hope, and don't depart,
For art is long and is, besides, of no import.

Liam Ō'Muirthile

Irish

Translated by Greg Delanty

Liam Ō'Muirthile *was born in Cork in 1950 and now lives with his family in Dublin. His most recent collection of poetry is* Walking Time. *He has also written fiction and drama. A selection from his weekly column in* The Irish Times *has been published in book form. He has received many literary awards.*

Greg Delanty*'s latest books are* The Hellbox *(OUP, 1998),* The Blind Stitch *(Oxford Poets, Carcanet, and Louisiana State University Press, 2001). His next book,* The Ship of Birth, *is due in November from Carcanet. Delanty was born in Cork in 1958. He lives now most of the year in Vermont and teaches at St Michael's College.*

Today In Ireland

A spell of heat from the south,
the shell of the distant haze
today in Ireland.

An uplifting beauty of a breeze,
the birds free wheeling in the heavens
today in Ireland.

The lithe swift becomes its name,
the sun highlights secret plumage
today in Ireland.

Blithe flocks move in unison on the sea,
a wing-spur at last to our step
today in Ireland.

Living Together

The way you order everything,
every saucepan scoured and dried
and set back in its proper place;
fork lies with fork, knife with knife,
the bottom of every spotless pot
outshining every plate.

Every plastic flower is delirious
with the floweriness of plastic.
The door shutters
under its lock as if nothing happened;
as if history does not exist
and the whole oblivious lot
sits perfectly still in its ordained order.
Woman,
I would rather
the monk's habit
to the blinding pots and pans
of this kitchen cell.

The Flying Shoes

It must be the whiff of polish
as I buff shoes . . .

our shiny shoes,
trailing pair by pair
step by step
up the stair,
soled by my own father,
the loosened tongues lolling.

One morning a nest of daws
dropped down our chimney.
Each fledgling hoppedskipped
and, caw by caw,
toddled up the stairs.

As he caught the birds
and released them one
by one out the landing window
the vamps of each shoe flapped
and our clodhoppers
flew away with the daws
vamp by wing, vamping it,
winging it.

Salvatore Quasimodo
Italy

Translated by Patrick Milan

Salvatore Quasimodo *(1901-1968) was born and remained a Sicilian, despite training as a civil engineer in Rome and then working in his profession in Tuscany and, later, in the foothills of the Alps under a boss who 'couldn't stand poets'. He subsequently gravitated to literary journalism and then, for twenty-seven years, the teaching of Italian literature (at the Conservatorio Musicale 'G. Verdi' in Milan). He was also an extremely productive translator from Greek and Latin, and from Shakespeare. In 1959 he was awarded the Nobel Prize for literature.*

Patrick Milan *works as a database consultant, based in London.*

Already is with us rain

Already is with us rain,
it ripples the silenced air.
Swallows swoop to kiss dead-water
as it lies by Lombard lakes,
dropping like gulls on the tiny fish;
the odour of hay through wicker-fences.

Another year's burnt out,
nor shriek of protest or complaint
raised on a sudden to reclaim a day of it.

Written, perhaps, on a tomb

here, far from anyone, the sun beats
upon your hair, luminates the honey of it,
and we're reclaimed for the living
by summer's last cicada on his bush,
and by the siren, howling out its alarum
across the plains of Lombardy.
O dried-up voices of the air,
what is it that you require of us?
Weariness shimmers from out the soil.

An Open Arc

Evening fragments itself into earth
in thunderings of smoke, and an owl
echoes its 'you', voicing only
the silence. Islands high and dark
crush the waves, and on the beach
night enters inside the shells.
And you measure out the future,
the beginning we have left behind;
you divide up in careful steps
the balance of a time already absent.
With the pebble-sucking sea-foam
you dispel a sense of the irresistible
momentum of destruction.
The old song of the owl knows
nothing of death even as it dies away
as it tracks the curve of its search for love
as it traces the line of an open arc
to reveal its own aloneness.
But someone will come.

Angel Rupérez

Spain

Translated by Joan Lindgren

Angel Rupérez *was born in Burgos in 1953. Educated in Romance Philology at the University of Valladolid, he is now professor of Literary Theory at the Universidad Complutense de Madrid. Rupérez has published four books of poetry:* En otro corazón *(1983),* Las hojas secas *(1985),* Conversación en junio *(1992, a finalist for the National Poetry Prize), and* Lo que han visto mis ojos *(1993). He has also published an anthology of poetry translated from the English:* Lirica inglesa del siglo XIX. *In 2002 he published a novel,* Vidas Ajenas *(Debate) and edited the Austral Collection of the poetry of Luis Cernuda. He is a regular contributor to the Spanish daily,* El Pais.

The poems that follow come from the poet's recent book, Una razón para vivir, *which the Barcelona publisher Tusqets chose for publication in its series,* Nuevos Textos Sagrados/New Sacred Texts, *thus placing Rupérez in company with Claudio Rodriguez and José Angel Valente. (Work of the three poets is featured in Lindgren's manuscript* Relinquishing Permanence, *an anthology of New Sacred Texts.)*

Of his poems Antoni Marí comments as follows: 'They surprise us with their vigorous cadences but are nonetheless grave and reflective for their conversational tone. These are poems that create and contemplate a landscape right before our eyes, inviting us to enter.'

Joan Lindgren *has edited and translated a collection of the poetry of the Argentine writer, Juan Gelman, in the University of California Press volume,* Unthinkable Tenderness *(1997). Her years in Argentina have been dedicated to others among the families of the Disappeared, whose work she has translated and collected in* Translating Argentina. *Her own work, sometimes called literary ethnography, and her translations have appeared in many magazines. At home on the border between Mexico and the United States, she has taught cross-border translation workshops as a Fulbright Border Scholar. Presently she is organizing a program with the support of San Diego State University's Latin American Studies Program and the border's Children's Museum Without Walls, 'Twice Told Poems', which introduces Spanish language literature to bilingual school children and develops their innate ability to translate.*

Joan Lindgren's translations of Mexican poet Aurora Aranjo Story appeared in MPT *5, of Argentinian poet Juan Gelman in* MPT *11 and below, and of Spanish poet José Angel Valente in* MPT *13.*

Life Has Not Fallen

Day may have fallen, but not life.
It was an error to have supposed that autumn
would bury all leaves for all time,
in the brief tunnel between the window
and the back garden where, on occasion,
when light lay sleeping on a pool
of water and shipwrecked leaves, I believed
myself dead, a being caught in the drift of his destiny.
How wrong! That was not death
but an accident of vision, a mere pooling of rain
where autumn had painlessly dropped a few leaves.
Now, the same puddle, the same leaves,
and I know that nothing has ended, that this light
rekindles to relight the candle of our lives
in that corner where once I thought I saw death.
If it be so, protect the flame with your hands
and follow in the direction of autumn's ladder
where today, under the clouds, I have witnessed
life, as it came to me from the hands of branches
which yearn for nothing because they wait,
not in despair, but sure resuscitation is at hand.

Counterfeit Coins And Precious Stones

Morning sun and an afternoon sky so gray
that who could tell if the clouds had given up
their heaviness to the wind or if the last light
there at the crossroad had given way
to the vacant blue that presages the night.
In the morning I abandoned myself to the sun,
there in the plaza where rays of another season
linger on the sand that my eyes commit
to sifting through to sort the counterfeit coins

                              from precious stones.
Now, the sun fled, a naked tree draws me to it
as if it were singular, my one-and-only of days gone by.
A row of trees, a dream-like single branch,
a sort of confidence, of calm clarity,
a measure of gray patience, of drought
and clarity, clarity and drought confused.
An unknown virtue, perhaps, unknown to me

or a link uniting days with days
in this plaza frequented by children where
with the sun's help my eyes research to learn
if the sand in fact still keeps the gems
I buried there one far gone winter day
when I believed in life; some January day
come full term as if it were a harvest.

Novembers

They're still watching me, the black poplars. The red
berries of the flowering fence watch me also. The sun
dissolves the snow, voices are diluted, time
is winning its battle against time and we're still here
just as life meant for the faithful to be.
Yet everything dies and the calendar says nothing
and no dates are foreign to the exile of living
with the loss of what I know I've lived.

To Think Of You

Its song has made me think of you,
field afire with bonfires of poppies
that suffocate forgetting, and also of you,
promise lost in the drops of dew
in February, that bespeak a tiny glow to come,
dew which soon would have me drink of life itself.
Its song: thrushes mixed among the other birds,
the withheld breath of winter, the regular
beating of my unconscious heart just now become aware.
Its song: sun invoked by faith, the streets,
windless but afire with light, or with a wind
that tastes of needed snow to come,
or wind that brings its memory of mountains
intact, yesterday intact, the two of us united
in our common promise of rebirth.

The Monk And The Rain

It's cold in the cell and the monk is learning
a lesson in why he loves the rain so much.
He rises, goes to the window and looks out
poppies, today a fire extinguished, their splendour
withered, almost resigned, and beside them cornstalks
gone to seed, their being claimed by the downpour.
His eyes straddle the distant plains
fertile fields of flowers, but also of dreams
that he can't quite make out and does not understand.
Patiently, he draws that field in his mind's eye,
little by little he paints it, absorbs it tenaciously,
melts himself into it, but an anxiousness remains,
an unfulfilment that even the rain cannot fill.

What can it be? The fact is, he loves the rain,
of that he is sure, and he needs the whole landscape,
exactly as he sees it, all of it, the poppies
that yesterday were fire and today smell of ash;
the chestnut that only yesterday seemed lifeless
and today gives its leaves for shelter from the wind;
the rainswept distance, where sunflowers, once austere
are buffed to a shine, the slate of rooftops polished
to a matt finish that shouts renouncement of the world,
retirement at once presence, harmony, surrender;
that far-off sound from the sea of wheat fields
whistling their songs that one after another
the rain organizes into waves
and sometimes buries in the earth.

He loves it exactly as it is, and if a bell
were to announce the slipping by of the hours
he would face up, lament nothing, concede to his life
a diffused sentiment of belonging to something,
not knowing exactly to what,
to the landscape, perhaps, to time as it passes
to the poor poppies, the poor rocks, maybe,
and it might be that all that keeps him alive,
the not knowing to whom he belongs, nor knowing
either what belongs to him of all that he sees.
He speaks not of ownership but of belonging,
of faith in time past, of knowing
that things are not dead milestones
of yesterday, obligatory burials of today itself.

Something else, he asks, a greater safety,
a full confidence, absolute conviction
that the rain promise him what he dreams,
that endless wandering born of not knowing
which is the territory of love, which of ashes.
And that's what keeps him going, in suspense,
absorbed, concentrating, to the point that
he loses within himself the notion of being alive
because he seems to have come to a mysterious threshold,
the door that opens on a superior world
where nothing happens except the rain itself,
the soft patter, the constant agreement, the slow spray,
the drop that will come to be the salvation of the dead poppies.

And he sits down to think, to meditate perhaps,
he remembers, he feels and he knows nothing.
He only dreams that tonight his fatigue
will find in sleep a promise of certainty:
that the journey be repeated endlessly,
the journey of his eyes over the sown fields
and the rain of always, his sleepless passing
through what he believes is his, not knowing it his,
until the day of perpetual rest arrive, the day
when the rain no longer obsesses
because at last he has understood what it means:
a belated calm, ambition at rest,
a triumph equivalent to knowing above all
that at last he is satisfied, that now he can die.

My Normal Routine

I wanted to vary my normal routine
and I took a different road home
and I saw the park
illumined by autumn's gold and by a silence
perfumed by smoke from a bonfire someone had lit
to burn the leaves that fall day after day in November.
I wanted to reach that distant place lit by the sun
where the houses are wrapped in the gold of the poplars
houses lived in to dream of a life re-
signed to the sweet adventure of dying,
a life in the debt of the man who is burning the leaves.
The trembling of the poplars, the gusts of wind

the gold that fused with fugitive light and my dream,
my desire to catch forever the shimmering gold
that the invisible bonfire could not consume.

And that memory remains with me, continues in me, fixed.
The memory of reaching the top of the hill, not
looking for anything, given that I was travelling by car
with nothing more than the pretension of remaining a little apart,
in the direction of an inevitable horizon,
towards the secret nostalgia of a timeless journey,
towards an uncertain paradise where I'd never arrive.
And then I had this dream:
I saw the houses and the leaves falling from the trees
and the sun extracting shining fragments from them,
brilliant sparks, nearby fires that
instead of frightening me drew me to the flames.
Yes, houses in the distance – possible houses
and impossible houses – that I longed to go to
knowing that among them was my house.

But in what memory was I, in what years
that light I viewed, in what direction was I driving?
Here, nearby, where the gold of autumn rustles, where
the sun dissolves into the sparks it creates? There,
far off, where the smoke from the fire
floats upon the air, where the rake drags the leaves
with the distant sound of death and
the din of madcap gusts can be heard,
the great windmills of a perpetual November?
There, where one time or another there was a light
for anyone who had ever been afraid of being lost?
I didn't know, couldn't know; my eyes demanded
certainty, nothing less, and what they got
was the nearby residences with the same old hosts:
the rhythmic sparks of the sun in the leaves,
the cascade of light lost among the branches,
the compass of the rake, the faithful wind song,
the perfume of smoke from bonfires everywhere,
and all I had imagined autumn would be when
I was at the age of not yet believing in death.

Rafik Schami

Germany

Translated by Stefan Tobler

Rafik Schami, *born in Damascus in 1946, has lived in Germany since 1971. He is the author of numerous novels and collections of stories and has won many prizes, including the Hermann Hesse Prize and the Adalbert von Chamisso Prize.*

When God was still a Grandmother

As a small child I was often at my grandparents' house. I spent days and weeks there. It was nice to get out of the over-populated squeeze of my parents' flat and to enjoy the endless peace, which smelt of thyme.

My grandfather and I often sat at the fireplace. He would tell me things and think as he stared into the crackling fire, until he drifted asleep. Often I would fall asleep too, soon after him. When I woke again, he was normally already awake, would smile embarrassedly and ask, as he gathered some sticks and put them on the fire: "Where was I?"

Grandfather must have spent his whole day at the fireplace. It's the only memory I have of him. If it got dark, we stayed in the dark until grandmother came. She knocked gently on the wall and then it was light. If I got afraid in the dark, then grandfather comforted me. 'Gran is coming soon. She'll turn the light on. She's good at that', he'd say with admiration. He couldn't turn the light on, neither in summer nor in winter.

And in summer, when it got hot, he politely asked grandmother if she could kindly turn the wind on. Grandmother knocked on the wall, and an old propeller on the ceiling magicked up a fresh breeze. Grandfather lent back with his eyes closed. 'Heavenly', he sighed and fell asleep. I vividly remember how one windy morning, as I was standing at the window, I asked him who turned on the light and wind outside. 'God', he replied. I was sure then that God was a grandmother too. I later studied chemistry, physics and mathematics. But often, when my fingers touch a light switch, I think about my grandmother and, just for a moment, I curse the sciences, every one of them.

George Seferis
Greece

Translated by Roderick Beaton

Poet, essayist, diarist and professional diplomat, **George Seferiadis** *was born in Smyrna (Izmir), then part of the Ottoman empire, in 1900. He took the pseudonym Seferis with his first book of poems,* Strophe, *usually translated as* Turning Point *(1931). 'Love's Discourse' is the longest poem of that volume, which predates the poet's turn to free verse with* Mythistorema *(or* Novel), *published in 1935. During WWII his diplomatic duties took Seferis far from Greece: between 1941 and 1944 he served in Pretoria, Cairo, Jerusalem and briefly in southern Italy. He became internationally known with the publication of* The King of Asine and Other Poems, *translated by Lawrence Durrell, Bernard Spencer and Nanos Valaoritis and published in London in 1948, and was awarded the Nobel Prize for Literature in 1963. Seferis died in Athens in September 1971.*

His work has often been compared to that of T S Eliot, which he was instrumental in introducing to Greece; Seferis stands in the same 'High Modernist' tradition. But he always kept aloof from either the religious or the political conservatism of Eliot; his observations and his intuitions of the forces at work in the history of nations were honed by the exigencies of a lifelong service to the 'drudgery' of a diplomatic career, and he emerges early in the new century as one of the most humane and authoritative literary witnesses to the last one, into which he was born.

Roderick Beaton *is Koraës Professor of Modern Greek and Byzantine History, Language and Literature at King's College London. He has published books and articles on Greek literature and culture of the 12th century onwards; he has also translated both poetry and fiction. His biography of Seferis, provisionally entitled* Waiting for the Angel, *is to be published by Yale University Press in autumn 2003.*

Note on 'Love's Discourse'

'Love's Discourse' is a poem of renunciation. Its language is dense, often allusive, using rich rhymes, assonance and alliteration, in the suggestive manner of the French Symbolists. It is markedly in contrast with the lapidary incisiveness of Seferis' later, and better known, poems in free verse. The first, second and fifth parts are addressed to fate; the loved woman appears directly only in the third, central section, which is also the longest. The strange fourth part may allude to the myth of Tiresias, the hermaphrodite seer punished by the gods for watching the coupling of snakes. Finally, the moment of erotic epiphany is out of reach, and the poem closes with a paradoxical affirmation of loss, and an acceptance, tinged with the language of religious faith, of life as it is: 'the world is simple.'

This and other poems in strict metrical form were relegated to an appendix, and rendered into free verse, by Edmund Keeley and Philip Sherrard, translators of the *Complete Poems* of Seferis (1995) [reviewed by Roderick Beaton in *MPT* 8]. That volume is justly regarded today as the standard version of Seferis in English. This version is offered in the hope that something of the rich musicality of Seferis' Greek can after all be captured in English, using roughly equivalent formal means.

Love's Discourse

> There exists a most foolish race of men
> those who despising what is theirs seek things far off,
> with vain hopes chasing the wind.
>
> *Pindar*

I

O rose of fate, you sought the way to wound us
but yielded like a saint before the glory
and good was the decree you deigned to grant us
your smile above us like an unsheathed sword.

Your old wheel rising brought the world to life
your thorns blocked thinking of the road ahead
desire dawned sweet and naked to possess you
the world was easy then, a simple heartbeat.

II

Forgotten on the shore the sea's secrets
forgotten in the foam the dark below;
a sudden memory blood-red like coral
gleams . . . Oh, but peace . . . take care to hear its soft

stirring . . . you touched the apples and the tree
the hand outstretched and there the thread to guide you . . .
Dark shudder to the root and trembling leaves
could *you* but bring the long-forgotten dawn!

Could lilies bloom once more upon the place
of parting, days be ripe in heaven's embrace,
could but those eyes alone reflect the gleam
the soul be pure inscribed by the flute's song.

Could it have been the night that closed her eyes?
Embers remain, the buzzing of the bowstring,
ashes and dizziness on this dark shore
dense fluttering of wings closed to surmise.

Rose of the wind, you knew but we knew not,
you took us just when thought was reaching out
to interlace our fingers, join two fates
and plunge as one into the placid light.

III

Dark shudder to the root and trembling leaves!
Come forth, o wakeful shape, into the fount
of silence, raise your head from your crouched fingers
thy will be done and say to me again

the words that touched and mingled with my blood;
spread out your longing like a tree's deep shadow
and let the abundance of your hair engulf us
your downy kiss reach into the heart's leaves.

You lowered your eyes with such a smile as once
in times gone by was humbly wrought by painters.
Forgotten lesson from an aged gospel
your speech had breath and this ethereal voice:

"Time's passage is a silent, otherworldly thing
and suffering moves gently in my soul
dawn pales the sky, the dream remains unsinkable
as though sweet-scented shrubs were passing by.

"The sudden movement of the eye, the body's flush
can wake and make descend a flight of doves
that beat their wings in circles round me and embrace me
the stars with human touch caress my breast.

"Like waves inside a seashell comes to me the adverse
far off, impenetrable world's lament
but moments too of stillness when bright-forked desire
is all my thought, desire and none but that.

"Perhaps in memory you see me risen, naked
as when you came, my dear, familiar stranger
to lie down by me and deliver me for ever,
as was my wish, from the swift rattling wind."

The shattered sunset faded and was gone,
it seemed a cheat to seek the gifts of heaven.
You lowered your eyes. The moonlight cast a thorn
that bloomed, you shrank back from the mountain's shadows.

. . . How love's reflection in the mirror fades
in sleep and dreams, school of oblivion
and how time's emptinesses shrink the heart
and love is lost, lulled in another's arms . . .

IV

Two fair and sluggish snakes, the shape of parting
slide seeking one another through the trees' night,
for secret love in undiscovered dells
they seek unsleeping without drink or food.

Coyly they coil: insatiably their will
weaves, multiplies, turns, binds in chains the body
that governed by the stars' unspoken laws
is raised to whitehot pitch of quenchless passion.

The trees, night's tentpoles, stand erect and trembling
the silence is a silver bowl wherein
the minutes fall like echoes whole, distinct,
a careful chisel chipping sculptured lines.

A sudden dawn: the statue. But the bodies
are lost to sea to wind to sun to rain.
Just so are born those beauties nature gives us
but who can say if any soul has died.

The parted snakes are but imagined now
(The trees aglow with birds and budding shoots)
the traces of their coils remain, the same
as fortune's turning wheel that brings us grief.

V

Where now the two-edged day that changed our lives?
Will ever river be for us to sail?
Will ever sky let fall its cooling comfort
on souls so numbed from nurture on the lotus?

Upon the stone of patience we still wait
for heaven's miracle to make all well
still waiting for the angel like the age-old
drama, the hour of evening when the open

roses fade . . . Scarlet rose of wind and fate,
you are but memory, a heavy rhythm
o rose of night you passed me by, a storm
of purple, storm at sea . . . The world is simple.

[*Athens, October '29 –December '30*]

Volker Sielaff

Germany

Translated by Stefan Tobler

*Born in the Lausitz hinterland of Eastern Germany, **Volker Sielaff** now lives in Dresden, where he works as a critic and stage manager. He has read at poetry festivals throughout Europe.*

*

On a hot day
in the bakery (Reitbahn-
straße) I sit
and drink coffee.

Around noon she steps
out of the shop
with a red
plastic bucket,

goes across to the flowers
stands
bent over the little pots
of greenery:

I hold my breath.
Just for a second now
I'd like
to believe in a miracle;

the way she stands there
and taking each pot in turn
dips them into glass-
clear water.

The birds' bickering

The birds' bickering
in the trees quarter
past three.

Cioran
complained about insomnia
all his life.

I throw myself blindly
into this morning's arms.

No experience
can be shared.

Afternoon Moon

for Kerstin and Hilda

It lay above us, and she pointed
at it with her finger. There, she said.
It scarcely stood out from the grey
afternoon sky. It was the first day
of the winter sales, people
were running into department stores
and arguing violently
over parking space.
They had lots to carry
because absolutely
everything was reduced.
There, said the girl.

Sometimes
you wake up in the night
you can't sleep and go
over to the window
probably slowly
so as not to wake anyone.
Then you see it
you see it
above the chimneys
no trouble seeing it now
(it's so bright and somehow far off)

But during the day
during the day it's different
then it's pretty difficult
then you have to be a kid or think
of nothing, of absolutely nothing
else.

Lennart Sjögren
Sweden

Translated by Robin Fulton

Lennart Sjögren *(b.1930) has spent most of his life on Öland, a Baltic island off the south-east coast of Sweden. He is both a painter and a writer, his books of poetry and prose (almost thirty of them) having now gained him a special place in Swedish writing. The poems here are from his latest collection,* Sent, Tidigt *(Late, Early) (Bonniers, Stockholm, 2001). Short selections of his work, in Robin Fulton's translation, were included in* Four Swedish Poets *(White Pine Press, New York, 1990) and in* Five Swedish Poets *(Norvik Press, Norwich, 1997).*

Robin Fulton *is a Scottish poet and translator who has lived for many years in Norway. The latest edition of his* Tomas Tranströmer: New Collected Poems *(from Swedish) came from Bloodaxe Books in 2002. A selection from the Danish of Henrik Nordbrandt (Dedalus Press, Dublin, 2002) is to be followed in 2003 by a revised and expanded gathering of his versions of the Norwegian poet Olav H Hauge (Anvil Press Poetry, London). Robin Fulton contributed translations of Sjögren, Aspenström and Rose Ausländer to MPT 5.*

The Urn

Night came and asked:
where is your face? I want to paint it.

And the painter surrendered himself and his soul
to the night.

At the time when even the flies are asleep
and the voice of silence is the only one
heard clearly.

The painter held out the urn
where the dead live
the night scraped away all the paint that was
and put there his black light.

Note: After a painting by Bror Ingemar Fröberg

If

If I only had the bat's teeth
sitting there in the little human face
between the lizard wings
and if I had the female snake's knowing eyes
when she squirts poison into the human foot
which has unwittingly got in her way

and if in my lungs
I had the beautiful veins of the hills
with secret metals
and if I had the dragon-fly's body
which lacks a mouth:
no need to hunt, no need to eat
already by next morning it'll be loosened
from its life.

If I had that voice which is in the wind
and is abandoned at the moment of birth.

For Another World

I don't think
any birds are singing today
for a better world.

But if my ear
were tuned in more deeply I might well have thought
the birds are singing today
for a better world.

And I don't think
those who let themselves
die today
are dying for a better world.

But if my ear
were tuned in more deeply
I might well have thought
those who let themselves
die today
are dying for a better world.

A Clear And Late Summer Evening

Inside the ash-trees
which the years have scooped into mortuaries
holes of dark light wait.

The night more imprisoned than any time
before.

The stones on the road say
they met a man
going in the direction of the end of his life.

Someone carries a basket of sorrow.
Here's my life, she says
this is what my life came to.

Birds that were no longer birds
died on the branches at the same time as the sunlight
but sat on there.

The Mirror

In the water-mirror we see a world
that's not there
above we see a world which
most certainly may be questioned.

The trees, which in this landscape have large crowns,
let themselves be doubled
the children play beside a precipice.

The great wars seem far away today
but others are drawing near
though the mirror continues to divide the world.

It's hard for us to know what

It's hard for us to know what
to think of the dead
but they do seem at least
significantly more alive than we are.

On certain aimless afternoons
when no-one says anything
and no-one dares to think
the dead approach us and say to us
clearly and methodically what we don't dare to say

until we woke up
and the wind resumed its flow in the grass.

October Dusk

A dusk richer than usual
falls over the shore
gold tongues rise on the horizon
licking the sky
the black and gold exchange voice and face.
Boats on their way into harbour
are caught in the fine-meshed net
the sun throws over them –

Night, brighten us in the dark
as you brighten the dead at their new entrance.

A place far away on the map
a day in the middle of October
regains the gloss otherwise mostly
to be seen on medieval paintings
where the varnish has deepened and time says
loud and clear:
I belong only to the surface
whatever's beneath I don't touch.

The New-Born

The new-born who still travel around
in the leafing boats
– their eyes have been fetched from the coal's
innermost depth

with them they observe us
before the black light fades out
in their pupils
and they see the world only as we see it.

Esaias Tegnér and Charles XII

by Charles Harrison Wallace

Charles Harrison Wallace *was born in Sweden in 1937, and educated in Scotland, England and Sweden, as well as for short periods in France and Germany. In 1962 he obtained a degree in English Language and Literature from Brasenose College, Oxford. After various occupations in the Canadian Arctic, Iran and London, he was employed in 1986 as a lecturer in management theory at the London Institute, from which he was happy to retire in 2002. He has translated three books from Swedish to English, and several samples of Old Norse and Anglo-Saxon poetry. Currently he is engaged in research on the life and work of Peter Monamy (1681-1749), the founder of English marine painting.*

> 'On the 27th June 1682, was born King *Charles* the Twelfth, a Man the most extraordinary, perhaps that ever appear'd in the World.'

With these words in 1732, from the first English translation of Voltaire's vividly readable *Histoire de Charles XII*, the legend of the adamantine warrior received an indelible imprint. The French original was first published in 1731, and remains one of the most frequently re-issued and re-translated works in literary history. Rigorously nurtured in the Protestant religious ethic by devoted parents, Charles placed his deceased father's crown on his own head, at the age of fifteen. Three years later, in 1700, Sweden's then extensive Baltic and North German territories were opportunistically attacked by a coalition of three kings ruling four countries, Russia, Poland, Saxony and Denmark. Charles spent the remaining eighteen years of his life at war, leading the resistance to this onslaught in person. The first nine of these eighteen years were attended by unparalleled success, followed by nine years of virtually unremitting defeat. By 1721 a diminished Sweden was left to lick her wounds in peace. Charles had been killed in 1718, murdered, according to the latest investigations, by a ball fired from close range, encased in the brass or silver metal of one of his own coat-buttons.

Voltaire set the mould for an enduring legend, but the panegyrists were engaged from the moment of Charles's shattering first victory over the Russians at Narva on the Baltic coast in the early months of the war, the news of which spread rapidly throughout Europe. In 1951 Olov Westerlund published his doctoral dissertation at the University of Lund, *Karl XII i Svensk Litteratur*, a 350-page study in the ways of poetic iconography from Dahlstierna (1661-1709) to Tegnér (1782-1846). This analysis of myth-making could rank with *The Road to Xanadu* by JL Lowes, and it demonstrates that virtually every line of Tegnér's poem on

Charles XII has its origin in the effusions of the preceding hundred years.

Tegnér's centenary verses were a milestone in the long process of debate on the character and historical significance of Charles and his Great Northern War, in which the human individual has now almost vanished under successive layers of hagiography and censure. Westerlund reveals that one of the king's most virulent critics in the mid-18th century was a man at least as extraordinary as himself, Emanuel Swedenborg. Attitudes to Charles XII within Sweden, which hardened against him as his star began to fall, have always been subject to swings of hero-worship and denigration. It has proved almost impossible for Swedes to reach a consensus in weighing reverence for their boy David against the fact that his obsessive pursuit of his hydra-headed Goliath merely led to the collapse of their 17th-century European status. A well-judged biography by Bengt Liljegren, published in 2000, may finally have achieved the desirable balance of passion and objectivity.

In a trenchant article in *Tidningen Boken*, 1998, a Swedish historian and novelist, K Arne Blom, expressed his concern about the devaluation of Sweden's historical and literary heritage. In his view a major victim of this revisionism is Esaias Tegnér, who can fairly be described as his country's first international best-selling author. Within 15 years of its appearance in 1825 his principal work, *Fritiofs Saga*, had been translated, partially or completely, twenty times, and the present reckoning is reputed to be once at least into every European language, as well as twenty-two times into English, and twenty times into German. The basic theme of this verse epic is the continuity of human values underlying the transition, during the Viking age of Scandinavia, from paganism to Christianity. Tegnér ended his life as a bishop, albeit of an unorthodox sort. Apart from his poetry, his work centred mainly on education and pan-Scandinavian cultural enfranchisement.

Until about the mid-1960s Tegnér's summation of the memory of Charles XII would have been known to every Swedish schoolchild. Although anthologies of pre-modernist Swedish poetry occasionally appear in English, one of the latest being *The North! To the North!* by Judith Moffett, published by Southern Illinois University Press in 2001, the only known previous attempt to translate Tegnér's extremely familiar lines has been by JED Bethune, in his *Specimens of Swedish and German Poetry*, 1848.

Few translators of formal, rhymed, metric, 18th- and 19th-century verse seem able to resist expressing their contempt for the efforts of their predecessors, and Bethune is no exception. Disingenuously admitting that 'I have not myself attempted a version of Frithiof', he rides into an attack on those that have, with 'I am ready to allow that all the previous English translations of Frithiof are indeed very bad', and singles out that of George Stephens, 1839, as the worst of the lot. It is true that Stephens, a pioneering runologist who spent most of his life in Denmark, appears to have no ear whatsoever for the rhythms of English verse. A much later translator, CD Locock, 1924, agrees that Stephens's 'versification can only be described as ludicrous', but concedes that as regards the first essential prerequisite, 'the reproduction . . . of the author's meaning', it is 'almost too unimpeachable'. In Stephens we perhaps have a significant forerunner, in the advocacy of literal translation, to no less a practitioner than Vladimir Nabokov.

The fact is that a poet, whatever s/he writes and whether in a style of the strictest traditional formality or the most outré avant-garde, is expressing his/her love-affair with his/her mother-tongue. For any poet older than about fourteen there can be no fully acceptable surrogate in this relationship. How then is the well-meaning translator to tackle his/her self-imposed and thankless task? Another of Tegnér's translators, Clement B Shaw, in 1908, set out a number of rules, of which the following are only a sample: 'A translation should produce the effect of the original. But this identity of emotional effect is by no means always to be secured by literal rendering . . . Moreover, the translator must translate – must faithfully reproduce the matter of the original, – no more, no less . . . One must not depart from his course for a rhyme too good to be lost; must not employ 'mountains' to rhyme with 'fountains', when the original does not allude to mountains.' Shaw's native origins are plainly evident from this excerpt. He, too, can only disparage his predecessors: 'no European English paraphrase of Frithiof's Saga preserves the Tegnerian measures with enough felicity even to evince literary courtesy to the great poet. Yet each translator claims to have done this very thing'. However, he reserves 'very high indorsement (sic)' for two American translations, 'the works of Mr and Mrs Holcomb, and of Professor Sherman. No consideration of nationality prompts the opinion that these two translations have not been equaled (sic) in England.'

Devotees of Nabokov's masterpiece, Pale Fire, may surprise themselves with a start of recognition at Shaw's instancing the rhyme of 'fountains' with 'mountains', and might wonder if the well-read polyglot was also familiar with the numerous English paraphrases of Fritiofs Saga. Yet another of its British translators, in 1872, was Captain H Spalding, of the 104th Fusiliers – a gentleman too upright to belittle his rivals. By 1881, when he translated Pushkin's Eugene Onegin, he had been promoted to Lieutenant-Colonel, and he is jocularly referred to in Nabokov's own impeccably non-paraphrastic 825-page conundrum as 'bluff Spalding', or 'matter-of-fact Lt Col Spalding'. Nabokov's dissection and 'literal' translation of Eugene Onegin in 1964 produces an effect on the English reader at least as ludicrous as Stephens's Frithiof's Saga. My suspicion is that the roguish genius was consciously constructing a monumental academic joke at the expense of lickspittle scholarship. Pale Fire is the obverse of this performance: a comic novel which is deeply serious, and the prankster's shade may now somewhere be chuckling at the Kinbotes he has spawned.

In the foreword to his three volumes devoted to *Eugene Onegin* Nabokov asserts: 'To reproduce the rhymes and yet translate the entire poem literally is mathematically impossible. But in losing its rhyme the poem loses its bloom . . . Should one then content oneself with an exact rendering of the subject matter and forget all about form? Or should one still excuse an imitation of the poem's structure to which only twisted bits of sense stick here and there, by convincing oneself and one's public that in mutilating its meaning for the sake of a pleasure-measure rhyme one has the opportunity of prettifying or skipping the dry and difficult passages?' . . . 'A schoolboy's boner mocks the ancient masterpiece less than does its commercial poeticization, and it is when the translator sets out to render the 'spirit', and not the mere sense of the text, that he begins to traduce his author.'

To coagulate a poem's spirit, sense, metre, verbal tropes, rhymes and meaning, into a language other than its original, would be a supernatural achievement. Mortals are left to compromise. While agreeing that 'in losing its rhyme the poem loses its bloom', I can only dissent from Nabokov's opinion that the translator who sets out to render the spirit of the text 'begins to traduce his author'. What other objective should s/he have, which could not otherwise be accomplished by handing the would-be reader several dictionaries, a selection of grammars, the rest of the literature in the source language, and locking her/him up for a year or ten? Clement B Shaw, in my view, is correct to say that 'a translation should reproduce the effect of the original'. Spirit is certainly communicable, and its inter-cultural transfer has been the aim of translation since poetry first began – the only issue is the translator's ability to prioritise from those factors that are irreconcilable. In the end it is a matter of taste and judgement and, *pace* Nabokov, the verdict of the consumer.

The modern reader might wonder that a military man, at the apogee of Queen Victoria's Empire, addressed himself to translating verse masterpieces from Swedish and Russian, and be curious about what he was doing between 1872 and 1881. It is recorded that on 22nd January, 1879, a Brevet Major Henry Spalding, of the 104th Regiment, rode out of a tiny British supply depot in Southern Africa, leaving Lieutenant JRM Chard in command, with the memorable words 'You will be in charge, although, of course, nothing will happen. I will be back by evening.' The defence of Rorke's Drift during the following 24 hours is one of the most astonishing actions in the annals of military history, unmatched since the Battle of Narva. I must try to emulate the disciplined restraint of 'bluff Spalding' by limiting myself to remarking that JED Bethune seems to have been mesmerised by his overwhelming compulsion to reproduce Tegnér's rhyme-scheme.

Charles XII: *on the centenary of his death* 1818

Kung Carl, den unga hjelte,
han stod i rök och dam.
Han drog sitt svärd från bälte
och bröt i striden fram.
"Hur Svenska stålet biter
kom låt oss pröfva på.
Ur vägen Moscoviter,
friskt mod, I gossar blå."

Och en mot tio ställdes
af retad Vasason.
Der flydde hvad ej fälldes,
det var hans lärospÂn.
Tre konungar tillhopa
ej skrefvo pilten bud.
Lugn stod han mot Europa,
en skägglös dundergud.

Gråhårad statskonst lade
de snaror ut med hast
den höga yngling sade
ett ord och snaran brast.
Högbarmad, smärt, gullhårig
en ny Aurora kom:
från kämpe tjugoårig
hon vände ohörd om

Der slog så stort ett hjerta
uti hans Svenska barm,
i glädje som i smärta,
blott for det rätta varm.
I med och motgång lika,
sin lyckas överman,
han kunde icke vika
blott falla kunde han.

Se, nattens stjernor blossa
på grafven längese'n,
och hundra årig mossa
betäcker hjeltens ben.
Det herrliga på jorden
förgänglig är dess lott.

King Charles, the conquering boy,
Stood up in dust and smoke;
He shook his sword for joy,
and through the battle broke.
How Swedish iron bites,
We will make trial new;
Stand back, you Muscovites;
Forward! my own true blue!

Not ten to one appal
The angry Vasa's son;
Those fled, who did not fall:
So was his course begun,
He drove three Kings asunder,
Who leagued against him stood;
And Europe saw with wonder
A beardless Thundergod.

Old grey-haired schemers muttered
Their plots with wily care
The brave young hero uttered
One word, and burst their snare.
High-bosomed, goldhaired, slender,
A new Aurora came:
From his throne's young defender,
The temptress turned in shame.

So great a heart was heaving
In his true Swedish breast,
In gladness, or in grieving,
Justice he loved the best.
Though fortune smiled or lowered,
He dauntless kept the field:
He could but be o'erpowered,
He knew not how to yield.

The stars have long been glowing
On his sepulchral stones;
A century's moss is growing
Above the hero's bones.
Thus glory passes forth,
So soon its records fall:

Hans minne uti Norden
Är snart en saga blott.

Dock – än till sagan lyssnar
det gamla sagoland
och dvergalåten tystnar
mot resen efterhand.
Än bor i Nordens lundar
den höga anden qvar
han är ej d^d, han blundar:
hans blund ett sekel var.

Böj Svea, knä vid griften,
din störste son göms der.
Läs nötta minneskriften,
din hjeltedikt hon är.
Med blottadt hufvud stiger
historien dit och lär,
och Svenska äran viger
sin segerfana der.

Esais Tegnér 1818

Their echo in the North
Is but an old man's tale.

Still is the old land hushed,
The tale still calls up wonder,
Low dwarfish sounds are crushed
By the old giant thunder.
Still in our Northern numbers
The lofty spirit burns;
It is not dead, it slumbers,
Its hour of pride returns.

Kneel, Sweden, where reposes
Thy greatest, noblest Son;
The crumbling stone discloses
The honour thou hast won.
There bards, to read his story,
Come reverently bare;
And Sweden's flag of glory
Is dedicated there.

JED Bethune, 1848

King Carl, the youthful hero,
In smoke and dust he stood;
He drew his sword from harness
And into battle strode.
'Come, let us try its war-bite,
What Swedish steel may do:
Make way, you Muscoviters,
Fresh heart, the lads in blue!'

So one at ten was pitted
By Vasa's angered son,
And all unfelled had fled when
Their lesson's day was done.
Three hostile kings united:
The boy stood like a rod,
And calmly faced Europa,
A beardless thunder-god.

As grizzled statesmen plotted
With hasty craft their trap,

The lofty stripling uttered
One word their snare to snap.
Full-bosomed, slender, golden
Aurora came one day:
The warrior of twenty
Turned her unheard away.

So great a heart was beating
Within his Swedish breast,
In gladness as in anguish
Alone for what is Just.
Alike at flood or ebbtide
Too resolute to quell,
The overlord of fortune,
He fought until he fell.

See! Stars of night an epoch
Upon his grave have shone,
And mosses now centennial
Bedeck the hero's bone.
All glory that is mortal
Is fated so to fade.
His name in Northern story
Will soon be just a shade.

Yet – to the tale may hearken
This ancient saga-land,
And dwarfish talk fall silent
When giants rise to stand.
Still in the Northern forest
The noble spirit stirs,
Not dead, but sleeping merely:
His sleep, one hundred years.

Kneel, Svea, by the graveside,
Thy greatest son here dwells;
And scan the worn memorial
Thy epic story spells.
All history, bare-headed,
Will to this place repair,
And Swedish honour hallows
Her victory-banner there.

[CHW 1998]

Alberto Blanco

Mexico

Translated by Joan Lindgren

Jose Emilio Pacheco calls **Alberto Blanco** *a dynamic and influential voice in the new poetry of Mexico. Musician, artist, essayist, translator and story-teller, Blanco writes poetry that explores connections and frontiers between the verbal, visual and aural experience. He is both innovator and classicist, materialist and mystic, visionary and chronicler of everyday life. He speaks of a world far beyond language and borders, and his love of nature is both genuine and artificial – without contradiction.*

The Shadow of Everyday, *from which the poems below are taken, is part of* Trebol Inverso, *one of the twelve books of poems written between 1973 and 1993 and collected in* El corazon del instante *(Fondo de Cultura Económica, 1998). Alvaro Mútis called it 'a loving catalogue of the minutiae of moments, plants, animals, beings, suns, and nocturnal revelations.'*

What These Flowers Want

1

What these flowers want
is to drink from your hands. Water

They need your shadow as they need
the round light of the sun

they long to turn back
and retrace your steps

Look, look, and don't be alarmed
these flowers want your friendship

2

In the mirror of the corollas
is the day's tumult

The shadow of every day
is the body of the city

War breaks out
in every one of the flowers

A volcano on the brink
of awakening every night

3

When the eye moves away from the treetop
it finds a flower on every branch

when the ear moves from the branch
it finds a memory in every flower

Now it is time for stones
to set out from zero and flower

As shells flower or
hurricanes flower in every season

The Trunk Of Language

1

The tree agreed upon as the place
for a halt on the road

The tree where two hearts
entwined turned dark

Solitary tree on whose trunk
names take on the flesh of life

Language of the bark of the ages
not all of a tree is foliage

2

Trunk of neon, foliage of crystal
fragile ashes of transitory humus

No one denies a tree is an iceberg
arrogant conqueror of the tides of time

Nights repose in this tree that
the daytime flower grow wise with sap

Crow and pigeon sweetly rock
awaiting the longed-for song

3

Every tree lighthouse of an inner sea
of shadows to guide us among the lights

that dizzy us on our course
from earth's one extreme to the other

To follow their imperceptible dance
is to recall the coitus of the hours

Like cradles rocked at midnight amidst
rattling of bones, rustling of dry leaves

A Spider On High

1

Out of the precarious balance
of a tragedy about to happen

A spider observes the world
a prisoner of motion

A drama whose plot involves
more affinities than betrayals

And whose pain reveals
more answers than questions

2

Her quiet between parentheses
she shrieks, rips, stomps

The thousand transformations
of a carpet lit by a vegetal moon

There is a darkness that
even in dreams won't be erased

A candelabrum of sugar
that lights up a statue of salt

3

When silence signs its contract
when day decides to end

And the numberless legs of the spider
take a first step into the unknown

A multiplication of fear will issue
from every imprecation, a hymn of praise

And a spider in a corner somewhere
will weave itself a dream rose to dream by

Juan Gelman
Argentina

Translated and introduced by Joan Lindgren

Joan Lindgren *writes:* Those who read of the *Argentinazo*, the angry popular roar rising up out of Argentina's latest descent into degradation (*The Guardian*, January 16, 2003, Naomi Klein), may want to revisit the work of **Juan Gelman**. Argentina, the country said to be lost in the vastness of its own possibilities and unmanageable wealth, has always maintained twin flames: the one of the crucible where its people periodically get melted down, and its parallel, the bright flame of stunning and rarified literary fire. The irony of their co-existence should not be lost on us.

Juan Gelman, said Eduardo Galeano, fires off from his country 'his incessant shots of beauty and melancholy. Juan . . . outlaw poet . . . has committed the crime of marrying justice to beauty . . . To read Juan Gelman with impunity is impossible.'[1]

The families of Argentina's Disappeared maintain that the country has not been able to recover from the Dirty War / military dictatorship which took their loved ones, because in fact the Disappeared, including the children of Juan Gelman, were the yeast, the cream, the heart and brains of the nation. Gelman's voice had reached deep into the historical suffering of his people and in the intimate, conversational tone of the tango had sung their dilemma for decades. In 1997 the poet was awarded Argentina's National Poetry Prize. In the year 2000 Mexico, where he continues to live in exile, awarded him the Juan Rulfo Prize, placing him for posterity among the many masters of Latin America's prodigious literary force.

Though *Unthinkable Tenderness, Selected Poems of Juan Gelman* (University of California Press, 1997) is a difficult book to lay hands on, the Argentine people continue to resonate with Gelman's language:

"us the poor who fed on patience..."[2]

57.5% of the populace are living below the poverty line today and children are dying of hunger daily in the world's fourth largest food producing nation.

"When we are born they cut the umbilical cord. When we are exiled nobody cuts the memory, the language, the blood supply . . ."[3]

Much of the nation is made up of new immigrants and their offspring with hardly time for the ripening of families, the securing of the social order.

> "I am a monstrous plant. My roots are a thousand miles from me and no stem connects us . . ."[4]

Reverse immigration is in process now to Spain and Italy with 27.5% unemployment and rampant crime.

> "Here nobody washes his mother's diapers . . ."[5]

In other words the Argentineans are a people still haunted by the shadow of the left-behind as well as by the absence of the Disappeared.

But if the soldiers – "my country, disappeared into a soldier's cap" – are gone now, the current genocide is economic. Argentina's descent from its place as foster child of neo-liberalism to broken cast-off toy of that global movement further humiliates the national self-image. And Gelman, not, of course, retired from his poetic reflection upon the fate of himself and his country, continues to write what Julio Cortazar refers to in his introduction to *Unthinkable Tenderness* as poems that are 'a permanent caress of words upon unknown tombs'[6], and others that explore and question the 'general uneasiness of the dangerous and fertile embrace' of Galeano's justice and beauty.

Returnings

So you're back.
As if nothing had happened.
No concentration camp.
As if for 23 years
I've not heard you or seen you.
The green bear is back, you
in that coat two sizes too large
and me still a father. We've gone back
to our incessant father-and-son-ship
in those irons that never end.
Will they never cease?
You'll never cease your ceasing.
You come back and come back
and I have to explain that you're dead.

The Bird

Saying bird I destroy him
and that's an unpardonable sin.
The bird goes on flying.
I have destroyed him in me, that's all.
He's not flying now, already
not building his nest in the tree
that I'm not nor stirring up thoughts
in me. He's lost among the branches
and the incense.
Who am I to him?
Nothing in fact.
Before they used to visit me the ones
I lost and the memory of what I lost.
Now they are silence deciphered
and certain hopes have died.

Travels

He goes into his poems as one goes into his cave.
Penelope
never will knit him a sweater
never mind unravel him one.
He has no Achaean urgencies.
The loves of Priam and Arisbe
are nothing to him and thus
he's always listening for cymbals
and other aerial adventures,
displacement, maybe, or dis-time-ment.
The light of the stars touches him
by some random whim of the universe.
Dry leaves fall from him
which he contemplates stupidly.
He is naked and trembling. There is
no justice to be found and
what he looks for is not.

Spittle

The vanquished dress in suits made of nothing.
Have they become a sign of absurdity?
Has utopia congealed in their heads?
You see them in afflicted cafés, where
they bother and babble
a shabby shine on their lips
that can't be turned off. Do they
keep up their passion for raping the world
and not being raped by the world?
Do they rage against stupidity?
Or do they quietly wipe off the spittle
that time has let drool on them?
They write papers no one will read.
Their bones already silent,
they have unspoken names.

*

It would seem that Gelman recognized long ago the work cut out for an
Argentine poet. Back in the eighties he wrote these lines in the poem 'Sayings':

. . . I met the two tasks of the caged bird
which are to both tie and untie itself
to wound life with love and to suffer the wound
to be purified by silenced love and to use that silence
to burst the world's eardrums[7]

Speaking of pockets of resistance in his book The Shape Of A Pocket *(Pantheon*
Books, 2002), John Berger cited a poem of Juan Gelman's with the introductory
words: 'Much pain is unshareable. But the will to share pain is shareable. And
from that inevitably inadequate sharing comes a resistance.'

The Deluded

hope fails us often
grief, never
that's why some think
that known grief is better
than unknown grief
they believe that hope is illusion
they are deluded by grief[8]

Gelman is not deluded by grief. A poem from the recent collection Valer la pena *(Visor, 2002), from which these recent poems are taken, refers us back to the twin flames:*

The Flame
to Eduardo Galeano

The old flame does not go out.
The storms, the
impieties, all that surrenders
these do not prevent it from trembling
like a body desired.
It insists on the breakdown of evil
though various and unstanchable blood
stain the first heart, the one
that changed furies daily.
The flame is written, not lost.
It frequents unnamed places
and goes on burning.

Such a flame, of course, has fuelled the blazing hopes of the Argentinazo. And its roar may yet burst some eardrums.

Notes

1   Juan Gelman, *Unthinkable Tenderness*, Berkeley, 1997, xi

2   Ibid., 41

3   Ibid., 72

4   Ibid.

5   Ibid., 77

6   Gelman was able to find and bury his son's remains and is presently searching for those of his daughter-in-law. His grandchild, a woman then of twenty-four, he located in Uruguay in 2000.

7   Ibid., 127

8   Ibid., 167

Lya Luft
Brazil

Translated by Arthur M Lipman

Lya Luft, *born in Porto Alegre, Brazil in 1938, is one of the country's major contemporary writers. Since 1964 she has produced fifteen novels and collections of poetry and over one hundred translations from the German or English into Portuguese, including Goethe, Schiller, Rainer Maria Rilke, Hermann Hesse, Doris Lessing, Günter Grass, Thomas Mann and Virginia Woolf. In 1988 she published* O Lada Fatal *(The Fatal Side), a collection of forty-two short poems dealing with the trauma of untimely death and personal grief. These poems, originally written without any intention of their being published, continue to be widely read in Brazil, and a theatrical version was subsequently produced as a one-woman show in Rio de Janeiro. The poems printed below are from this collection.*

Arthur M Lipman *was born in England in 1914 and educated there. He lived in Brazil for twelve years. Poems by him have appeared in Brazil, Canada, England and USA. A collection of his Brazilian sonnets,* Saudades, *was published in Rio de Janeiro in 1939. Lipman has translated the works of many Brazilian poets, notably Vinicius de Moraes, Carlos Drummond de Andrade, Cecilia Meireles, Mario Quintana and, more recently, Lya Luft.*

*

When my loved one died, I could not believe it:
I would walk around the room alone repeating in a low voice
'I don't believe it, I don't believe it.'
I kissed his mouth still warm,
caressed his curly hair,
took off his heavy silver wedding-ring with my name
and slipped it on my finger.
It was much too big, but still I wear it.

Many people came and went.
They stared, they embraced me, they cried,
behaving as if it were they, incredulously, who were orphans.

He of whom they talk and write about today
(who little by little is being forgotten)
is much less than the person who rests within my heart,
my lover and my little boy still.

*

My loved one carried the weariness of many centuries.
He would lie on the sofa, head resting on my lap:
'With you I have found peace.'
But he was tired. He yearned for more peace
than I could give him with all my limitless love.
He would say:
'Today I am tired as the devil and for no reason.'

The reason was he was an exile in this life
and his soul a flame
which could be assuaged only in God.

So it was necessary that he should go.

*

Everything appeared to be so routine:
I even remembered to take both our toothbrushes
and the book we were reading together.
Everything as usual:
that morning at breakfast we had discussed
the latest news in the paper.
We went to the place where you were to die
less than two days later,
and it was one of those clear, sunny Rio de Janeiro mornings,
I in the back seat, leaning forward,
stroking your face.
(You had even shaved.)
Everything absolutely normal:
you speaking and laughing, disguising the fact you were not
feeling well.
I am trying to find out, but have not discovered
whether crouched within my heart
was the forewarning that in a few hours
it would be all over.

(In some deaths this is the ultimate betrayal.)

*

When my loved one died
this hole opened up in my chest

out of which they tore my heart
and replaced it with a strange machine
which keeps me alive,
full of blades and sharp points.

(Each beat cuts into me
and forces me to live.)

*

My loved one was young and old
brusque and candid
passionate and lonely
and understood my
restless soul.

Sometimes he found me amusing.
But when in the middle of the night I would tell him
that for no reason I felt afraid
(without doubt anticipating the separation which would come
to pass)
he would embrace me, silent and sombre, saying:
'You have good reason to be afraid.'

Then we would never mention the dreaded word
which perhaps was lurking in the corners of the room.
But on these occasions he would explain nothing to me.

*

Still I don't believe you are dead.
I visit your grave under the Rio de Janeiro sun,
where we were happy and unhappy and loved each other so much.
But I refuse to believe it.
I put my hand on the stone which hides
some little part of you that remains;
yet I won't believe it.
I leave flowers on the rough stone slab,
get up and walk among anonymous and familiar graves,
alone under the sun of a city where I no longer live.
I guess you must really be dead
or you wouldn't allow me to walk there all alone.

(Once I truly believe you are dead
what will my heart do?)

Sitesh Aloke
Hindi

Translated by Debjani Chatterjee

Based in Delhi, **Sitesh Aloke** *is a leading poet and short story writer in Hindi. He is co-editor of* Pratibha India, *a quarterly devoted to the arts. The translation here is of a poem from Sitesh Aloke's collection,* Yatha Sambhav (For the Reason), *published in Delhi by Medha Books (2000).*

Debjani Chatterjee *is a well-known poet, editor and children's writer. Her recent anthologies include the award-winning* The Redbeck Anthology of British South Asian Poetry, Who Cares? Reminiscences of Yemeni Carers in Sheffield, My Birth Was Not in Vain *and* Rainbow World: Poems from Many Cultures. *Sheffield Hallam University conferred an honorary doctorate on her in 2002.*

Progress

The news states:
twenty years have elapsed
since our victory
over smallpox.

And we know
this too,
that in the meantime,
terrorism and fanaticism
have each year
delivered thousands
from the bondage of living.

We are making progress:
humanity no longer dies
at the hands of insects and vermin.
It has achieved the distinction
of death at the hands of human beings.

Saleha Chowdhury
Bengali

Translated by Debjani Chatterjee

Saleha Chowdhury *was born in Rajshahi, Bangladesh, in 1943, but has been living in London since 1972. After retirement from teaching, she has concentrated on writing novels, plays and poetry. She has also written two bilingual books for children. Her poetry collections include:* Judas Ebong Tritiyo Pokkho (Judas and the Third Party) *and* Dewaley Cactus Phool (The Cactus Flower on the Wall).

Translations of poems by Saleha Chowdhury have been published by Sheffield Libraries in a bilingual anthology: My Birth was Not in Vain: Selected Poems by Seven Bengali Women *(2001).*

After The War

This time I met
the labourer, Shamchhu,
after twenty-five long years.
He had lost an arm
when injured by a mortar shell
in the War
twenty-five long years ago.
His eyes were clouded with cataracts.
His body was bent with age.
I asked: 'How are you?
Having lost everything,
what did you gain from our nation's independence?'

'I don't worry about myself,'
said Shamchhu, stitching an umbrella
in spite of his filmy eyes.
'I worry for Akbar,
rendered bedridden forever by the War.
His back is broken
and his whole body is riddled with maggots.
Azrael has forgotten him
in his lonely room.'

War creates many such cases.
Akbar, Shamchhu and so many others

don't die, yet lose their lives.
But those whom Fate
has showered with prosperity today,
did they – on that day – smell the reek
of gunpowder in the air ?

Notes:
The War referred to is the Bangladesh Liberation War of 1971. Azrael is the Angel
of Death in Islam.

Yet Another Birth

Rebati and Radhika bowed their heads
at God's feet
for many years.
Thereafter on a storm-lashed morning
a resplendent child
proclaimed the news of his arrival
with a piercing scream.
The rain poured all over the house then.
Rebati and Radhika thought:
God is not false.

Arjun grew up
and succeeded to his father's caste occupation –
pulling the Municipality's
rubbish cart.
Unceasingly he sings:
'*Patita pavana Sita-Ram . . .*'

Note: '*Patita pavana Sita-Ram*' is a line from one of the most popular Vaishnava Hindu
hymns in praise of Rama and Sita, the avatars of Vishnu and Lakshmi who are the hero
and heroine of *The Ramayana*. Arjun is the name of a heroic prince in *The Mahabharata*.

The Story of *Kaw, Khaw, Gaw* and *Ghaw*

In some reckless Raja's reign,
for some reason during a destructive phase
Kaw, Khaw, Gaw and *Ghaw* were about to lose their lives.
Such things happen so often.
Whenever a careless Raja pleases
he can shower down his disapproval

in diverse forms of destruction,
if he so chooses.
After this a common human occurrence,
an inevitable display,
is the defiance of a cluster of youths.
In a herd those innocent rebels
lose their lives in a passionate and tumultuous war.
When the entire world is waiting,
various hands are raised in invitation,
calling them.
What happens next?
Everyone knows.
And what news of those defiant youths?
Deep flow the cloudy waters
of the Padma, the Tishta, the Jumna.

What can stop me speaking on this 21st February?
My birth was in that innocent land
of ardent devotion to some lost impulse.
People are called to assemble
in this city on this one occasion every year.
The discussion is of the same insoluble matters.
Here too *Kaw, Khaw, Gaw* and *Ghaw* cry and die.

Note: *Kaw, Khaw, Gaw* and *Ghaw* are the first consonants of the Bengali alphabet and, therefore, the equivalent of 'A, B, C and D'. Here the Bengali letters refer to the language as a whole. 21st February is Bengali Language Movement Day, an annual commemoration of the day in 1952 when many youths were martyred for their devotion to their mother tongue.

Shared Pain

Rohim Miah's two wives
pull the plough in his field;
Rohim Miah enters
his field for work at midnight.
His house is shut in the daytime –
Rohim Miah's womenfolk are learning the Shariah.
From time to time a cane
swishes sudden welt marks on backs.
Heads ache, blood is vomited –
alas! God is the witness.

From time to time the two women
hold each other and weep.
People marvel at such friendship
between the two wives.

Note: The Shariah is the canonic law of Islam, but in popular speech it refers to any of Allah's commandments.

Mangalesh Dabral

Translated by Robert A Hueckstedt

Mangalesh Dabral *has published four collections of poetry* – Pahāṛ par lālṭen *(1981),* Char kā rāstā *(1988),* Ham jo dekhte hain *(1995) and* Āvāz bhī ek jagah hai *(2000). He has also published one travelogue,* Ek bār Iowa *(1996) and a collection of prose,* Lekhah kī roṭī *(1998). He was awarded the Om Prakash Smriti Samman in 1982, the Shrikant Varma Puraskar in 1989, the Shamsher Samman in 1995, the Pahal Samman in 1996, and the Sahitya Akademi Award in 2000. His work has been translated into all the major Indian languages as well as Russian, Spanish, German, Polish and Bulgarian. He works for the Hindi daily newspaper* Janasattā.

Robert A Hueckstedt *teaches Hindi and Sanskrit at the University of Virginia, Charlottesville, Virginia. His translations form the Hindi have appeared previously in* Concerning Poetry, raddle moon, Pig Iron, Paintbrush, Indian Literature, Nimrod, Other Voices *and* Comparative Criticism. *His translation* The Hunted, *of Mudra Rakshasa's Hindi novel* Dandavidhan, *was published by Penguin Books India in 1992. In 1998 he was a prizewinner in the annual literary translation prize sponsored by the British Centre for Literary Translation and the British Comparative Literature Association.*

Return

If you were to return home like a lost and long-forgotten child, then, though you had become quite old, your mother, father, or some other relative would recognize you as if you had never left. Your true love, combing out the hair of your unborn child, would spread it out like the sheet of your nuptial night. If you go to the jungle, better go as a tree than a hunter. A taller tree will hide you below it. From your tread a light dust will rise and twinkle in the sunlight. Shaking your leaves will make a sound setting off the ripples of a breeze. A story will be there, or some preserved fragment of it, in the ruins of which you can live. Rain will pull you out; snow will send you back. It will be good to follow for some distance those things you do not understand. You will be able to enter into old, broken mirrors immersed only in their own memories. There you may see a dream, or within you may be born something indistinct, and you will experience again that moment before which you were what you did not remain.

[1998]

In *Āvāz bhī ek jagah hai* (New Delhi: Vani Prakasan, 2000).

The Seven Day Journey

First, Monday flaps open like a freshly washed sheet
Hope snuggles up and says, This time
We can take a different approach
So we map out the problems along the way
And where the detours have to be.
Tuesday's like a cliff,
A blind either-or,
Ahead, do we turn or slide down the descent
And how much concentration and courage do we need?
Through Wednesday's binoculars we can see far ahead
It won't be as easy as Hope first had said
There he was, just as before,
Unsettling, indefinite Haze in the head.
Thursday's like an inn along the way
Half the distance we've already travelled
And now we know exactly where we stand
And perhaps, in these difficult times, there may just be a way out.
Coming along that very path Friday gives us patience
But it's clear that so far we've accomplished nothing
And now it's getting late
And we haven't even sent a postcard.
With that anxiety we enter Saturday
A subterranean space where it's difficult to know
If we're moving or not
And when someone asks how I am
I say there's nothing to tell.
The next morning Sunday comes
Day of rest and things
Assume their prehistoric immobility
Books lie open
The tea's gone cold
Over there the pile of dirty clothes
On the table the phone rings and rings
And on my door someone's hesitant knock.

Note: The Hindi original was written in 1998, and first appeared in the March 1998 issue of *Kathades*, a literary magazine published in Delhi. It was later published in the collection *Āvāz bhī ek jagah hai*. This translation first appeared in *Hindi: Language, Discourse, Writing*, a journal of the Mahatma Gandhi International Hindi University, New Delhi, published by Rainbow Publishers, Noida, UP, India.

A Poem on Childhood

The older I get the more a child I become. For a minute I'm angry and petulant, then I'm suddenly happy. In front of the toy store I stand for hours. My eager eyes want to know what's behind every lock. In the morning I look all around in amazement as if seeing the world for the first time.

I want to return to my childhood. But I have no map to get there. It is a riddle-like, complicated path. Often filled with smoke. At the end of it is a cave where a demon lives. Sometimes a boy hides there who's run away from home. Pieces of hard rock and glass by his legs.

People from home keep shouting for me. I write them letters. I'm coming I'm coming I'll be home soon.

[1990]
In *Ham jo dekhte hai* (New Delhi: Radhakrsna, 1995).

Lantern on Mountain

In the jungle are women
Unconscious under bundles of wood
In the jungle are children
Buried before their time
In the jungle barefoot old men
Afraid and coughing disappear in the end
In the jungle hatchets always fly
In the jungle blood has slept.

Behind the cliffs heated in the sun
The cries of centuries of pain
And just a little grass – quite ancient
Swaying in the water;
Trees reaching the jaws of the next season
Night after night become naked;
In the stillness like the point of a needle
The burning earth rolls on her side
And the sky revolves like a huge millstone.

The mountain your ancestors brought this far
Every year breaks more and more, like grief
All the years all the centuries

Freeze like ire in dreamless eyes
In your soul
In the domestic darkness of the hearth
Your helpless words are spread
Like grain gathered in a famine.

In the distance glows a lantern on a mountain
Like a luminous eye
Twinkling slowly becoming a fire –
Look at your mortgaged field,
The jewelry taken off sobbing women,
Look at all the people dead
From hunger, from flooding, from disease
Who've risen up on the cliffs
Wiping away infinite snow with their hands,
Look at your own hunger
Becoming a quick claw;
From the jungle comes a constant roar
And desires sharpen their teeth
On the rocks.

   [1974]
In *Pahāṛ par lālṭen* (New Delhi: Radhakrsna, 1981).

Exhaustion

In the evening, having shaken off the world,
Face down on the bed, in the end
What's left but misery riding one's shoulders
What's left in the end
But mould on the soul

Slowly, kept down by daily routine,
Darkness rises,
The parks' breezes return to the parks,
The children are incarcerated at home,
The women watched all day
Reverberating late in the brain
Go off to sleep,
Like a roaring river
A hush descends from the sky

When night mutely
Crouches on my chest,
Black exhaustion climbs into bed
Negotiates the curve of muscles
Raises its hand from the abyss

The years stand like silence,
In them, in haze-filled rooms, is sleep,
The past there is like burning candles,
On the years' roofs ice has formed,
Over them walk whistling screaming dreams
Trailing lines of blood

In the light in the middle of the night
Trees quietly keep dropping their leaves,
In the minds of animals in the middle of the night
The constrained earth spreads out to infinity,
In the middle of the night
Ruin-risen ash falls
On my bones.

[1974]
In *Pahāṛ par lālṭen* (New Delhi: Radhakrsna, 1981).

A Child

He remembered exactly
Every year how many toys he broke
How many times he cried left alone
How many times he fell on the stones
And got up and ran fast for home;
He remembered every dream individually
In which only children appeared
Coming his way
The taste of each thing one by one
Rested on his tongue
Till the next one had come.

Gradually he became older,
And suddenly he was an adult.
Now he laughs
That he's forgotten how many times
The place of his dream

Was a land on fire
Where sometimes he could hear
His mother and father crying.

[1977]
In *Pahāṛ par lālṭen* (New Delhi: Radhakrsna, 1981).

Final Incident

Flicking out their tongues the days
Slither past my head
And daylight makes me even duller
And leaves me in the middle of the city
In a peculiar haze.
I'm startled and clear my eyes,
The city drifts on in a perpetual flood
Tossing me to the side
Like a stone or piece of wood.

My glasses, often giving me
An indifferent and imposing air,
Plumb my bottomless soul and smash
At night when I light a cigarette
While lying on the bed;
An obscene wheeze
Rises from my throat
And I feel around
For jagged horns of desire
Taken root on my face.

For many years I've seen numb girls,
Like cut saplings,
Exit their offices and disperse
Looking at nothing on the streets;
I've seen hunger rising behind houses;
I've seen the insane screaming
In the ruined night's wooden cage;
And I've heard an insensible clopping of hooves
Resounding in my rattled brain.

*

Within a final incident
Green trees are swaying all around
The dust is settling in the city
People elbow one another aside
And slip out ahead;
In the darkness a big-bellied woman is drowsy,
Her three sickly children
Beat each other
And I, hands clasped,
Stand at the bus stop
Where a fresh poster waits for me
And an unknown bird is
Eager to sing into my memory.

[1975]
In *Pahāṛ par lālṭen* (New Delhi: Radhakrsna, 1981).

Debarati Mitra

Bengali

Translated by Debjani Chatterjee and Ashoke Sen

Debarati Mitra *was born in Kolkata, India, in 1946. A leading poet and poetry critic in Bengali, she has won the Krittibas Purashkar and the Ananda Purashkar prizes. Her poetry is modern in style and her eight collections have earned her a distinctive place in contemporary Bengali literature.*

Ashoke Sen *lives in Kolkata where he is a freelance journalist and writes for serious Indian newspapers and journals. He is also a short story writer, translator and anthologist.*

Translations of poems by Debarati Mitra have been published by Sheffield Libraries in a bilingual anthology: My Birth Was Not in Vain: Selected Poems by Seven Bengali Women *(2001).*

The Compassionate King

On his crow-wife's death anniversary, a king
tied a small pitcher to the branch of a *pituli* tree,
drew clouds and a peacock's cry on its surface,
painted the forest's collyrium
so that the rains would come.
May rain water gather there throughout the year.
Crows suffer greatly in this life:
at least after dying in the searing sun, beak and head dipped, may
they drink the plentiful water.
This was his earnest prayer.

The compassionate king had human, animal
and various other wives.

    [DC]

My Daughters

My daughter is dark, quite dark really, wears her hair in a topknot.
At dawn, seated on the clothes-line on the terrace,
she swings to and fro and says:
'Went to Argentina to see the clouds,
but it rained in torrents, I couldn't find shelter,
so I am back.'

I tell her: 'My pet, I couldn't teach you anything properly:

not dance, song, painting or the three Rs.
So, in sorrow, you turned into a bird!
Come, eat a little grain, drink a little water
and remain here.'

'Will you be able to keep me forever?'
she asked, darkening the morning. Floating on air,
the girl suddenly flew off.
Storm, thunder and lightning are her walls, windows and doors,
but she's in a fix the moment she wants to land –
for the earth keeps shifting like an escalator –
where will she perch?
Where can I find her a home?

I think on and on
when one day from the skies
come gusts of wind to tell me –
'Don't worry, Mother, don't worry so.
I, we, who are your daughters,
will float from land to land –
trees, words and life itself
cannot even be born without us.'

[AS]

Bhashani, Mangala and Independence

In July nights on the tin roof
there is only the pattering sound of rain.
At the crack of dawn there's a bus to be caught,
a factory at Rajpur that I must rush to –
why does the finger ache so badly
when putting continuous white stitches on black bags?
Lemon flowers don't find it painful
to bloom in the pitch dark.
For humans why is there such dislike, misery and disquiet?
In the mornings as I leave home I see
slimy monsoon mud on roads and pavements,
as though some innocent creature's blood is flowing,
like the agony of a slaughtered goat in the air.
In our village of Kotalipara, they say that happiness
used to float about like the light clouds of the Puja season.
Mother would tell so many stories.

Where have they all gone now!
Biting on the nation as on a custard apple,
who made it the earthen bowl of the goddess of misfortune?

When, after two girls, the youngest girl was born,
her father grudgingly named her Bhashani.
With much struggle I'm sending her to school, she takes her
Madhyamik
next year.
The other day, standing in the courtyard, she was showing me a
      comet –
long like her own hair;
such a big comet, it seems, has not risen in a hundred years.

At night, lying next to me, Bhashani babbles so many things.
Hugging me, she says: "Ma, you're the same age as Independence."
Perhaps, but I'm not independent, I never was.
I only recall that in Father's house in my childhood village of Mophoswal,
milk flowed profusely like tears from Mangala the cow
and drenched the dummy calf of straw under her udder.
Is our Independence like that?

    [AS]

Notes

Puja season: the festive season in autumn when Bengali Hindus celebrate their most
important festival, the Durga Puja festival in honour of the Mother Goddess Durga.
Bhashani: *Bhashan* means immersion, so by naming his third unwanted daughter
Bhashani, the father is suggesting that she arrived drifting on floodwater or even
that she should be immersed in the river. The name is also suggestive of the ancient
practice of female infanticide in Bengal when infant girls would be drowned in the
Ganges.
Madhyamik: Secondary school examinations.
Mangala: *Mangal* means good fortune and auspiciousness.
Goddess of Misfortune: *Alakshmi* or the Goddess of Misfortune is the opposite of
Lakshmi the Goddess of Good Fortune. Lakshmi normally carries a miraculous
vessel containing riches. So the poet imagines *Alakshmi* carrying a poor earthen bowl.

Kabir
India/Hindi

Translated by Arvind Krishna Mehrotra

Arvind Mehrotra *writes:* Very little is known about **Kabir**, outside what can be culled from his heavily interpolated poems, or from hagiographies and legends. According to the latter, Kabir lived for 120 years, from 1398 to 1518. Modern scholars, however, take a more realistic view, but are divided as to whether his *floruit* is the first or the second half of the fifteenth century. Kabir (whose name is a Quaranic title of Allah meaning 'great') was born in Kashi into a Muslim family recently converted to Islam. The family belonged to the *Julaha* – or weaver – caste, and it is safe to assume that the chief reason for its conversion was its low status in the Hindu social system.

There are occasional references to the family profession in Kabir's poems. In one poem in particular, addressed to his anxious mother, he talks of dismantling his loom because, he says, he cannot both thread the shuttle *and* hold the thread of that supreme reality, which he called Ram, in his hand. Someone who is the lord of three worlds, he says, is not going to let them starve . . . Kabir was married and had a son and daughter, perhaps two sons and two daughters.

Kabir's hagiographers, who have been active since c. 1600, approve neither of his marriage nor, indeed, of his lowly origin, and it was in order to disguise the latter that the birth legends were created. However, the legends ended up highlighting precisely what they were meant to conceal. In one of them, a Brahmin widow once accompanied her father to the shrine of a famous ascetic. Pleased with her devotion, the ascetic prayed that she be blessed with a son. The prayer was answered, and in due course a son was born to her. But there was one problem: Brahmin widows are not supposed to get pregnant, and she had to abandon the infant. The wife of a weaver, who was passing that way, discovered the child and took him home. The child was Kabir.

It is said that Kabir chose to spend his last days not in Kashi, the holiest of holy Hindu places, a city that promises salvation to all those who die there and where he had lived all his life, but in an obscure town called Maghar, a place that from ancient times has been associated first with Buddhists, and later with Muslims and the lower castes. 'He who dies in Maghar is reborn as an ass', Kabir says in one poem, expressing a popular belief. The move to Maghar has a clear message: the place of one's death is of no consequence; salvation can be found anywhere. It was Kabir's last act of defiance.

In his distaste for humbug, Kabir can remind you of Diogenes. He was born in a Muslim household, but poured scorn on their *kazis*, or lawgivers, at every opportunity. He had Hindu followers, but reserved his sharpest barbs for pundits. In the end, Islam and Hinduism caught up with him. A famous story about Kabir tells how, following his death, both Hindu and Muslim mobs laid claim to his body. The Hindus were adamant to cremate, and the Muslims to bury him, but when the shroud was removed they found instead of the cadaver a heap of flowers. The two communities peacefully divided the flowers and performed Kabir's last rites, each according to its custom.

Described as 'A great many-sided shift . . . in Hindu culture and sensibility', the movement called *bhakti* began in South India, in the country of the Tamils, in the sixth century AD. It moved to Karnataka next (tenth century), then to Maharashtra (twelfth century onwards), but it was in North India, between the fifteenth and seventeenth century, that it found perhaps its fullest expression. During this long period of over a millennium, in which there were great political and cultural changes within India, there was one aspect of *bhakti* that remained constant throughout: its opposition to religious and social orthodoxies. The degree and nature of opposition varied, but it was never wholly absent. *Bhakti* favoured the informal over the formal, the spontaneous over the prescribed, and the vernacular over Sanskrit.

The poet-saint, who was often a low-caste cobbler, tailor, or weaver, was at the vanguard of this movement. Not content to worship him from a distance, he wanted to taste God, that 'chemical called Ram', on his tongue. The poet-saint could, of course, also be a woman. *Bhakti* is derived from the Sanskrit root *bhaj*, and one of its meanings is 'to serve, honour, revere, love, adore'. The *bhakta*, the 'devotee' or 'lover of God', looks upon God with a certain intimacy. It was a relationship based not on ritual but romance, and like any close relationship, it sometimes reached breaking point.

Of all *bhakti* poets, Kabir is the most outspoken. He is ever ready to engage the reader, to harangue him, using the vocative to grab his attention: Mulla, Pundit, Kazi, Yogi, Fool. A Kabir poem has no time to waste; it hits the ground running. And yet, despite the thousands of poems ascribed to Kabir, not one can be attributed to him with certainty. His is a collective voice, which is so individual that it cannot be mistaken for any one else's.

The numbers in brackets refer to *pads* in *Parasnath Tiwari, Kabir Granthavali* (Allahabad: Hindi Parishad, 1961). It was the first critical edition of Kabir to take into account both manuscript and printed sources, and is still unsurpassed.

Arvind Krishna Mehrotra *is the author of four collections of poems, the most recent of which is* The Transfiguring Places *(Ravi Dayal, 1998). He has also translated* The Absent Traveller: Prakrit Love Poetry *(Ravi Dayal, 1991) and edited (with Daniel Weissbort)* Periplus: Poetry in Translation *(Oxford UP, 1993). Other books edited by him are* The Oxford Indian Anthology of Twelve Modern Indian Poets *(Oxford UP, 1992) and* A History of Indian Literature in English *(C Hurst, 2003).*

1 [8]

Like a sharp arrow
    Is the love of Ram.
Only someone struck by it
    Knows the pain.

You look for the wound,
    But the skin is not broken.
You bring out the ointment,
    But have nowhere to rub it.

When all women
    Look the same,
Who among them
    Will the lord choose?

Fortunate is she,
    Says Kabir,
In the parting of whose hair,
    And hers alone,

Is put vermilion.

2 [11]

My husband is called Hari,
And I am his young wife.
My husband is called Ram,
He's an inch taller than me.

Looking my best,
I go in search of Hari,
The lord of three worlds.
He's nowhere to be found.

We live under the same roof,
Even sleep in the same bed,
But seldom meet.
Fortunate the bride, says Kabir,

Whose husband loves her.

3 [19]

Lying beside you,
I'm waiting to be kissed.
But your face is turned
And you've dropped off to sleep.

Though a saw blade on my neck
Would sound sweeter than your snoring,
My arms put around you
I'll make my submission:

I have one husband: you.
You have one wife: me.
Who's there to come between us?
Beware, says Kabir,

Of the man you love.
He can be a tricky customer.

4 [29]

Chalo,
Chalo,
Everyone keeps saying,
As if they know where Paradise is.
But ask them what lies beyond
The tips of their noses
And they'll look at you blankly.

So long as Paradise is where they want to go,
Paradise is not where they're going to reach.
And what if all talk of Paradise is hearsay?
Best you check out the place for yourself.
As for me, says Kabir, if anyone's listening,
The company of the good is what I seek.

5 [38]

When the lord of three worlds
    Is the lord you serve,
Those other gods
    Need no looking after.

They're like branches,
    Says Kabir,
Kept green by the water
    The tree receives.

6 [62]

Why so much fuss
About something so false,
So quick to deteriorate?

Once dead,
The body that was fed
The kilos of sweets
Is taken out and burnt,
And the head on which
A bright turban was tied
Is jabbed at by crows.
The bones burn like tinder,
The hair like a pile of hay.

But your sleep, says Kabir,
Is deep, unbroken.
Even death's bludgeon,
About to crush your head,
Won't wake you up.

7 [77]
Try as you may,
If the heart's elsewhere given,
Nothing will bring you
To the four-armed god.
Not explication, or fasting,
Or telling beads, or sleeping
On a bed of nails.

Greed, anger, lust,
Get rid of them first,
And wipe that bootlicking smile
Off your face.
Praying to a stone idol's
Of no use otherwise.
Be without guile, says Kabir,

It'll get you to Ram quicker
Than anything else.

8 [78]

Death has them in its sights,
Both beggar and king.
Man's life is a tree's brief shadow,
Amounting to nothing.

But the body is a lake,
The soul a swan,
If on your tongue, says Kabir,
Is a chemical called Ram.

9 [81]

Listen carefully,
As neither the Vedas
Nor the Koran
Will teach you this:

Put the bit in its mouth,
The saddle on its back,
Your foot in the stirrup,
And ride your wild runaway mind

All the way to heaven.

Sanskrit, Pali and Hindi Poems
India

Translated by R Parthasarathy

R Parthasarathy *is a poet, translator, critic and editor. He is the author of* Rough Passage, *a long poem (OUP, 1977), and editor of the anthology* Ten Twentieth-Century Indian Poets *(OUP, 1976), which is now in its twenty-second printing. He has translated into modern English verse the fifth-century Old Tamil epic,* The Tale of an Anklet: An Epic of South India *(The Cilappatikaram of Ilanko Atikal, Columbia UP, 1993). The Tale of an Anklet was awarded the 1995 Sahitya Akademi (National Academy of Letters, India) Translation Prize and the 1996 Association for Asian Studies AK Ramanujan Book Prize for Translation. His poems and translations have appeared in many journals. His forthcoming books are* A House Divided, *a long poem, and* The Forked Tongue: The Indian Writer and Tradition. *Parthasarathy teaches Indian and the New English literatures at Skidmore College.*

R Parthasarathy writes: The Rtusamhara [A Cycle of the Seasons] *and the* Srngaratilaka [The Mark of Love] *are attributed to Kalidasa (5th c.), regarded as the greatest of the Sanskrit poets. The poems by Amaru, Ksitisa, and Vikatanitamba are from anthologies compiled between the seventh and sixteenth centuries. The 'Song of a Former Courtesan' by Vimala is from the* Songs of the Elder Nuns [Therigatha, ?6th c. BC], *possibly the earliest anthology of women's religious verse. 'When Will You Come, Beloved?' by Mira is from her 'Songbook' [Padavali, 16th c.]. Mira, traditionally believed to be a Rajput princess, is the most famous woman saint in the history of north Indian devotional Hinduism (bhakti). Vikatanitamba and Vimala are women poets.*

Aubade

The fever of passion spent, but nipples still erect
from her husband's close embrace,
the young woman at daybreak views her body
that had given him such pleasure,
and smiling to herself, leaves the bedroom
for another part of the house.

Anon, Sanskrit / *Rtusamhara*

The Traveller

My husband is away on business.
There's been no word from him.
His mother left this morning for her son-in-law's:
her daughter has had a child.
I am in the full bloom of youth.
But being alone, how can I meet you tonight?
Evening has come on. Traveller, go elsewhere.

Anon, Sanskrit / *Srngaratilaka*

Who Needs the Gods?

Watch how she straddles her lover!
Her face breaks out in a sweat
smudging her dark mascara;

her forest of black hair turns limp;
the solid gold earrings swish back and forth
even as her bright eyes flicker and grow dim.

When you have her sweet face
watching over you night and day,
who needs the gods anyway?

Amaru, Sanskrit / *Amarusataka*

The Seal

When will I see her generous thighs again,
shut tight at first out of modesty,
then opening slowly, prompted by desire,
disclosing, as the silk wrap around her waist comes loose,
the fine, purple marks of my nails,
like a red seal inscribed on a treasure?

Ksitisa, Sanskrit / *Subhasitaratnakosa*

A Word of Advice

Come now, stop fretting about this girl
being young and fragile.
Whoever has heard of a flower
Snapping in two from the weight of a bee?

Squeeze her hard, throwing all caution
to the winds, when the two of you
are alone together. Sugarcane,
pressed gently, will not release all of its juice.

Vikatanitamba, Sanskrit / *Subhasitavali*

Song of a Former Courtesan

Young and overbearing –
drunk with fame, beauty,
with my figure, its flawless appearance –
I despised other women.

Heavily made up, I leaned
against the brothel door
and flashed my wares. Like a hunter,
I laid my snares to surprise fools.

I even taught them a trick or two
as I slipped my clothes off
and bared my secret places.
O how I despised them!

Today, head shaved, wrapped
in a single robe, an almswoman,
I move about, or sit at the foot
of a tree, empty of all thoughts.

All ties to heaven and earth
I have cut loose forever.
Uprooting every obsession,
I have put out the fires.

Vimala, Pali / *Therigatha*

When Will You Come, Beloved?

How can I sleep without my Beloved?
Wrenched from his arms how can I survive?
I drown in the flames of love.
Without him my house is dark and unwelcome.

Of what use are lamps in his absence?
Not for me the pleasures of the bed.
I spend my nights sleepless.
Will my Beloved ever come home?

Frogs and peacocks, cuckoos and koels
call out to one another. Lightning thrashes about
in a net of black clouds. Thunder fills me with terror.
In vain I fight back the tears.

Tell me, friends, what shall I do? Where shall I go?
Send for the physician, I beg of you.
Like a venomous snake, his absence has bitten me:
in wave after wave, my life ebbs away.

Go, bring me the herb at once.
Who among my friends will return with my Beloved?
You stole her heart, Lord. When will you meet her?
When will you come to talk and laugh with Mira?

Mira, Hindi / *Padavali*

Rabindranath Thakur
(sometimes anglicized as Tagor)
India (Bengali)

Translated by Prasenjit Gupta

Rabindranath Thakur *(1861–1941) is the leading Indian literary figure of recent times. He was a prodigious writer who over the course of sixty years produced more than thirty large volumes of poetry, novels, short stories, plays, and essays. He wrote more than two thousand songs, which are extremely popular under the collective term* Robindro-shongeet. *He also took up painting late in life and is a painter of considerable merit. In Bengal, his influence is omnipresent even fifty years after his death; over the rest of Indian literature his influence is not as overwhelming, but still it is enormous.*

Prasenjit Gupta, *son of Pratima Gupta and the late Dr Paresh Ranjan Gupta, is a graduate of the Iowa Writers' Workshop and a former Fulbright scholar. He translates fiction and poetry from Hindi and Bengali into English and writes fiction in English. His book of translations of short stories by Nirmal Verma,* Indian Errant, *was published in 2002, as was his collection* A Brown Man and Other Stories.

Tagor's translation of One Hundred Poems of Kabir *was published in 1915. It was the first selection of Kabir's poems to be published in English and has been reprinted many times. Readers may be interested in comparing Tagor's versions with those by Arvind Mehrotra, published in the current issue of* MPT. *Meanwhile, we are glad to publish one of Tagor's many short stories below, newly translated by Prasenjit Gupta.*

Bolai

The story of humankind forms the conclusion to the many chapters that tell the history of the earth's many creatures – this we have heard. In any human society we sometimes encounter the various animals that live hidden within us – this we know. In reality we call that human which has blended all the animals within ourselves, combined them into one: penned our tigers and cows into one enclosure, trapped our snakes and mongooses in the same cage. In the same way we give the name *raag* to that which combines all the *sa-re-ga-mas* within itself and creates music – after which the notes can no longer make trouble – but still, even within the music an individual note may stand out from the others: in one *raag* the *ma*, in another the *ga*, in yet another the flat *dha*.

My nephew Bolai, my brother's son: in his nature, somehow, the fundamental notes of plants and trees sounded the loudest. Right from childhood he had the habit of standing and staring silently, not exploring places like other boys. When dark clouds massed themselves in layers in the eastern sky, it was as if his soul became dense with the moist fragrance of the forest in July; when the rain came thrumming down, his whole body would listen to what it said. When the sunshine lay on the roof in the afternoon, he walked about bare-chested, as if gathering something into himself from all the sky. When the mango trees bloomed in the month of Magh, a deep happiness would enter his blood, in memory of something inexpressible; his inner nature would spread itself in all directions, like a grove of sal trees flowering in Phalgun, would become suffused, become deeply coloured. At these times he liked to sit alone and talk to himself, patching together whatever fairy-tales he had heard, the tales of the pair of aged tattlers that had built their nest in a crevice of the ancient banyan tree. This wide-eyed-always-staring boy didn't talk very much; he would stay quiet, thinking things over in his head. Once I took him into the mountains. When he saw the green grass that covered the slope all the way down to our house, he was delighted. He didn't think the coverlet of grass was any fixed thing; he felt it was a playful, rolling mass, always rolling down. Often he would climb up the slope and roll down himself – his entire body itself become grass – and as he rolled, the blades of grass would tickle the back of his neck, and he would laugh out loud.

After the night's rains, the early-morning sun would peer over the mountain tops, and its pale golden rays fell on the deodar forest; and without telling anyone he'd go quietly and stand awestruck in the motionless shadows of the deodars, his body thrilling all over, as if he could see the people within these gigantic trees – they wouldn't speak, but they seemed to know everything, these grandfathers from long ago, from the days of 'Once-upon-a-time-there-lived-a-king.'

His eyes, deep in thought, weren't turned only upwards: I often saw him walking in my garden with his head bowed, searching for something. He was impatient to watch the new seedlings lift their curly heads towards the light. Every day he would bend low to them, as if asking: 'And now what? And now what? And now what?' They were stories always unfinished – tender young leaves, just arisen; he felt a companionship towards them that he didn't know how to express. They too seemed to fidget in their eagerness to ask him something. Maybe they said, 'What's your name?', maybe 'Where did your mother go?' Maybe Bolai replied, in his head, 'But I don't have a mother.'

It hurt him whenever someone plucked a flower from a plant. But he realized his concern meant nothing to anyone else. So he tried to hide his pain. Boys his age would throw stones to knock amlokis off the tree; he couldn't speak, he turned his face and walked away. To tease him, his companions would stride down the garden, slashing with a cane at the rows of shrubs on either side, in an instant would break a branch off the bokul tree; he was too ashamed to cry, lest someone think it madness. His most troubling time was when the grass-cutter came. Every day he had walked among the grass, peering closely at it: here a green tendril, there an unknown purple-and-yellow flower, so tiny; the occasional nightshade and its blue flowers, in their hearts a speck of gold; along the boundary wall, a kalmegh vine; elsewhere an onontomul; the small shoots just emerged from neem seeds pecked off the tree by birds, how pretty their leaves – and all these would be weeded by the ruthless weeder. These weren't the fancied plants of the garden, and there was no one to listen to their complaints.

Sometimes he would come and sit on his aunt's, his Kaki's, lap, and wrap his arms around her neck. 'Tell this grass-cutter, won't you, not to cut down my plants.'

Kaki would say, 'Bolai, sometimes you talk like a madman. All this is becoming a jungle, how can we not clear it away.'

Bolai had learnt a while ago that there were some griefs that were his alone; they sounded no chord in anyone else.

This boy's real age was the age, those millions of years ago, when, from the womb of the ocean and the newborn layers of mud, the earth's would-be forests rose and first cried out; that day there were no animals, no birds, no babble of life; – on all four sides only rock and silt and water. The trees, leading all other creatures on the path of time, raised their hands to the sun and said, 'I shall stay, I shall survive, I am the eternal pathfinder; after death and amidst death, endlessly, I continue my pilgrimage of growth, my journey in sun and cloud, through night and day.' Even today that murmur of the trees rises in every forest, on every hill and grassland; and from their branches and leaves, the life-breath of the earth speaks out, again and again: 'I will stay, I will stay.' These trees, the mute foster-mothers of earth's life, have through endless eons milked the heavens to gather into the earth's nectar-cups the radiance, the essence, the grace and power of life itself; and endlessly they raise their eager heads high: 'I will stay.' And in some way Bolai had heard that call of the earth-being, heard it in his blood. We'd laughed about it no end.

One morning I was pondering the newspaper when Bolai ran up and hurried me into the garden. He showed me a seedling and asked, 'Kaka, what plant is that?'

I saw that it was a tiny silk-cotton plant that had taken root in the middle of the gravel path.

Bolai had made a mistake in showing it to me. He'd noticed it when only a small shoot had come up, like an infant's first incoherent word. After that he watered it every day, checked it anxiously morning and evening to see how much it had grown. The silk-cotton grows rapidly, but it couldn't keep up with Bolai's eagerness. When it had risen a hand's breadth or two, he saw its rich leafage and thought it was a prodigious tree, the way a mother sees the first hint of an infant's intelligence and thinks, a prodigious child. Bolai thought it would astonish me. I said, 'I must tell the gardener, he'll uproot it.'

Bolai started. What a terrible thing. He said, 'No, Kaka, please don't, I beg you, don't have it uprooted.'

I said, 'I don't know what gets into your head. It's right in the middle of the path. When it gets bigger it'll spread its cotton all around and drive us crazy.'

Unable to prevail over me, this motherless child went to his Kaki. He sat down in her lap and hugged her. Whimpering and sobbing, he said, 'Kaki, you tell Kaka not to, not to have the plant cut.'

He'd found the right approach. His Kaki called me and said, 'Oh, listen! Do leave his plant alone.'

I left his plant alone. If Bolai had not pointed it out in the beginning I might not have noticed it at all. But now it leapt to my eye every time. Within a short year it grew shamelessly large. And Bolai lavished all his affection upon it.

The plant began to look more and more loutish to me. Standing there, in the wrong place, without a by-your-leave, just growing taller and taller by the hour. Whoever saw it wondered what it was doing there. Twice or thrice I proposed the death penalty for it. I offered Bolai the enticement of replacing it with several rose bushes of high quality.

Then I said, 'If you must have a silk-cotton plant, I'll have another seedling put in near the boundary wall. It'll look very pretty there.'

But whenever I mentioned cutting it he would flinch, and his Kaki would say, 'Oh, it doesn't look all that bad.'

My Boudi had died when Bolai was an infant. I think the grief of it unbalanced my brother somewhat: he went off to England to study engineering. The boy was raised by his Kaki in our childless home. About ten years later Dada came back, and to prepare Bolai for a Western education he took him to Shimla; from there they would go to England. Bolai, crying, left his Kaki and went; our house was empty.

Two more years passed. Meanwhile, Bolai's Kaki wiped her eyes in secret, and went into Bolai's empty bedroom to arrange and rearrange his torn pair of shoes, his cracked rubber ball, his picture book of animals. Bolai has left all these relics behind and grown much older, she sat and thought to herself.

One day I saw that the wretched silk-cotton tree had grown beyond all reason; it was so overbearing that it could not be indulged any longer. So I cut it down. At this time Bolai wrote to his Kaki from Shimla: 'Kaki, please send me a photograph of my silk-cotton tree.'

He was to have visited us before he left for England, but that didn't come about. So he had asked for a picture of his friend to take along. His Kaki called me and said, 'Listen, can you go bring a photograph-walla.'

I asked why.

She gave me the letter, written in Bolai's unformed hand.

I said, 'But that tree's been cut down.'

Bolai's Kaki didn't eat for two days, and for many days after that she wouldn't say a word to me. Bolai's father had taken him from her lap, as if breaking off the umbilical cord; and his Kaka had removed Bolai's beloved tree for ever, and that too shook her world, wounded her in the heart.

The tree had been her Bolai's reflection, after all, his life's double.

Glossary

Dada, older brother

Kaka, father's younger brother

Kaki, Kaka's wife

Magh, the month from mid-January to mid-February

Phalgun, the month from mid-February to mid-March

Rabindranath Tagore
India (Bengali)

Translated by Carolyn B Brown

Rabindranath Tagore *(1861-1941) was awarded the Nobel Prize for Literature in 1913. Tagore's* Gitanjali: Song Offerings, *a set of prose poems in English derived from his* Bengali Gitanjali *(1910) and several other volumes, appeared in England in 1912 with an introduction by William Butler Yeats. Two English translations of the complete* Bengali Gitanjali *are now available. Joe Winter's rhymed version was first published as* The Gitanjali of Rabindranath Tagore *by the Calcutta Writers Workshop in 1998 and then reprinted as* Song Offerings *by Anvil Press (London, 2000). Brother James's free verse version, originally published in 1983 by University Press Limited in Dhaka, has not been widely available outside Bangladesh until its recent reissue as* Show Yourself to My Soul, *translated by James Talarovic (Notre Dame, Indiana: Sorin Books 2002).*

Carolyn B Brown *recently completed* Another Shore *(Kolkata: Sahitya Akademi, 2001), a collaborative translation with Sarat Kumar Mukhopadhyay of poems by Amiya Chakavarty (1901-1986). The Bengali poet was a close associate of Tagore's during the 1920s and early 1930s; he later settled in the United States, where he taught for more than thirty years before returning to West Bengal.*

from Gitanjali

20

Tonight   you're trysting with a storm
          friend of my heart oh friend
             the heavens rain despair
             eyes emptied of sleep
             I unlatch the door, oh love
                I look out again and again
             friend of my heart oh friend

          I can't see a thing outside
          can't guess your path
             far off on some riverbank
             at some forest's edge
             in thickest darkness

you're crossing over
   friend of my heart oh friend

['Padma' boat Srabon 1316]

26

Day   is done, shadows fall
         over the earth
now   let me go down to the ghat
         and fill my kalash
           the river's evensong splashes
           under a restive sky
   oh!   that melody is calling me
            down the path
           let me go down to the ghat
            and fill my kalash

Now   no one's coming or going
         on the lonely path
oh!   waves race along love's river
         as the wind rises
           I don't know whether I'll come back
           whether I'll meet someone tonight
   on a raft   by the ghat a stranger's
            playing the veena
           let me go down to the ghat
            and fill my kalash

[13 Bhadro 1316]

34

You've been coming for me
   forever
hiding behind
   your sun and moon
       your footsteps always ringing
      at dawn or dusk
      a messenger whispering
        in my heart

Oh voyager, today
    waves of joy
set my whole being
    quivering quivering
            as if at last
            my work's ended
            oh maharaj, the breeze
                    is spiced with your scent

[16 Bhadro 1316]

44

I was invited to the world's festival
blessed my life's been blessed
    images flooded my eyes
    my ears drowned in sounds
    I roamed till my hunger
            was sated

my job at your festival
    was to play the flute
to stroll composing songs
    of life's laughter and tears
            has the time come?
            if I see you holding court
            I'll trumpet triumph
                    this is my humble offering

[Shilaidah – 30 Aswin 1316]

56

You   climbed down, lord
                    from your lion seat
    and stood at the door
            of my lonely room
                    I was sitting by myself
                        singing a song
                    when a note caught your ear
                        you climbed down, lord
                    and stood at the door
                        of my lonely room

countless skilful songs
    fill your court
today's unskilled song
    echoed your love
        a tentative note
            tapped the world's harmony
    garland in hand
        you climbed down, lord
    and stood at the door
        of my lonely room

[27 Choitro 1316]

61

He came and sat beside me
    but I didn't wake
poor girl
    overcome by sleep
he came in the hush of night
his veena in hand
and left a dark ragini
    echoing in my dream

your maddening scent
    seeds the south wind
fills the darkness
    and wakes me
why won't he take me
when he comes at night
oh why don't I feel his garland
    against my breast

[Bolpur – 12 Boisakh 1317]

83

You promised we'd go just you and I
    adrift   in a boat just drifting
no one on earth neither above nor below would know
    where   our journey would end at which altar in what realm
        in the middle of that shoreless sea

I would sing a ragini for you alone
        like waves on wordless waves
you   would smile silently and listen

Is it time yet? is there still work to do?
    love   look, night is falling over the sands
shorebirds spread their wings in the twilight
    homeward   they all fly
                    when will you come down to the ghat
                    and cut the line?
                    like the sun dropping beneath the horizon
        our boat   will slip away through the night

    [Bolpur – 30 Jyoistho 1317]

103

I started out to meet you
    by myself
so who's following me
    in the muffled dark?
I want to get rid of him
I circle and backtrack
and decide the stalker's gone
    but there he is again!

he's a walking earthquake
    the way he stomps along
whenever I try to say a word
    he butts in
lord, it's me, my self!
he hasn't a shred of shame
I'm so ashamed of him
    how can I come to your door?

    [14 Asarh 1317]

125

My song has cast off
     its bangles
no point preening
     when we meet
   bangles just get
   in the way
   their jangling
     drowns out your voice

I shed my pride
     when we meet
great poet, let me
     sit at your feet
   if I spend my days making
   a plain bamboo flute
   and fill it with my breath
     will you give me the notes?

[Kolkata – 1 Srabon 1317]

132

   my whole life long
     I've sought you through song
  within myself, beyond
     song has carried me
    room to room, door to door
      I've glossed all the world
       with song

such lessons learned
such secret paths found
   such stars I've greeted
     in my heart's orbit

     I've explored the hinterlands
     every region of joy and pain
       which mansion have I reached
       at nightfall?

[10 Srabon 1317]

148

Let me bow down, lord
    let me bow down
so I can touch the ground
    of your creation
As monsoon clouds
lower their burden to earth
    let me bow down, lord
        let me bow down
    so I can lay my heart
        at your door

As tangled notes weave
a river of song
    let me bow down, lord
        let me bow down
    so my mind can dissolve
        in the silent sea

As geese fly onward
day and night
    let me bow down, lord
        let me bow down
    so my soul can cross over
        to death's other shore

[23 *Srabon* 1317]

157

If day should die, if no birds sing
    if the wind's too weary to fly
then draw the darkness over me
    thicker than thickest cloudcover
        as you'd blanket the earth
        softly, secretly, with dreams
    and close the lotus petals of night
        as if kissing eyelids shut

that vagabond with a crop of bruises
    clothed in grime and dust
strength shattered, near collapse
    last coin spent long ago
                wrap his wounds, hide his shame
                in a cloud of compassion
soothe him with dark nectar
                let dawn blossom anew

[Calcutta – 28 Srabon 1317]

Translator's Note:

Numbers The translations follow the numbering of Tagore's Bengali *Gitanjali*. In the following list, the second number in each pair corresponds to the number in his English *Gitanjali: A Collection of Prose Translations Made by the Author from the Original Bengali*: 20/23, 26/74, 34/46, 44/32, 56/49, 61 /26, 83/42, 103/30, 125/7, 132/101, 148/103, 157/21. Of the 157 poems in the original collection, the poet included only 53 in the English version; the remaining prose poems come from other volumes.

Dates   The twelve poems were written in 1909 and 1910. Tagore often noted the date of composition, using the Bengali calendar. Boisakh, beginning in mid-April is the first month of the Bengali year; other months in the poet's annotations for these poems are Jyoistho (May/June), Asharh (June/July), Srabon (July/August), Bhadro (August/September), Aswin (September/October), and Choitro (March/April).

Places   Tagore also sometimes recorded the place of composition as he travelled from place to place in Bengal. The 'Padma' is the Tagore family's houseboat, named by the poet after the river Padma; Shilaidah (or Shelidah) is a village in East Bengal (now Bangladesh), location of the family estate; Bolpur is the railway station closest to the village of Santiniketan (the site of Visva-Bharati, an educational institution that Tagore founded); and Kolkata is the Bengali name (now officially readopted) for Calcutta.

Listening to *Gitanjali:* **Parables for Translators**

by Carolyn B Brown

'Now, I ask, has the time come at last when I may go in and see thy face and offer thee my silent salutation?' This question closes one of Tagore's self-translated prose poems. The corresponding Bengali poem (*Gitanjali* 44) promises not a mute gesture but *jaidhoni,* shouts of victory. The mutation from Bengali to English might serve as a parable for the translator's plight: the poet/musician's 'instrument' goes silent; he can no longer play the *banshi,* his bamboo flute, in another language.

It takes only a line or two of Tagore's Bengali verse to demonstrate the celebrated 'music' of his poetry. The poet/translator renders the first line of *Gitanjali* 20 in English as follows: 'Art thou abroad on this stormy night on the journey of love.' In Bengali, the poet writes: *aji jharer rate tomar abhishar.* Even in this simplified transliteration, the characteristic consonant linking is apparent, as *j*'s give way to *r*'s and *t*'s, then the labial *m* and *b*, with the final *shar* a softened echo of the earlier *jhar.* The line contains no verb – Bengali does not need one – just a storm, night, a person ('you'), and a lovers' meeting. The spare simplicity of the line and the general legibility of elliptical constructions in Bengali serve to amplify the distinctive texture, the 'music', of the original poem. In his English version, Tagore turns to rhetorical artifice – and often excess. Through the 'mazy depths of gloom', the shore is 'dim', the river 'ink-black', the forest 'frowning'. The evocative Bengali lines work primarily through sound patterns, large and small, without 'adjectival insistence': – *sudur kon nodir pare / gohon kon boner dhare / gobhir kon ondhokare* (where Sanskrit-based transliteration uses an *a,* I have used *o*'s for initial vowel sounds to represent more closely the actual pronunciation; *s* is almost always pronounced *sh*). Line by line, the sound deepens and darkens into the low rumbling of the paired *gobhir ondhokar* (the *k* is almost indistinguishable from *g* here), 'deepest densest darkness'.

The very compactness of the poems in Bengali is a challenge: Could an English version possibly come close to their frugality, allowing only a few words within a line? The twelve translations from *Gitanjali* in this issue of *MPT* are an experiment in minimalism, shaped as well by a second question: What if the translator were to insist on listening to each line – following the lines not only with the eye but also with the ear – in Bengali *and* in English. Another parable for translators takes the stage, first in Tagore's version: 'My song has put off her adornments. She has no pride of dress and decoration. Ornaments would mar our union; they would come between thee and me; their jingling would drown out thy whispers.' The music of the Bengali poem (*Gitanjali* 125) is in fact rather harsh. The central words (for 'adornments/ornaments', 'decoration', and 'jingling') are *alangkaar*, *ahangkaar*, and *jhangkaar*, and throughout consonants such as *k*, *kh*, *chh*, *g*, *j*, *jh*, *t*, *th*, and *dh* dominate (the *h*'s indicate aspiration; most consonants in Bengali are paired in unaspirated and aspirated forms). The lesson for the translator is not only to strip down but also to listen, to hear the entire range and all the collocations of expressive sound.

The intricate rhyme schemes of Tagore's *Gitanjali* are a significant temptation for any translator interested in retaining some small portion of what Joe Winter calls 'the great song of the *Gitanjali*.' He renders the first stanza of *Gitanjali* 125 as follows:

> This my song has cast off now
> all adornment and frill:
> proud apparel, in your presence,
> it must not wear still.
> Trinket-jinglings fall between
> our time-of-closeness, like a screen . . .
> and all you say to me is lost
> in that loud thrill.

Winter has translated all 157 poems in the Bengali collection in English, restoring its 'poetic format' – a formidable accomplishment, and yet perhaps also a misguided one. That is, Bengali has far greater resources for rhyme than English does, not simply because it is a highly inflected language, but also because it has a much greater allowance of phonemes. The English consonant -*t* is no match for Bengali's set of four phonemically distinct consonants (a dental and a retroflex *t*, each with an unaspirated and aspirated form). Entire sets of consonants are available for rhyming syllables in Tagore's practice. With the addition of -*e*, for instance, as a final vowel, the poet can alternate locative and dative case endings with a frequent verb ending (infinitive, conditional participle, past participle, and for second and third person in multiple tenses); in Bengali verbs come at the end of lines and sentences. Rhyme, then, seems to happen almost as naturally as exhaling, without the strain and unavoidable interpolations evident in attempts to replicate Tagore's rhyme schemes in English.

Driven by rhyme, Winter must find something to chime with the final word of the first stanza, ('unseen') to end *Gitanjali* 34: 'O great king, fragrance-charged with you a wind / arrives, is keen.' In Brother James's free-verse translation, 'Zephyrs play about, great King, carrying Your fragrance.' Tagore's prose version, 'I feel in the air a faint smell of thy sweet presence', subdues the original *batash ashe, he maharaj / tomar gondho mekhe*. With bare literalism, the lines might be rendered: 'Wind comes, oh great king / your smell spreading.' Although it compensates with compound forms, Bengali is relatively verb-poor; thus, a single verb may be highly resonant with multiple meanings and associations. *Mekhe* suggests smearing, daubing, rubbing –oil on a body, whitewash on a wall, spices into food – inviting my own 'figuratively literal' lines, 'oh maharaj, the breeze / is spiced with your scent', justified as much by the ear as by the dictionary.

In any case, the musical cadence and texture of Bengali poetry, even in contemporary free verse, lies mainly within the line, not at its end. The sound play can be constantly surprising, a steady source of delight. Consider three attempts to render the first stanza of *Gitanjali* 26, in which a woman is about to go to the river to fill her pitcher with water. Tagore writes, 'The evening air is eager with the sad music of the water'; Talarovic (Brother James), 'The sound of rippling water / disturbs the evening air'; and Winter, 'Dusk is restless in the sky / with the water gurgling by'. All are plausible, but perhaps no English phrase can approximate the felicity of the Bengali, in which the sound of the flowing water is neither sad nor gurgling; the 'low musical sound' is *koloshshor*, which both states and imitates the sound of water filling the woman's earthen water jar, her *kolosh*. Bengali is a language that savours its own sounds in 'reduplicative' forms of various parts of speech, on-the-spot rhymes that add a playful echo to a word, and pairings that, no matter how often they recur, still strike a nerve. In the final stanza of *Gitanjali* 132, for instance, 'joy and sorrow' or 'pleasure and pain' is *sukh-dukh* in Bengali, yoked together as permanently in language as in life.

Within such a repertoire, individual poems remain quite distinctive in tone and voice – the music is infinitely variable. The speakers of the Bengali *Gitanjali* would not recognize the elevated, 'poetic' eloquence of Tagore's English versions. For instance, *Gitanjali* 103, spare and plainspoken in Bengali, is also informal, personable, even funny. The poem has a distinctly 'bumpity' rhythm. Lines stop short of full length and contain little catches or hiccups – *jai je, se chai, se je* – that are commonplace in themselves yet have a cumulative effect that contributes to the poem's drama. The poem seems to be written against smoothness, fluidity and fluency; it is very much 'about' listening with acute attention. Someone is following the speaker: *apod*, 'danger' or an unpleasant, irritating person, a word that Tagore surely entertains as a pun. Orthographically, and sometimes as pronounced, *apod* can vary freely with *apad*, 'from the feet' (*pad* is foot or step). If so, can a 'stalker' be far behind? Indeed, here is another parable for translators! We try so earnestly to track a poem, we put it into our own words. This is our pleasure. And then, when we hear our own voice, we wonder when we have made fools of ourselves. This is our plight. Even if my own experiment is not altogether persuasive, I would still urge its premise. We may know we cannot sing, but if we keep listening to the poem when we shape a line, perhaps the poet will give us the notes.

Love Poems of Tukaram
India (Marathi)

Translated by Dilip Chitre

Dilip Chitre *(see also his 'Keynote Address' below) was born in Baroda, Gujarat, India in 1938 and educated in Baroda and Mumbai. He writes in Marathi and English and also translates either way. His books of poetry in English are* Ambulance Ride *(1972),* Travelling In A Cage *(1980),* The Mountain *(1998) and* No Moon Monday On The River Karha *(2000). His collected Marathi poems are in the three volumes* Ekoon Kavita-1 *(winner of the Sahitya Akademi Award in 1994),* Ekoon Kavita-2 *(1995) and* Ekoon Kavita-3 *(1999). He has edited and translated into English* An Anthology Of Marathi Poetry, 1945-1965 *(1967);* Says Tuka: Selected Poetry of Tukaram *(1991, winner of the Sahitya Akademi Translation Prize 1994);* Shri Jnandev's Anubhavamrut: The Immortal Experience Of Being *(1996).*

Chitre spent his early twenties in Ethiopia, teaching English as a foreign language, and two-and-a-half years in Iowa City, 'which we shared with itinerant poets and writers, and exuberant American students'. From the 1980s, he made several trips to Europe – and of course England. He also visited Hong Kong and Japan. He writes: 'Travel triggers something in the polyglot translator: just the sound of unfamiliar or half-familiar languages works on the adrenal glands, as I suspect happens in my case. Excitement tinged with anxiety followed by fatigue, so you want to 'retire into translation'. Each long spell of exile into a foreign language whets my translator's appetite. Perhaps, a poet-translator's bio isn't complete without such details?'

Dilip Chitre *writes:* Tukaram has transparencies in Marathi that are difficult to 'translate' into systems of culture other than his native Marathi, the language that I share with him as mother tongue. But isn't the term 'mother-tongue' itself a deeply embedded cultural metaphor? What sense, for instance, would 'father-tongue', 'brother-tongue', 'sister-tongue', 'spouse-tongue' – and all like expressions – make?

Degrees of intimacy – and their opposite, degrees of distance – are part of a deeper grammar or otherness inherent in all world-views. Hindu mystical poetry derives from many traditions, and not all of them are 'Hindu' except in an inclusive South Asian sense.

'Marital' and 'extra-marital' are categories that have sensitive and explosive connotations. 'Marriage with One's God' sounds like a taboo violation in which God is conceived as the male patriarch, father of the world and its ruling authority. Making love to one's father would be a shocking act of incest, even though Hindu mythology is replete with tales of incest told in a non-judgmental way. I am often tempted to compare Tukaram's erotic metaphor with that underlying San Juan de la Cruz's famous long poem that is an exquisite erotic epiphany. But I have resisted that compulsive Complit kind of temptation because I believe that in the end a translator must evoke in the reader's mind the idea of a source meta-text rather than the more obvious foreign-language source-text.

Tukaram touches upon the illicit and the clandestine aspects of sexual love that make dissatisfied persons seek 'love' outside their licensed marital bed. He also touches upon the cliché of a nymphomaniac and the stereotype of the adulterous woman going out into the woods to secretly meet her lover. He evokes the 'home' and the 'household' – the one with its duties and responsibilities and the other with its material effects and possessions.

In my 'other-tongue' English and in my 'mother-tongue' Marathi, I experience a continuous tussle between two quite distinct and separate cultural worlds attempting to penetrate one another and produce a few sparks of sense enough to kindle meaningful coherence and poetic resonance that can only be called 'cross-cultural'.

I hesitate to write this kind of note because, after all, like every translator I have burnt my boats all my life and lived neither here nor there. I have found out that translators are not transporters who 'move' anything from one space to another. I know that translators and translations are in a space of their own in uncharted literary territory. So this note could be actually self-defeating, irrelevant, unnecessary, meaningless – or all of these.

A new three-volume edition of Chitre's selected poems of Tukaram in English translation was launched in February 2003 with SAYS TUKA-I: *Selected Poetry of Tukaram. Each volume contains about 250 of Tukaram's poems. Volume 2 is scheduled for publication in late 2003 and volume 3 in early 2004.* SAYS TUKA-I *can be ordered from: Sontheimer Cultural Association Shobhana, Survey no. 51, Plot no. 235, Bhairav Nagar, Dhanori Road, Pune 411 015, India. Price (inclusive of postage) in India: hardcover Rs350; softcover Rs250. International: hardcover $17.50; softcover $15.00, pp.260 demy 8 vo.*

from SAYS TUKA –II

1

I don't care if they call me a whore
I will not let go of my lover in the forest.
I've cast aside all worldly cares, raised above them
I hope for no life or fear death.
I no longer hear what these people say of me
Says Tuka I'm lost in Hari's love.

2

The one I married didn't satisfy my desire
In sheer desperation I sought adultery.
I wanted Him by me all day and night
I would not rest a moment without Him.
Forget who I am, what name I have,
Says Tuka I am making love to the Infinite.

3

This now is my workaday setting
Sitting next to Govind.
I've trespassed his house to become the chief Queen
I've made the dark end of the universe my home.
I've lain with the mighty one, now,
Says Tuka; I have no worry or fear.

4

I've nothing to do with you now
You've made known to me the secret.
My illicit affair has been revealed to all
I've become a public embarrassment.
Don't expect anything from me now, Says Tuka,
My Lord possesses me.

5

I've forgotten my family, its manners:
What's a husband, a brother, a home, its ways?
No more am I clothed by concerns of this world – its fears, its taboos,
    and its cares:
My mind is locked with the love of the Infinite.
You may call me out with great urgency
Says Tuka, but I can hear no more.

6

I see not, I speak not, and I hear not a thing.
All that dwells in my mind is Hari.
Now I have neither kith nor kin
I've merged my home with his household.
I was called names for my brawling habit
Says Tuka; I proved it to be literally true.

7

Who else is mightier than Hari, the infinitely mighty one?
We've become his mighty mistresses lording over the world.
Says Tuka; we're the outrageous lovers of Govind
Who've become his darlings.

Translation: Problems of a Paralysed Republic

A keynote address to a national seminar on 'Translation and Empowerment' by Dilip Chitre

At the outset, allow me to touch upon some of the deeper concerns that motivate me as a translator. Though these concerns are not academically universal, they have for me defined my role as a translator within a certain literary culture and at a given time and place in history.

I was born just a year before the outbreak of the Second World War. Six years later, when that war ended, atomic bombs were dropped on the cities of Hiroshima and Nagasaki. Though world wars are fought between great military and economic powers that are always very few in number, they make the whole world suffer from their innumerable consequences.

During the Second World War, India's fight for freedom happened to be in its final phase. Mahatma Gandhi's non-violent opposition to British rule was on the verge of success. Two years after the war ended, the British prepared to leave India, but not before it was partitioned into two nations on the basis of religion. Our independence was born out of fratricide and genocide, mass-migrations and huge losses to property. It left a bitter taste in the mouths of people that has lingered longer than half a century.

The political partition of the Indian sub-continent along religious lines created cultural cracks that have taken too long to heal. It has damaged the identity of our common civilization as well as our more important identity as human beings capable of self-recognition. The partition of the Indian sub-continent created more borders than mere geo-political ones. It affected languages and literatures such as Panjabi, Sindhi, Urdu, Hindi and Bangla. You may add English to this list, too, though the role of English in India is much more complex.

Sindhi suffered loss of territory in India and became a secondary language in Pakistan. Panjabi was divided into 'Islamic', 'Sikh', and 'Hindu' and symbolically distributed over three scripts, the Arabic-Persian, the Gurumukhi, and the Devanagari. Bangla became a secondary language to Urdu, which became the official national language of Pakistan. The far-flung world of Urdu was divided. Lahore was in Pakistan and Delhi, Lucknow, and Hyderabad Deccan were in India. There was an attempt to Persianize Urdu in Pakistan and to Sanskritize Hindi in India.

The language my generation knew as 'Hindustani' and which was the *'lingua franca'* of the sub-continent was politically exiled from both the countries where it was widely spoken and understood. Both Hindi and Urdu were 'officially' expanded and colloquially strangled on both sides of an imaginary border that really began to hurt. I wonder how many people will agree with me if I say that Shamsher Bahadur Singh and Faiz Ahmed Faiz spoke and wrote in the same language, just as Premchand can be read and understood in two different scripts. Scripts and vocabularies were turned into political borders of sorts. They now seem psychologically difficult to cross.

Translation is about crossing linguistic borders and its triumph lies in proving them imaginary. It is about 'empathy' – which means: 'identification with and understanding of another's situation, feelings, and motives'. It also means 'the attribution of one's feelings to objects'. One can also define it as 'successfully reaching out to the other' or 'identifying with one's subject or object'.

Every mind-set has its own realm of privacy, which is enclosed and barred to 'alien' 'intrusion'. Every culture has its own subjective realm, its 'privacy'. Unless an urge is felt to transcend this realm – or cross the border and 'experience' the other side – there will be no translation. Literature – and in particular its extreme and purest form poetry – protects the 'subjective' or 'private' part of language which is 'empirical', 'aesthetic', and hermeneutically encoded.

'Hermeneutic' means, as everybody here knows, 'interpretative' or 'explanatory'. Within one's own culture, there are many words of which the context does not need to be explained because most people using the same language share it. But even within uses of language among the same people, there are areas of 'subjectivity' that require special tools to unravel. Empathy is a congenital faculty of humankind; it is not a 'tool'. 'Tools' are what translators use to break down the subjective elements of language into its universal elements. They attempt to reach, not the surface of a source 'text' but its underlying or 'deep' structure.

Debates concerning 'translatability' have been the basis of the history of translation as well as translation theory. The world over, these debates appear to have started with 'religious' texts that claimed descent from a divine, superhuman source and were 'directly spoken' or 'revealed' to some holy man, some sage, or some 'prophet'. Throughout history, translators have been persecuted, incarcerated, or even slain for their 'unfaithfulness' to a sacred text or revealed words.

At this point, translation connects with the theme of plurality – the plurality of messages and messengers, of texts and contexts, and most importantly to the plurality of *interpreters and interpretations*. The scriptures of every major religion in the world are texts. If we look upon them as 'revealed texts' then they are unalterable. They become fundamental. Either every possible reader, without any mediation, understands them or they are perennially misunderstood and

224 / Chitre

misinterpreted. The text may be a fixed given, constant as it is: but as long as its interpreters vary, it must go through specific mediations and modifications.

Translation practice and translation theory have both inherited a religious fundamentalist curse. Thus, to monopolize the interpretation as well as to freeze the text of the *Vedas*, the caste-system had to be invented and imposed. A priestly class had to be created. It had to proclaim to all the non-priestly others that only ordained or initiated members of the priestly class were fit to interpret the *Vedas*. It had to further proclaim that only children born into priestly families were fit to be initiated into the order of religious performers, interpreters, mediators, and counsellors.

If we look at the history of religions, however, we find that the politics of interpretation have resulted in the proliferation of sects and bitter sectarian feuds that assume the form of tribal wars, racial wars, ethnic conflicts, linguistic strife and cultural disharmony. We have a recurrence of prophets and impostors in every phase of human history. Interpretations lead to wars, if texts are treated as sacrosanct. But wars are fought only because one text is held more sacrosanct than all others. I speak to you as a practising translator and not as a theorist or a historian of translation. I am also a practising writer. I speak on the basis of my experience as a translator and as a creative writer. The relevance of my remarks is obviously limited by my own reading and writing, and the trials and errors of my own learning process. I believe that every text is interpretable and that therefore every translator is limited and fallible. For every text that is singular, there is a plurality of translators. Texts are like monuments that have survived their creators and have been neglected, rediscovered, or marvelled at by subsequent generations. Every subsequent generation of interpreters or translators of a text is aware not only of the text itself but also of the history of its interpretations and translations.

When I translated Jnandev's *Anubhavamrut* from a text believed to have been composed in the 13th century AD, I knew that the manuscripts of the text were themselves created in later centuries. They were either a copy of now-lost manuscripts that preceded them or were based on memorized oral traditions. The critical edition I used as my source text refers in its introduction and footnotes to more than one hundred manuscript variations of a lost 'original text'. These copies vary considerably. None of them can be treated as *canonical*. (The very word 'canonical' has the ring of religious 'authority').

The real question before me, as a translator, was: what was *I* looking for in my source text? In other words did I, as a translator, have an agenda? Did I have a specific intention in looking at *Anubhavamrut?*

I was unequivocally committed as a translator and yes, I had an agenda of my own. Jnandev is the founder of the Varkari tradition of Bhakti poetry in Marathi and I have been translating his 17th-century successor Tukaram's poetry since 1956. My translation agenda still has Varkari Bhakti poetry in Marathi as its first priority.

But the reason why my translation of *Anubhavamrut* took me more than four decades to complete needs to be explained. First, it was an 'early Marathi' text handed down through oral and (later) written transmission with a huge number of textual variations. 13th-century Marathi is as different from present-day Marathi as Middle English is from contemporary English. Again, although I treat *Anubhavamrut* primarily as a long poem of 3220 lines, it is traditionally treated as a mystical discourse in a translucent if not opaque esoteric code. It took me a long time to discover its connections with the Kashmir Shaivite discourse and decipher it coherently before transforming it into my English version. This whole exercise is riddled with complexity and occupational hazards. I had to stick my neck out at every stage of this process.

Our country must be full of potential translators. We are polyglot. Even the least literate Indian is likely to know more than her or his mother tongue. Dialects abound in India. Many of them do not even see print. There are full-fledged tribal languages spoken in India by tribes who are themselves culturally endangered.

The Anglophone Indian is placed in a precarious but challenging position in our huge language-scape. She/he is in a position to transform texts from Indian languages and their dialects into English and establish the presence of marginalized voices and vanishing registers in global awareness. Translation is necessary for cultural and political self-assertion and it is a pre-condition for the truly pluralistic and federal democratic state in India that our Constitution promises.

Our major languages have themselves been gobbling up dialects as well as minor languages. Language is a form of hegemony, after all, and like religion it has been the cause of much strife and bloodshed. Translation will continue to attract all sorts of enemies from all sorts of quarters.

And yet, much material invites a would-be translator in India, particularly the plurilingual among us.

I know people who are tri-lingual with combinations such as, for instance, Marathi-Gujarati-English, Urdu-Telugu-Marathi, Assamese-Bangla-English, Tamil-Malayalam-English, Urdu-Panjabi-English, Kashmiri-Urdu-English, Konkani-Marathi-Portuguese, French-Tamil-English – and so forth. These are our historical and geo-political legacies. Languages such as Hindi and Urdu have a variety of regional registers in the Indian sub-continent. Some of these have even been recognised officially as separate 'languages'.

Yet, our intra-lingual and inter-lingual 'borders' are as rigid as the 'jati-system' accepted by all our indigenous and naturalized religions and sects. We practise untouchablity at the level of language and choose to remain out of touch with our neighbours and contemporaries.

Here is where the theme of empowerment really enters the picture. There is a deep connection between democracy and translation. I do not have to elaborate this beyond a point because in all societies, the ruling elites exclude the rest by using language as a means of maintaining their hierarchical relationship with the rest of the people whom they rule, and we in India have our entire linguistic and literary history as a possible example of this. The terms 'vulgar', 'demotic', 'vernacular', 'native' and 'common' all have political connotations. The Vedas are 'revealed' in a superhuman voice that speaks 'Sanskrit' (Jibraeel brings the message of Allah to the prophet Muhammad in 'Arabic'. The Judaeo-Christian God 'spoke' Hebrew; and so forth). The binary opposition between the 'sacred' and the 'profane' is expressed in terms of an 'appropriate' language; and Sanskrit is no less than 'the language of the gods' even in their *Puranic* plurality. Women and servants in Sanskrit plays speak varieties of Prakrit. In a vertically structured hierarchical society, like our Indian model, there is also horizontal compartmentalization or *segregation*. And this is part of the linguistic politics we have inherited, through which we marginalize dialects and oral traditions of subjugated communities and classes, 'tribes' and 'castes' whose languages we *derecognize.*

A democracy whose language or languages are not demotic suffers from inequitable communication rules. Its very governance becomes suspect. Translation could become the necessary leveller in such a society – and again, our own is the best example I can think of. But language hierarchies require mediators and interpreters and that becomes the translator's role. When the governing class condescends to the governed, it creates an official register, a standard language that is a euphemism for its own language and its jargonised applications. In such a situation, translation becomes only a one-way, downward activity. The relationship between official Hindi or English and, say, the dialect of a tribal individual produced in a court of law, would be a poignant example of one-way translation-traffic with all its political and juristic implications. What the judges and the lawyers say in English, Hindi or the official language of the state needs to be translated 'downward' to the tribal who is an alien in their midst. What the tribal has to say needs to be translated 'upward' to the lawyers and the judges. Our courts of law have on their staff translators and interpreters. They can have an innocent hanged to death or sentenced for life by the sheer power of upward and downward translation and the tricks it involves.

What are the political implications of this in contemporary India? It is hard for me not to notice that ours is an anaesthetised, progressively paralytic republic where dialects are dying, and with them whole micro-communities are on the verge of extinction with their rich oral traditions, folklore and native knowledge systems erased forever.

In the context of empowerment, our lopsided view of translation only enables governing languages at the expense of increasingly disabled subject languages and their living variations. This is not merely an academic issue, because our pluralistic civilization owes its greatest strength to the variety of languages we are heir to, and I do not mean the 'dead' languages the orientalists celebrate but the living ones that even Indology has only recently discovered. My late friend, Gunther Sontheimer – who gave an entirely new dimension to Western Indology – made me aware of the richness of Marathi oral traditions and the critical state they are in. This has altered my own perspective on translation itself over the years.

Can India become a true Republic if we do not translate one another and thus ignore or blank out our diverse contemporaries? Can we grasp our plural past, our plural present and our plural future in any monolingual or monocultural steel frame?

[Pune, March 2003]

Wen Yiduo

China

Translated by Robert Dorsett

Wen Yiduo *wrote from the time of the collapse of the Ching Dynasty until shortly before the communist repressions. He was assassinated in 1946. As the main theorist of the Crescent Society, he advocated new forms, a diction close to the vernacular, and political involvement.*

Robert Dorsett *is a physician, poet and translator working in Berkeley, California.*

Hallucinatory Thoughts

Into the quiet dusk,
from my desolate mind,
strange thoughts scatter,
grotesque thoughts.

As if a swarm of jittery bats
erupted from a dust-choked, rain-spotted bell tower,
before an ancient temple,
strange beasts, almost birds but not.

And like those overly ambitious bats
my thoughts won't crawl upon the ground
but whirl all kinds of figures
throughout the sky.

From my desolate mind
unearthly thoughts scatter,
like a swarm of bats,
into the quiet dusk.

Defeat

Once, I cultivated a valuable flower,
which easily became pregnant with a bud.
But it remained half-hidden, unwilling to open.
I waited impatiently, peeled it harshly.
Day by day it wilted, wilted terribly,
and now I can't close it.
I haven't the flower I wanted.

Once, I dreamed a wonderful dream,
but I complained the dream was too vague.
I didn't care at all, let dawn break it,
waited till the moon fell and day brightened,
but it wasn't possible to weave a new dream,
and I couldn't patch the old.
I haven't the dream I wanted.

Last Day

The bamboo drain pipes swallow dew.
A plantain leaf licks the window.
The four plastered walls step backward.
I am too small to fill this room.

In my chest a fire begins to burn.
I quietly await a distant guest. I feed the fire
mouse shit, spider webs, hard scales
from spotted snakes like chips of wood.

A rooster crows. My chest fills with ash.
Stealthily, a cold wind wipes my mouth.
At last that distant guest is before me.
I cough once, follow him from the room.

He Zhizhang

China

Translated by Ouyang Yu

He Zhizhang *(659-744), poet, calligrapher and drinker, had only 19 poems included in quantangshi,* Complete Collection of Tang Dynasty Poetry.

    Ouyang Yu *graduated from La Trobe University with a doctoral degree in Australian literature and has had some twenty Chinese and English books published in the fields of fiction, poetry, literary translation and literary criticism, his most recent English novel being* The Eastern Slope Chronicle *(Brandl & Schlesinger, Sydney), his fourth collection of poetry,* Two Hearts, Two Tongues and Rain-colored Eyes *(Wild Peony, Sydney). He has translated into Chinese Robert Hughes's* The Shock of the New *(Baihua Publishing House, China).* Selected Poems of Ouyang Yu *is forthcoming from Salt Publishing (UK).*

A Casual Poem Composed After My Return To My Hometown

I left home young and come home old
my accent remains the same although my hair is grey
when kids see me they do not know who I am
and they ask with a smile: where are you from?

Some Recent Chinese Poems

Translated by Ouyang Yu

Wang Jiaxin

The Traveller

He is travelling in the landscape of the living and the dead,
you won't recognize him in a crowd;
sometimes in a train when the wind and clouds surge, I think,
he will take out a notebook or
on a candle-lit night, his shadow
will be thrown onto the snow-white wall of a convent.

Ants will crawl up his face when his forehead
is as bright and clean as the sand.
He is travelling in this world, travelling, or
he may have tied his shoe
lace in the human stream in the
busy Xidan;
and when he wakes up in the sky,
I have drunk too much beer in an underground restaurant.

For seven years there has not been a letter.
He is far away from us, travelling, travelling;
or he has gone back to the age of Dante,
exiled under the sky of his hometown; or, all of a sudden,
he appeared in a valley that spread wide open.
When the ocean shone, dots of white sails in sight,
he had come to a place where he could live.

For seven years my window has been repeatedly covered in
white frost,
and our fire has been replaced by the central heating – in
order not
to live in memory of him? And, as usual, I
go to work, write, have parties with friends?
Except that I am a little fearful when alone,
fearful that someone I no longer know will suddenly knock on
my door.

Song Xiaoxian

The Soil and the Letter

Father once sternly
intervened in my marriage

and so I wrote
a letter back with much force to hurt

According to Mother, after reading the letter
he did not eat for a day
but kept drinking all day alone

Later, I dug out
the letter and took it
to the straight road that led to Bazilao
where I tore it to pieces

Those fierce words
have now become part of the soil
in the ditch

At last the soil has accepted
the killer and the knife,
as well as countless ghosts and
hate
You can hardly imagine
how much poison the soil contains

Fei Ya

Born in 1965, **Fei Ya** *is now based in Nanning.*

The Waking of Insects

In the evening, at 7, the rain outside the window, the
lightning, lighting up everything
then thunderous noise, the spring thunder, the first rumbling
of thunder, crisp, sudden
I'd heard it, surprised, excited, and I ran towards the
window

I just wanted to have a look, at the way the thunder worked
in the sky
after winter. The wind was blowing, with more rain
the greenish curtain was also blowing, and I turned my head
in the darkened room, I seemed to see someone
looking angry running to us, rugged, tall
wearing old blue cloth
garments, as if saying: 'I have
emerged
from the icy-cold sea-bed and rocks
into the empty night, clouds, dirtying
everything, when people
come out of the winter with tightly closed doors
the wind, dishevelling their hair.
And I would rather stay on the mountain top so that
I can roll from one place to another
I sing, I dance, I twist my buttocks, so what
if I make a fool of myself in public?
unlike you who maintain decorum and silence
in such a rare spring.'
Early April, still raining, I remembered what I saw two days
when I went back to my village: the ground was wet
on the road to the outskirts of the city, the young pumpkin
fat and pretty, shooting out of the cabbage plots
a large group of swallows, drawing a curve, and others
in a row, like a crowd of country people
waiting for some work, standing on the tall wire poles
they are flying, crying, their heads twisting this way and that
so happy that they dismissed us on the road as the air, as if saying,
'so beautiful
so wonderful, what a lovely season, so many worms
emerging from the earth, too many to eat.'

Note: The Waking of Insects, commonly known as *jingzhe*, occurs in the 3rd solar term.

Song Yaozhen

Based in Taiyuan, Shanxi, **Song Yaozhen** *sounds like a woman's name but I don't know anything about him or her. [OY]*

Someone with Tooth-Ache

Someone with tooth-ache was pacing in the house
He cursed the wild wind outside the window, the wildly flying
torn pieces of paper
He cursed pain-killers, the doctors
the endless television commercials and news
and the plastic bag hanging on the top of the tree outside
the window for a whole spring
hanging there, flapping, never coming down
and now, in tatters, it pretends to have wings
practising flying, in a good mood
Alone, he was pacing in the house
He began to curse his newly wed wife
wondering why she is still not home. What is she doing
outside
This is an uncomfortable age
when chastity is as cheap as scandals of politicians
At dusk, he was as tempestuous as a lion in a cage
He was in pain and he wished to have all his teeth pulled out
and smashed into pieces with a hammer
He began to curse everything associated with teeth: the gum,
the tongue, the lips
and the whole head
and the whole world linked to the head
It had become completely dark
Exhausted by this pain
this pitiable person could not help but cry in pain, his face
in his hands

Luruo Diji

The name, **Luruo Diji***, sounds like an ethnic name in Chinese and the poet now lives in Yunnan Province.*

Wood Ear

is wood
is ears grown on the wood
ears of wood
what sounds have they heard
when they are torn off alive
does the wood utter a secret cry
we cook them
and the instant they are put in our mouth
there is a crisp sound
we feel as if we ate our own ears
in that instant
we become wooden

Note: Wood ear or *mu er*: an edible fungus.

Ahtna Athabaskan Poems

Translated and introduced by John E Smelcer

John E Smelcer *is the author of more than twenty books. His best-selling non-fiction books include* In the Shadows of Mountains *(introduced by Pulitzer Prize winner Gary Snyder),* The Raven and the Totem *(foreword by Joseph Campbell) and* A Cycle of Myths. *In 1994, he edited the anthology* Durable Breath: Contemporary Native American Poetry. *His work has appeared in many periodicals, including* The Atlantic Monthly, *and in numerous anthologies. A federally-enrolled Native American, he served as the tribally appointed Executive Director of his tribe's Heritage and Cultural Foundation and edited and compiled* The Ahtna Noun Dictionary *(1998). His poetry collections include* Changing Seasons, *published in Australia;* Riversong *(foreword by Joseph Bruchac);* Songs from an Outcast *(selected, edited, introduced and nominated for the Pulitzer Prize by the late Denise Levertov); and* Without Reservation. *The late Allen Ginsberg named him as "one of the most brilliant younger poets in recent American literature."*

In the Shadows of Mountains*
Preface to the Ahtna poems

Far, far away from any place you have ever heard of is a tribe of American Indians who were so isolated, that they were the very last indigenous People discovered in North America. The first Western European did not even set foot on our land until 1885, only some twenty years after my late grandmother, Morrie Secondchief, was born. Even then, the first sustained contact was not until 1899, at the end of the Yukon-Alaska Gold Rush.

That tribe is the Ahtna (pronounced *ot-naw*) People of the Copper River of south-central Alaska. Our tribal name comes from the Indian name of the river – Ahtna Tuu.

My grandmother was the last of the full-bloods in my family tree. My father is half-blood. Of the 1,068 enrolled members in my tribe, only some 40-50 elders still speak our endangered language. I am the only person left who can read and write in it as well. The handful of poems here are among the few written in my language and then rendered into English. As far as I know, no one has ever re-translated my English versions into any other major language, though I would welcome such an attempt.

Our language, like our culture and mythology, is almost gone. As the youngest speaker of Ahtna (at 39), there is little doubt that I will one day be the last living speaker. It is a great burden to know such a thing. And though I have worked hard to create programs, school curricula and bilingual children's books, and even a dictionary, there is little or no interest among younger members to learn the language. While some parents teach their children the names of a few animals, how to count to ten, or the names of body parts, there is no sustained effort to educate people to maintain a truly living spoken language.

So, the poems here come from certainly one of the rarest languages on earth. There exist only two dozen or so such poems. They come to you not simply from the heart of a poet, but from the inseparable entanglement of a man's life with a place. They could not arise elsewhere or from any other condition. Native Americans are defined, in part, through their connection to the land. While many rural inhabitants or farmers enjoy a life-long, even a multigenerational familiarity with their region, it is not as intense and culturally-determined as the bond between an Indian and his traditional land. When I look out across the Copper River, see the eternally snow-covered mountains rising over 14,000 feet above the wide flood plain, I see not only trees, water and soil, but the spirits of my great-grandfather's ancestors roaming the sand and gravel banks along the silty river's edge.

John E Smelcer
(Ahtna Athabaskan, Tazlina Village)

* Especially written for *Modern Poetry in Translation*.

The Prophet

Can you understand my language?

Almost no one does.
Almost no one remembers.

I am sick and lonely
and weak from crying.

Uni'di C'ilaenen

Nekenaege' di'its'ak da?

K'aagu kenaege' kole.
K'aagu kenaege' niic kole.

Tiye 'est'aat'el sneyaa
el' stiye' kole tsagh.

My Conversation with a Fox

When the startled fox
stepped from its leafy forest

I knelt in raven-coloured light
bleating like a wounded hare

until he came
nervous and reluctant

to question my patient hand
open like a tundra rose.

Baptizing the Last Shaman

On the day the boy was born
in Batzulnetas

a priest arrived carrying
spring water in a
tea pot.

When he baptized him
the boy's nose began to bleed.

Happiness

Happiness for the robin
and for the wolf,
      is to exist.

For Indians,
it is to know existence
      and to marvel in it.

**Mourning Song
For The Last Indian**

When the Indian People are no more
trees will sing and weep
mountains will shake
wolves will howl
and lakes and rivers will go dry.

When Indian People are no more
a red moon will rise forever.

The Widow's Dance

In January, the month of riddles,
beneath a red aurora –
'the fire in the sky that burns the cold',
a husband danced on the ice
beside the burning wick of a stone oil lamp.

He danced the mourning dance
until the light of dawn arrived
and he cried himself to sleep.

Ahmad Shamlu
Iran

Translated and introducd by Gholam Reza Sami Gorgan Roodi

Gholam Reza Sami Gorgan Roodi *was born in Tehran in 1968. He has taught Comparative Literature at various universities and colleges in Tehran, and has published many articles and translations on modern Persian and English literature in Iranian literary journals. He is now a researcher at the School of English and American Studies at the University of Sussex, England and is currently working on the radical US writers of the 1930s.*

We must hide the light in the closet
Ahmad Shamlu (1925-2000)

Ahmad Shamlu, Iran's most celebrated, prolific and prominent twentieth-century poet, and a nominee for the Nobel Prize in Literature in 1984, received the Freedom of Expression Award from the New York-based Human Rights Watch in 1991. On 5 June 1999, Shamlu received the Stig Dagerman Award (Sweden's highest prize for writers who emphasise human rights and freedom of expression) from the Swedish Academy. Shamlu was born in December 1925 in Tehran and spent his childhood in the poverty-stricken southern Iranian province, Baluchestan, and then in the city of Mashad. The Baluchestan experience, the impoverished Baluchi children and the ghastly, dictatorial and bad-tempered teachers of the province, stayed with Shamlu throughout his life and shaped his poetry. Shamlu failed to finish high school and decided to go to Tehran to start a career in journalism, during which time the allied forces invaded Iran. The allies put him in prison in 1943 for his political activities. Years later, in 1954, after the the CIA-backed coup in August, 1953 and the overthrow of the democratically-elected Prime Minister, Dr Mohammad Mosadegh (head of the most popular government since the 1906 revolution), Shamlu was imprisoned again for being a member of Iran's communist party. Later on, when the party members fled Iran to save their own skin, Shamlu abandoned the communist party and wrote scathing attacks on the party that had once nurtured his desire for a socialist utopia.

Shamlu, who adopted the pseudonym 'Baamdaad' ('Morning') is, in the view of many Iranians, a symbol of secular nationalism. He was a rebel humanist and a revolutionary force in the intellectual movement opposed to the former Shah of Iran before the 1979 revolution. The Shah had exiled him in 1970. On his return home, however, he seemed totally disillusioned with politics. His hopes for equality and social justice were once again awakened in the wake of popular opposition to the Shah in the late 1970s, which made him join other Iranian intellectuals to lead a secular intellectual movement against the monarch's dictatorship. With the abolition of monarchy in the country, however, Shamlu's expectations and hopes for freedom were not fully realized. After the religious hard-liners' crackdown on secularist groups, he grew more outspoken about restrictions on individual freedom: 'They smell your mouth / lest you should have said: "I love you." / They smell your heart. / What a strange world, my dear!', reads one of his poems. Shamlu lived in isolation in a Tehran suburb prior to his death, but on several occasions he travelled to the West for medical treatment. Although slandered by hard-liners as a 'traitor' and a 'Westernised writer', he has recently been rehabilitated under Iran's reformist President, Mohammad Khatami. Much to the hard-liners' disappointment and annoyance, Khatami's Culture Minister, Ayatollah Mohajerani, openly expressed his grief over Shamlu's death.

On 26 July 2000 Anthony Appiah, Chair of the PEN Freedom-to-Write Committee, and Diana Ayton-Shenker, Director of the PEN Freedom-to-Write Program, released a letter expressing their condolences over the death of Ahmad Shamlu. In this letter they referred to 'Shamlu's unique poetry' that 'celebrated humanity, freedom and beauty, enchanting all who encountered his work.'

Shamlu developed a simple, free-verse poetic style, known in Iran as 'Sepid' poetry (literally meaning 'white'), departing from the tightly balanced rhymes of classical Persian poetry. He democratised the language of poetry by employing the style and vocabulary of the common people. Having been influenced by Nimaa Youshij (1879-1960), father of modern Iranian poetry, the Spanish poet, Federico Garcia Lorca (1898-1936), the black American poet, Langston Hughes (1902-1967), and the French thinker and writer, Louis Aragon (1897-1982), Shamlu wrote increasingly of love, sacrifice, betrayal, desire, pain, the beauty of nature and the agonizing fragility of life and human misery. He was a socialist and a humanist who wrote modernist *engagé* poems and also passionate love poems with political overtones. He was a 'committed' poet. To him poetry was 'the people's weapon' that 'touches the wounds of the old city' and tells of a better world to come. Shamlu's books were banned for a long time before and after the Iranian revolution. However, since the early 1990s his poems have appeared in many literary journals and have been translated into many languages. Here is my translation of a poem which recalls years of tyranny and hardship:

In This Dead-End[1]

They smell your mouth
lest you should have said: 'I love you.'
They smell your heart.
What a strange world, my dear!

And they whip love
near the lampposts.
We must hide love in the closet.

In this zig-zag dead-end of coldness
they keep the fire alive
with song and poetry.
Do not be afraid of thinking.
Whoever knocks at the door at night
has come to kill the light.
We must hide light in the closet.

Now the butchers are
on each cross-road
with a tree trunk and a bloody cleaver.
What a strange world, my dear!
And they operate to put a smile on our lips
and a song in our mouths.
We must hide our pleasures in the closet.

They barbecue canaries on fire
made of lilies and lilacs.
What a strange world, my dear!

It is the triumphant drunkard Devil
who is celebrating our sorrow.
We must hide God in the closet.

[1980]

Notes:

1   Persian title, 'Dar in bon bast', from Ahmad Shamlu, *Taraaneh-haaye Koochee Ghor-*
bat; Tehran: Zamaaneh Publishers, 1980.

Michael Bullock

Michael Bullock, who celebrated his 85th birthday on 19 April of this year, was born in London and went to Canada in 1969, retiring from the University of British Columbia Creative Writing Department in 1983. He lives in Vancouver where he continues to write his own poetry, to translate and to paint. He has devoted himself intensively to writing and visual art since his mid to late teens. In 1936 he visited the great Surrealist Exhibition at the National Gallery and has remained a committed Surrealist writer and artist ever since. This was followed by a prolonged visit to India, which also made a lasting impression on him that can be clearly seen in his work. He is the author of more than fifty works of poetry and fiction and two plays, many of which have been translated into various European and Oriental languages, notably German, as well as Punjabi and Bengali and especially Chinese, into which language most of his works have been translated in whole or in part. These translations have gained him international renown as a writer. His paintings are less widely known, since the international dissemination of works of art was less easy than it is today. Now, however, his visual art is quickly gaining recognition. A retrospective exhibition of his art and books has been running at Volume Gallery Book Art and Architecture Bookshop, London, in April and May, where his new collection of poems, *Colours*, was launched in both printed and audio form (*all enquiries to Miriam Cartwright: miriam.cartwright@axianet.com*).

Michael Bullock founded the West Coast Surrealist Group in Vancouver, later to be called the Melmoth Group, and now describes his art as Abstract Surrealism. In so far as much of his poetry and all his fiction is characterized by images drawn from the unconscious through the free flow of the imagination, the description is apt (he has been described as 'one of the most wildly imaginative minds ever to reach the printed page' – (Wendy Jeffries, *Hamilton Spectator*)). However, his work is entirely coherent and finely wrought – the product of literary craftsmanship as well as an unfettered and fertile imagination – unlike most of what passes for surrealist writing. It can rarely be considered 'automatic writing', though occasionally the author does employ this technique. As one critic puts it: 'Talent and labour have produced these polished gnostic visions' (John Reid, *Canadian Literature*).

A profile of Michael Bullock, one of the most prolific translators (especially from French, German and Italian) in our time, is to be found in *MPT* 3, Summer 1963, which also contains a review of Jack Stewart's *The Incandescent Word: The Poetic Vision of Michael Bullock* (Third Eye/ Ekstasis Editions, London, Canada, 1990). Bullock is Max Frisch's official translator and is a recipient of the Schlegel-Tieck German

Translation Prize (1966), as well as of the Canada Council French Translation Award (1979).

Below, by way of birthday greetings to Michael Bullock, we publish another of his translations (one was published in *MPT* 3) from Gustav Meyrink's *Dr Cinderella's plants & Other Stories*. This story puts one in mind of the bumblebee, whose flight, rather like that of the translator, apparently defies the laws of aerodynamics.

Gustav Meyrink was born in 1868 in Vienna, the illegitimate son of an actress and a government minister, and died in 1932 in Starnberg. He was a banker in Prague, before becoming a writer while in prison under a false accusation for embezzlement. He stands in the fantastic and grotesque tradition of ETA Hoffmann and was a close friend of Kafka. His best known work is probably the novel *Der Golem* (The Golem). There has been a revival of interest in his work after a long period of neglect.

The Toad's Curse – Toad's Curse

Largo, andante moderato e pesante
Die Meistersinger

On the road to the Blue Pagoda the Indian sun shines hotly down – Indian sun shines hotly down.

The people are singing in the temple and strewing white flowers before the Buddha, and the priests are solemnly praying: *Om mani padme hum, Om mani padme hum.*

The road is empty and abandoned: today is a holiday.

The long kusha grass had formed a lane in the meadows by the road to the Blue Pagoda – by the road to the Blue Pagoda. The flowers were all waiting for the millipede that lived over there in the bark of the venerable fig tree.

The fig tree was the most high-class residential area.

'I am the venerable one', it had said of itself, 'and bathing trunks can be made from my leaves – made from my leaves.'

But the big toad that always sat on the stone despised the fig tree, because it was rooted to the spot, and nor did she think anything of bathing trunks. – And she hated the millipede. She couldn't eat him because he was very hard and had a poisonous juice – poisonous juice.

Therefore the toad hated the millipede – hated the millipede.

The toad wanted to ruin the millipede and make him unhappy and she had been taking counsel with the spirits of dead toads all night long.

Since sunrise she had been sitting on the stone waiting, and from time to time her back legs trembled – back legs trembled.

Every now and then she spat on the kusha grass.

Everything was silent: blossoms, beetles, flowers and grass. – And the wide, wide sky. For it was a holiday.

Only the orange-speckled toads in the pond – the unholy ones – sang godless songs:

> 'I don't give a damn for the lotus blossom,
> I don't give a damn for my life,
> I don't give a damn for my life,
> I don't give a damn for my life!'

Then there was a glittering in the bark of the fig tree and something came rippling down like a string of black pears. Turned coquettishly and raised it heads and danced playfully in the radiant sun light.

The millipede – the millipede.

The fig tree clapped its leaves together ecstatically and the kusha grass rustled delightedly – rustled delightedly.

The millipede ran to the big stone. There lay his dancing-place, a bright patch of sand – bright patch of sand.

And scurried around in circles and figures of eight, so that all things were dazzled and closed their eyes – closed their eyes.

Then the toad gave a sign and her eldest son stepped out from behind the stone and with a deep bow handed the millipede a scroll written by his mother. The millipede took it with foot number 37 and asked the kusha grass whether the document bore all the correct rubber stamps.

'It is true that we are the oldest grass on earth, but we don't know that; the laws are different every year. That is known only to Indra – known only to Indra.'

Then the 'spectacle snake', the cobra, was fetched and read out the letter: 'To the Right Honourable Mr Millipede,

'I am only a wet, slimy creature, despised on earth, and my spawn is thought little of among the plants and animals. And I neither shine nor sparkle. I have only four legs – only four legs – and not a thousand like you – not a thousand like you. O venerable one! *Nemeskar* to you, *nemeskar* to you.'

'*Nemeskar* to him, *nemeskar* to him', chorused the wild roses from Shiraz, joining in the Persian greeting – in the Persian greeting.

'Yet wisdom dwells in my head and deep knowledge. I know the grasses, the many grasses, by name. I know the number of the stars in the night sky and the leaves of the fig tree – the one that is rooted to the spot. And my memory has not its equal among the toads of all India.

'And yet I can count things only when they stand still, not when they move – not when they move.

'So tell me, O venerable one, how is it possible that when you walk you always know which foot to start with, which is the second; and then the third; which comes fourth, then fifth, then sixth; when the tenth follows on the hundredth; what the second is doing meanwhile, and the seventh, whether it stands still or goes on; when you have reached the nine hundred and seventeenth, whether to raise the seven hundredth and put down the thirty-ninth, to bend the thousandth or stretch out the fourth – stretch out the fourth?

'Oh please tell me, poor wet, slimy creature that I am, with only four legs – with only four legs, and not a thousand like you – not a thousand like you, how you do it, O venerable one!

Your humble servant,

the Toad.'

'*Nemeskar*', whispered a small rose that had almost fallen asleep. And the kusha grass, the flowers, the beetles and the fig tree and the cobra looked expectantly at the millipede.

Even the orange-speckled toads fell silent – toads fell silent.

But the millipede remained fixed to the ground and from that moment on could not move a leg.

He had forgotten which leg to raise first, and the more he thought about it the less he could remember – less he could remember.

*

On the road to the Blue Pagoda the Indian sun shone hotly down – Indian sun shone hotly down.

James Kirkup

Daniel Weissbort *writes:* I have written a survey essay on James Kirkup as translator ('The Party of Humanity: On James Kirkup', *MPT* 11, Summer 1997), but should like to quote from David Burnett's introduction to *An Extended Breath: Collected Longer Poems and Sequences by James Kirkup* (1996):

> As Goethe remarked to Eckermann in 1827, national literature is at an end. The essence of modernity and of the human condition today is that we are no longer rooted within particular countries and cultures but are increasingly and necessarily inter-dependent and can and should be free of the whole world. Kirkup is above all a modern in what is fundamental, an openness to the entire world and its cultures, languages and pasts. Like Whitman, he, too, contains multitudes. The relative neglect and want of full recognition for his work spring in part from his sturdy independence as well as his residence in many countries abroad and the general (although unjustified) disparagement of translation but also and principally from an unwillingness to encompass his diversity: it is not the difficulty of his work that inhibits but its range [. . .]

Apart from wishing this were so, I shall refrain from commenting. But I am reminded of Ted Hughes's remarks, introducing the first Poetry International at the South Bank in 1967 (see TH tribute in the present issue for the full statement):

> However rootedly-national in detail it may be, poetry is less and less the prisoner of its own language. It is beginning to represent as an ambassador, something far greater than itself. Or perhaps it is only now being heard for what, among other things, it is – a Universal language of understanding, coherent behind the many languages in which we can all hope to meet.

Mr Kirkup has supported *MPT* for many years and has regularly sent us translations, many of which are brilliant examples of the art. He has translated very widely from French, Italian, Catalan, German and Japanese, and many others. We include some of his work below.

As is well known, Kirkup is one of the very few Western poets who can be called a master of the Haiku form. I cannot resist printing again (from *MPT* 9 [1971] and *MPT* 11, New Series) the following haiku-like piece, translated from the Japanese of Takagi Kyozo. The title is 'Peasant':

I blew from my snitch
snot green as rice-pests

William Cliff
Belgium / French language

William Cliff *was born in 1940 in Belgium. He studied philosophy and
literature at the University of Louvain, where he graduated with a thesis on the
Catalan poet Gabriel Ferrater. Cliff began teaching, but gradually gave it up to
devote himself to writing and world travel. His first Gallimard collection,*
Homo Sum *(1973) at once established his sexual orientation and his poetic
reputation.* Conrad Detrez *(Gallimard) consists of a long sequence of 10-line
verses dedicated to the memory of his friend the novelist Conrad Detrez, who
died of Aids. Cliff has also published a volume of poems translated from the
Yugoslav poet Brane Mozetic:* Obsedenost (Obsession, Paris, 1999). *His
latest publication, from which the poems below are taken, is* L'État belge,
*(2000). A Belgian documentary about Cliff (1997) has been made by Geerard
Prestow (from James Kirkup's Introduction).*

*Other translations by James Kirkup of poems by William Cliff were
published in* MPT *18.*

Leningrad

near the exit to the metro what can it be this crowd
of youths not knowing where to go just staying put there
in a big bunch watching each other and smoking to
calm their nerves? there they stay not knowing where to go
but preferring to stay here rather than all alone at home

the cops from time to time walk slowly through the crowd
casting glances here and there but the youths don't give a damn
they disperse a little then form their groups again
looking at each other as if they'd nothing better to do
than take great gulps of smoke to calm their nerves

not knowing where to go they stay there and they linger
so as to feel a little more together they can feel a something
that hovers among them with the smoke that drifts away
out of their gullets but what? but what? they do not know what
it is and stay there in a big bunch near the exit to the metro

Mister President

do you know that in Lima on the outskirts there exist
innumerable rabbit hutches made of rotten planks
in which are crowded people who have nothing left to eat?
Mister Vargas Llosa wanted to take them all in hand
to be their president seemed to him a title
that should flatter them and allow this grinning
buffoon to parade his vanity all round
suddenly these poor wretches saw pop up from a hole
a certain Fujimori whose eyelids like their own
were dragged up at the corners by centuries of wrong

on seeing him appear they could not believe that he
could be any better at extricating them
from the foul pit that would receive their miserable lives
his powerful choppers no less guilty
of idiot self-satisfaction and they knew
they'd still have to perish in that wretched poverty
whatever president they elected so they felt
they might as well choose a yellow one rather than
the Spanish pedant who there and then went home to his rich ghetto
where at once he started partying again

did you know that in Lima they sell rice only
by the cupful? that henceforth they have to queue
in order to beg a bowl of charitable soup?
(there's no longer any water or any electricity)
and that people are very happy when because of his good looks
their child can prostitute himself to bring them food?

Saint-Hippolyte-du-Fort

clear away those tables set the tables out
pass the broom over the floor go and fetch
the wine laid away in the cellar be up
in the morning early to get these jobs done
go to bed late at night and sleep your fill
never knowing what it's like living somewhere else

cast a glance up there to see that traveller
spying on you from his window and never
be anything but you yourself without hope of a rebirth

in the skin of one looking down from his window
who watches you working and knows nothing about you
cast a glance up at him go and fetch the glasses

place them on the tables for the dinner
then you'll wash them in dirty water then
dry them on a dirty dishtowel then
go and set them on the tables for the supper
when two or three stonybroke diners will come and eat
and drink a quarter flask of the cheap stuff and go

and if a lodger turns a bit funny and
tries to make advances to you then
you pretend you don't know what he wants
you go and get the broom and set to work again
on what you always have to do and clear
the tables set them out again and get them cleared away

Larzac

Larzac you have given me air to drink
the air of your wilderness your fruit to eat
the black of brambles I've crouched beneath
your dolmens and embraced their stones
and their long existence and when lost
in your measureless wastes I asked
a farmer who on his bit of field
was burning piles of straw asked him the way
with his big finger loaded with earth he
pointed me to the path to take his face
filled with the drunken air of the plateau shone
in the light his long blond hair punished
his features ravined by the sun
(when I set off again I turned
to look at him he was back at work again
in the hollow heart of that vast landscape)

Millau down below afforded me
food and drink but oh! nothing
nothing to breathe for the air you get down there
is not the same as your desert's Larzac

Oscar Lubicz-Milosz
French language

James Kirkup writes: **Lubic-Milosz** *(1877-1939) was a distant relative of the great modern Polish poet Czeslaw Milosz, though he used to refer to him as 'my nephew'. He was born in Byelorussia in a region that had once been part of the Grand Duchy of Lithuania. Educated in France, Lubicz-Milosz held several diplomatic posts and wrote poetry and plays in French. At the age of eighteen, he had met Oscar Wilde at the celebrated American bar 'Kalissaya' in Paris. He also became acquainted with Jean Moréas and many other literary and artistic figures, including Raymond Duncan and Nathalie Barney, to whom he dedicated a suite of six poems,* Adramandoni, *in 1918, published by Menalkas (Raymond) Duncan. His play* Miguel Mañara *had its first, clandestine reading, in Polish translation, by a young actor, Karol Wojtyla, who was to become Pope John Paul II.*

Lubicz-Milosz was multilingual, and was fluent in English, German, Russian, Polish, Italian, Spanish and French. His 'nephew' Czeslaw Milosz, knew him well, and visited him at the end of his life in his retreat at Fontainebleau. An account of this meeting, and of his frequent contacts with Lubicz-Milosz, can be found in the La Nuit *(Gallimard), a well-selected anthology of his poetic works.*

All the Dead are Drunk

All the dead are drunk on dirty old water
In the strange cemetery of Lofoten.
The clock of the thaw tick-tocks far away
In the hearts of the poor coffins of Lofoten.

And thanks to the holes dug by a black springtime
The ravens are fat with cold human flesh;
And thanks to the snell wind with the voice of a child
Slumber is sweet for the dead of Lofoten.

I shall probably never behold
Either the seas or the tombs of Lofoten,
And yet as if deep within I feel love
For that remote speck of earth and all its pain.

You missing ones, you suicides, you far-flung ones
In the foreign cemetery of Lofoten – the name
Sounds gentle and curiously soft to my ears –
Tell me true: are you all sleeping, all sleeping?

– There are more entertaining things you could tell me
As I sip this good claret from my silver cup –
Stories more charming, less crackpot than this;
So give over, and spare me the dead of Lofoten.

It's cosy here. In the hearth softly lingers
The voice of the most melancholy of months.
– Ah! the dead, and the dead of Lofoten –
The dead, the dead are really less dead than I . . .

Lu Wen Ming
Chinese (XVII Century)

In the Ancient Manner

The moon falls in muddy water,
But remains pure.

By the twisting path, a lonely pine
Keeps growing straight.

He who is superior meets with setbacks
But his heart remains steady.

Friedrich Hölderlin

Germany

Translated by Michael Hamburger

Friedrich Hölderlin *(1770-1843) studied theology (with Hegel and Schelling) but worked mainly as a private tutor rather than becoming a minister. He worked in Switzerland and Bordeaux, returning home in 1802 both mentally and physically ill. From 1806 until his death he suffered from schizophrenia. Hölderlin's word-for-word versions of Sophocles and Pindar are among the most radical examples of translation in his own time and well beyond.*

    Michael Hamburger *has translated nearly all of Hölderlin's mature poetical works into English – the new Anvil edition will appear sixty years after the first selection of 1943 – and his translation must be regarded as one of the most important and influential poetry achievements of our time. As Hamburger himself states, he has moved 'towards a kind of translation that is neither free imitation nor strict metaphrase . . . but something in between . . . I do not appropriate my text to the extent of transposing it into my own idiom, my own favourite verse forms and my own favourite imagery, but treat it as a phenomenon different in kind from anything I could ever produce.' His versions of Hölderlin's poetry find an equivalent in English for the author's own radical strangeness and rigorous adherence to Greek metrics and idea content (see* The Oxford Guide to Literature in English Translation, *edited by Peter France, 2000, pp. 301-311). Michael Hamburger was born in Berlin in 1924 and came to Britain in 1933. He has been an adviser to* MPT *for many years and his translations have frequently appeared in its pages. His most recent collection of poems is* From a Diary of Non-Events *(Anvil, 2002). Anvil Press has published Hamburger's* Collected Poems, 1941-1994, *as well as many of his translations of German poets, including* Hölderlin: Poems and Fragments. *The translation published below of 'Die Nymphe' ('The Nymph') is from the revised edition of the latter, to be published shortly by Anvil.*

Michael Hamburger writes on 'The Nymph': This is DE Sattler's reconstruction and conflation of the three drafts previously known as 'Mnemosyne', published in his edition with a title also considered by Hölderlin for a poem of which there is no final, definitive version. I have taken the text from DE Sattler: *Hesperische Gesänge* (Neue Bremer Presse, Bremen, 2001), and it is published here with his permission. Sattler believes that all the poems previously known as 'hymns' – and the fragments of these published by Hölderlin before he became Scardanelli – were intended to constitute a single twelve-part work which he calls 'hesperian cantos' or 'canticles'.

    My Hölderlin translations, done over a period of fifty years, could not be based on Sattler's reading of the manuscripts or his construction of what might or might not have become the definitive texts. Not only did Hölderlin leave no fair copies of most of the poems and fragments in question, but there was virtually no end to his reworking even of poems that were finished once, but superseded, if only for him, by new insights, experiences and visions. I have made an exception of 'Die Nymphe' because Sattler's conflation has made a coherent poem of what were fragmentary drafts in Beissner's Stuttgart edition, on which most of my texts were based.

What has become clear from DE Sattler's admirable and devoted work on manuscripts not so much as legible to him when he began the work, is that there never will be one authentic and definitive text of poems not finalized by the poet – unless lost manuscripts reappear, as the fair copy of 'Friedensfeier' did in London as late as 1954. This is the justification for Sattler's conflation of the successive drafts of the poem formerly known as 'Mnemosyne' – and mine for adding it here, with thanks to him.

The Nymph

Ripe are, dipped in fire, cooked
The fruit and tried on the earth
And a law that all goes in
Like serpents is
Prophetic, dreaming on
The mounds of Heaven. And much as on the shoulders a
Load of logs is
To be retained. But evil are
The paths. For crookedly
Like horses, wrongly go the imprisoned
Elements and ancient
Laws of the earth. And always into
The unbound a yearning goes.
But much must
Be retained. And loyalty
Is needed. Forward, however, and back
We will not look. Abandon ourselves to be rocked as
In a swaying skiff, on the sea.

But not all too timid, rather be
Unseemly and, with the Erinnyes, rush off,
My life. For all things a demigod
Or a human being must grasp, in the way affliction,
By hearing, alone, or by being

Transformed in person, foreknowing from afar the horses of
The Lord, and
The watchman's bugle by day
And gives away the most loved,
To the fruitless,
For never from now on
The sacred is good for use.
A cipher we are, no key decodes it,
Painless we are and almost
Have lost our speech in the alien lands.
For when there is a dispute about mortals
Up in Heaven, and planets move
With mighty strides, then loyalty goes blind. But One
Is beyond doubt. He
Daily can change it. Hardly he needs
Laws, that is, how
With mortals it is to remain; and the writ resounds and
The leaf resounds. Many men wish
To be there in the true cause.
Then oaks flutter beside
The pear-trees. For the heavenly
Cannot achieve all things. For mortals too
Attain the abyss.
So then it turns,
The echo,
With these. Beautiful is
The wedding day, but we are anxious
On the score of honour. Terribly it goes,
Misshapenly, when One has been
Taken from us too greedily. Long is
Time, but the true thing
Occurs.

Always, dear one, the earth
Moves and the sky holds. Sunshine
We see on the ground and dry dust
And the woods deep with shade and on roofs
There blossoms smoke, by the ancient tops
Of towers peaceable, and lost
In the air skylarks trill and under day
Well led on the sheep of heaven crop.
And snow, like lilies of the valley marking
The noble-minded, where
It is, glistens with

The green meadow
Of the alps there,
Speaking of the cross that once was set
On his way, for those who died,
On the steep path walks
A travelling man, angry with
The other, but what is this?
Beside the fig-tree
My Achilles died and is lost to me,
And Ajax lies
Beside the grottoes of the sea,
Beside brooks that neighbour Skamandros.
In the blast of winds, according
To his native Salamis's constant
Custom, in foreign parts
Great Ajax died,
Not so Patroclos dead in the King's own armour, and
Many others also died. By their own hands
Many sad ones, their courage driven wild, but divinely
Compelled, in the end, but the others
Standing fast in fate, on the field. For the heavenly
Are angry when someone, not sparing
His soul, has failed to collect
Himself, but he must, nonetheless; like him
Here mourning is at fault.

National Academy for Gifted and Talented Youth

Translation Day

Introduction by David Hart

In 2002 the University of Warwick was host to the pilot summer school of the Government-sponsored National Academy for Gifted and Talented Youth. Being given responsibility for the writing course, I knew it should be three weeks of practical writing, that guest writers and their books would be vital to it, and that the course should include translation.

For a day to bring these three aims together, I invited Daniel Weissbort and we had a fascinating time learning from his life and writing experience, and having a go at making versions of poems. The eighteen 14-16 year olds, and the three of us staff, entered into quite new insights about poetry, and experienced something of what can come through to us from the variety of traditions and languages we have been fortunate to inherit.

And of course once we embarked on opening up the possibilities, we discovered several other fluent languages amongst the students, whether inherited or through education, so that the voices we were hearing amongst us were richer.

The notion that all poetry is a form of translation has seemed true to me in much of my own writing. The title poem of my first book of poems was 'Setting the poem to words', as if in some sense the poem pre-exists and our job is to find it. So one might think that in translating poems by poets writing in other languages, the task is many-layered, not simply working from the surface words but recreating as empathetically as possible that poet's initial discovery, and behind that again the culture – or shifting cultures – that gave rise to it.

The National Academy's aim is to give encouragement and practical support, engagement and stimulus to those school students who feel variously undernourished, impatient, locked inside themselves (and so on). Perhaps very many children-pupils-students feel these things, at all levels of paper achievement, and in advance of the summer school I had some political doubts. I can only say that faced with this particular group, with these particular individuals, I did get to understand some of their unfulfilled desires and needs: 'I've never had this kind of conversation before', 'I get bullied because I want to write well', 'I get pats on the back but am not helped to move on'.

The pilot summer school welcomed 100 students across five subject areas. In 2003 it is 900 at this and other locations, rising to 3,000 next year. We were the first year selecting from top grades, and I'd like to see the local encouragement-to-apply and the selection process opening up to students with a special gift but who may not be showing it in academic results. The mystery (and graft) of poetry – and a flair for the heard language, and for making connections across languages – may lurk in other than A grades.

The A-grade students in 2002 were a delight and worked hard. I wish all the students' versions of poems could be included here, but Daniel has had to make a selection from those that were handed in. We had no gradings of work, we were a peer group from beginning to end, so the poems here represent just some of what was equally achieved.

David Hart has worked as a university chaplain, a theatre critic and an arts administrator. He now works as a poet and among his part-time connections is an Honorary Teaching Fellowship at Warwick. His books of poems include *Setting the poem to words* and *Crag Inspector*, the latter a poem of Bardsey Island.

Daniel Weissbort *writes:*

I was advised that it would be most productive to come equipped with a number of hands-on exercises. Accordingly I brought along a few translation 'kits' (transliterations, literal and literate translations, plus some notes) and invited the students to have a go.

I had prefaced this by attempting to give students some sense of the variety of approaches to translation, showing them, for instance, different versions of Homer (*Odyssey*) and of Genesis (the Babel story). I went on to emphasize that in this workshop there were no set rules, but that participants should try to be aware of what they were doing, i.e. that they should also give some thought as to why they were approaching the translation in a particular way. I encouraged them to be as free as they liked. They might feel inclined to follow closely the literal text supplied in the handout, or they might wish to divert from it radically, even to the extent of producing parodies. They should be prepared to share their thoughts with the rest of us. The students responded enthusiastically, and made off with the 'kits', reappearing after half an hour or so with their own versions. Some, whose mother tongue was not English, produced versions in their first language, rather than in English. They paid a price for this 'privilege' in that I then asked them to give the rest of us some sense of the problems encountered in working between *English* and another language, bearing in mind that the English they had worked from itself had its source in another language. I believe we all enjoyed this vertiginous trip among languages.

To motivate the students even more – although, as it turned out, this was hardly necessary – I told them that I would try to publish some of the results in *MPT*, having talked a bit about the journal, of which the *Mother Tongues* issue (*MPT* 17) was available to them, by courtesy of the

Academy. Below are a few of the versions produced in the workshop, together with the 'kits' on which they were based.

A few words of explanation. The first exercise concerned a vividly propagandistic poem by the Russian Vladimir Mayakovsky (1893-1930), 'Our March'. I chose this because of the importance in it of onomatopoeia, generally believed to be untranslatable. In other words, though a readily comprehensible poem, here was one which seemed to defy translation. I suggested, though, that it is as true to say that nothing is untranslatable as it is to say that nothing is translatable. I felt that this poem, whatever one's politics, might appeal to youthful translators; furthermore, its obvious dependence on sound made it quite imperative that the translator do *something*. I mentioned the extreme experiments of the Zukofskys in their translation of Catullus, what the late André Lefevere called 'phonemic translation', trying to reproduce the sound of the Latin, while at the same time making some kind of sense in English. The value of this exercise is to oblige the 'translator' to listen very, very hard. Interestingly, perhaps, none of the participants in this workshop chose this extreme option, although many did opt for rhyme.

Anyway, here are some results. First, a literal, word-for-word version of the first two stanzas, without the alternative words that I offered as well:

Beat in the square the tramp of revolt!
Row of proud heads, higher!
With the surging waters of the second flood we
shall wash the cities of the world.

The bull of days is skewbald.
Slow is the bullock cart of the years.
Our god is speed.
The heart is our drum etc.

The poem continues as follows:

Is there a god more celestial than ours? / Will the wasp of bullet sting us? / Our songs are our weapons. / Resounding voices are our gold. / / Meadows, be covered with grass, / spread out a ground for the days. / Rainbow, harness / the fast-flying horses of the years. / / See the starry heaven is bored! / We weave our songs without it. / / Hey, Great Bear, demand / that they take us up to heaven alive! / / Drink joys! Sing! / Spring flows in our veins. / Beat to battle, heart! Our breast is the copper of a kettledrum.

And here is a transliteration of the second stanza ('The bull of days is skewbald' being line 1) giving some idea of what the translator is up against sound-wise: series of emphatic monosyllables; driving, three-stress lines:

Dnei byk pyeg.
Myedlenna lyet arba.
Nash bog byeg.
Svertsye nash baraban.

Now, a few versions, some showing a distinct reluctance to follow Mayakovsky along the path of revolution! I have included some of the comments acccompanying these versions. The present selection, I should add, is arbitrary. A few participants gave their age, others didn't.

Anna Bodicoat

After rebellion the sound of dying,
deafening wails flood the street.
Mothers, fathers, children crying
scrounging around for scraps to eat.

The hunger and pain that follows the fighting
defeats ideas of a better world.
Rebels that were, now conforming
forgetting all thoughts of flag unfurled.

[*Written after looking at 'Our March' by Vladimir Mayakovsky.*]

Kate Shipton

Revolution
Beneath my feet reverbs the sound of revolt.
Russia trembles with the sound of the drum.
Where our defences? The army? Okhrana?
Come preach for your emperor. O free churchmen come.

The aristocracy fails, our blood falls to dust,
where the command to call peasants to work?
The colours of mutiny raised from the towers,
to inflame the high heavens: those stars shadowed in murk.

The tramp of those feet and the cool of the air,
hold tight to your children in the crisp, broken dawn.
The moon is still large in this early fast moment,
and the march of the workers on the palace's lawn.

[Translation and interpretation of 'Our March' by Vladimir Mayakovsky.]

Caleb Klaces
(aged 18, volunteer assistant in the course)

Our march
Come out with pots and pans banging
to be noisy, up and at it.
bang loud enough to shake the sky
to crack and wash us into the new days.

Come with horses,
with wit and a fiery tongue,
the gods of doing
and our big heart a music box and thunder.

Paint over in gold emulsion
the old road signs,
smother with blue and purple songs
the pop and wasp of gun,

lie on the grass;
get the fields to lie down.
Roll back the sun roof of the stars and
bark at the heavens nakedly.

Dandelion come and bathe with me,
we will watch the horses.

[My Our March *began as an attempt at a faithful, direct translation of the original poem, but ended up as something that, although I think similar in some respects, could only very loosely be called a* translation. *I picked out what seemed like interesting and important words from the literal translation of each line and worked around them, used them as grounding points. And what could be called the* literary *version was a rough guide to how the poem could look, and work as a whole. I tried to keep to the basic form of the original, that seemed important even in a wandering springboard sort of translation, and something of its forcefulness, while perhaps leading into something very different. I wanted some sort of parallel poem, a poem that leads the reader in the same direction as Mayakovsky's but with different signs, and with my voice.]*

Issy McCann
(aged 15)

Our March

Parade the sound of revolt through the city.
The arrogant, wealthy and proud must fall.
Our second flood will sweep without pity –
we'll free the world of slavery and thrall.

> Days are long.
> Years are slow.
> God is speed –
> our heart's glow.

No gold is more holy than ours.
    No bullet leaves us cold.
Our weapons are our joyful songs.
    Our voices are our gold.

> Green grass grow!
> Days go by!
> Each year's horse,
> harnessed, should fly.

The sky is bored with our stars.
    Our lives are but her mirth.
    So without celestial help
we'll make our heaven on earth.

> Wine of joy.
> Hearts that sing.
> Breasts of steel.
> Blood of Spring.

[In this translation or version I have tried to retain the sound *of Mayakovsky's original, because I felt that it was the alternately staccato and drum-like rhythm which made it so stirring.]*

Sophie Taylor-Gooby

Run, break free!
Wash over the world with your frenzied hate.
Beat it into the earth
with your proud bayonet.

Write ballads for your bullets.
Deny death.
You are united, invincible.

You need no heaven,
no stars,
and love will cause strife,
the glorious revolution,
will feed you all your life.

[This is a re-translation of the Vladimir Mayakovsky poem. I was interested by the idea of taking a poem and translating it into a poem with a different slant on the same subject. A retrospective view on the Russian revolution is bound to show a different opinion to the contemporary one. I used some of the original imagery but this is predominantly a response rather than a translation.]

Božo Lugonja

Rebel against what is wrong
fight for the good in every man
do not let your eyes be fooled
the liquid will spur us on

blood will flow
lives will go
but our cause shall live on

contradict our views
when we fail
the leader we hate
we hail

And here is a version of the same poem by a graduate student with a taste for parody, in an Iowa of two decades ago:

John Rogers

Our Country
(A drinking song dedicated to the Philadelphia Police)

Beat the heads in the square!
Scram revolting scum!
there's commies everywhere!
the keg is our drum.

Biff, bam boom!
the paddy-wagon's slow.
Zim, zam, zoom!
A whack an in ya go!

God bless the dollar!
God bless all we get.
Go ahead and holler!
We'll just kick the shit.

Out of youse! Splitski! Vamoose!
Dis is no joke.
The Red Peril's loose.
How you like a poke

In the eye, chump?
Hey you, Great Bear,
Butkis, lend a lump
Outta charity!

Chug it!
Down the hatch!
Fuck the faggots!
Get some snatch!

Count your blessings!
Count 'em twice!
Count the money!
Throw the dice!

Among one or two other similarly 'challenging' items, for a change, I handed out a haiku (i.e. 17-syllable poem, arranged in a 5-7-5 pattern, classically containing a 'kigo', or word that expresses a season) by Basho, which I had stolen from another workshop. Here is the 'kit':

The Original Japanese, transcribed:

> fu ru I ke yha
> ka wa zu to bi ko mku
> mi zu no o to

literal version:

> the old pond
> a frog jumped into
> sound of water

literate version:

> Breaking the silence
> of an ancient pond,
> a frog jumped into water
> —
> a deep resonance.

interpretation of the original:

> a frog jumped into an old pond at Basho's hermitage. Even the slight sound of the water could be heard, so quiet was it there.

Two problems:

1. frog (in Japan the frog was a 'kigo' of spring, i.e. it was associated with spring. In English it isn't!
2. the 5-7-5 form may present problems.

There followed a biographical note on Basho (1644-94) and a brief technical one on the haiku.

Issy McCann

A Basho Haiku
ancient silent pond
a green frog jumps into it
sudden shocking splash.

Seasons (*inspired by Basho*)
when you live your life in a reclusive Hermitage
days
weeks
months slip away

But you notice instead

winter: draughts creep under your door

Life in the city moves in seasons too.

Chloe Stopa-Hunt

Haiku
stillness, silent water
frog leaping loud in wetness
soft sound, deep sound

wake water echoes
ancient pool song, frog leaping
and long sound, distant

Božo Lugonja

skin of water cracked

               green of animal leaps down

   silent thought echoes

Original Translations

On Arthur Jacobs
by Daniel Weissbort

A belated comment on AC Jacobs's *Collected Poems & Selected Translations*, edited by John Rety and Anthony Rudolf, foreword by John Silkin; Menard Press/Hearing Eye (in association with the European Jewish Publication Society), 1996, £13.99.

Each time I saw John Rety of Hearing Eye, and long after he had given up mentioning Arthur Jacobs's *Collected Poems & Selected Translations*, which Hearing Eye co-published with Tony Rudolf's Menard Press, I experienced a twinge of Jewish guilt. I had promised to write a piece on this book and to try to get it published somewhere, failing which I would publish it myself in *MPT*. So, seven years have elapsed since this remarkable collection of poems and translations appeared, and this may be my last chance . . .

I begin to look for an angle, one that might justify the delay. There are no angles . . .

Arthur was a quiet man and his poetry is firmly quiet as well. So quiet that it seems to have escaped the notice of all but those who were tuned to him in the first place, like Tony Rudolf, the late Jon Silkin, John Rety, and, well, myself, and a number of others of course, who accidentally, as it were, became aware of Arthur's writing. In a letter published in the Menard catalogue, Ted Hughes wrote: 'Tony Rudolf sent me the volume two days ago and I've been reading this. Amazing what we can be wholly unaware of, in the writing of one's contemporaries. We cover our ears from the din, perhaps, and miss crucial signals. Certainly I'd missed Jacobs whom now I'm getting to know with great pleasure.'

Generationally, Arthur Jacobs and I are related. Our life paths even crossed or almost crossed. For instance, he shared the top floor of 10 Compayne Gardens with Jon Silkin at the time when the West Hampstead house was owned by Bernice Rubens and Rudi Nassauer, from whom I bought it.

And then there is the book by Arthur that Tony Rudolf published at Menard, *A Proper Blessing*. It is among the half-dozen or so Menard titles – along with, for instance, Primo Levi's poems – that indelibly marked my literary sensibility, if that's not putting it too grandiosely.

But I suppose it was Arthur's involvement in translation that connected us, to the extent that we were connected. *Modern Poetry in Translation* 22 (First Series, Autumn 1974) was devoted to Israeli poets and was guest-edited by the late Robert Friend, another Menard author I would not be without. The issue kicked off with translations by Arthur of all eleven poems published by Avraham Ben-Yitzhak during his life. This was followed by a few poems, again translated by Arthur, of another founding father of modern Hebrew poetry, David Vogel. Ben-Yitzhak was born in Galicia in 1883, Vogel in Podolia, Russia, in 1891. The translations, as English poems, struck me at the time as utterly convincing, lucid, precise, though the 'subject' matter was sometimes quite oblique, mysterious even. I was proud to be able to publish Ben-Yitzhak's *collected* works, although these were not actually all the poems he had written. When I told Tony Rudolf that I was finally writing something about Arthur Jacobs and was, of course, alluding to Ben-Yitzhak, he drew my attention to a note in the *Collected Poems and Translations*, quoting Leah Goldberg (another notable Menard author): 'He (Ben-Yitzhak) was the first Hebrew poet whose watch displayed not merely the specific Jewish time, but rather the time kept by world literature at the same hour.'

Both the Ben-Yitzhak and the David Vogel translations are reprinted in the collection under review, including, among others, Bialik, Amichai, Ravikovitch (all Menard authors), Zach, Carmi. The editors talk of the difficulty sometimes of determining whether they were dealing with a translation or an original poem by Jacobs (some '*sounded* like translations'). Robert Friend wrote: '. . . It is hard to believe that his translations of David Vogel are translations . . . He has made Vogel's tone, the delicate nuances, his very own.' It seems to me that the boundary between Jacobs's own poems and his translations is indeed quite indeterminate. Perhaps the same could be said of other poet-translators of this calibre, insofar as a poet will translate, if at all, those poets with whom some empathy is felt or whose work in some way complements – one might almost say completes – their own work.

The Menard / Hearing Eye book, bringing together both original work and *original translation*, to coin a phrase, is particularly interesting in this regard. I was struck by the similarity between Jacobs's Jacobs and Jacobs's Vogel or Ben-Yitzhak. The translations read altogether like original texts, which is not quite the same as saying that 'they do not read like translations'. Is this simply to do with the affinity Jacobs felt for these poets? A problem may seem to pose itself that has exercised contemporary translators and translation theorists, i.e. the contrast or opposition between domesticating and foreignizing translations. I doubt whether Arthur Jacobs was much concerned with such questions. To my mind, his essential humility and the fact that he was well employed doing what he was doing surely render all such discussion irrelevant.

And yet I continue to be bothered! If what I have hinted at above makes any sense, then clearly Jacobs domesticates. The translations and his own poems are, in a general sense, indistinguishable. And we are told that translations now, if they are to avoid the stigma of having, as it were, tamed (domesticated) the foreign beast, should not shrink from sounding foreign. As suggested above, injunctions or instructions drawing their inspiration from this version of political correctness sound problematical if not simply dogmatic when one is dealing with a devoted writer like Arthur Jacobs.

I think it is Arthur's oddness or uniqueness, noted by Tony Rudolf in his AC Jacobs obituary (*The Independent*, 1 April, 1994), when he quotes Forster on Cavafy, 'at a slight angle to the universe', that guarantees the authenticity of his translations as well. Which, alas, is to say that there may be another obstacle in the way of a more general appreciation of this poet's work. His circumstances, as a Jew and a Scotsman, are perhaps not so unusual but they are unusual enough. He is twice marginalized, and what is more each marginalization, as it were, cancels the other out. So it comes about that he or his reputation does not benefit from the light being shed on the borderlands of our literature, 'a bit east of the Gorbals / in around the heart', as Tony Rudolf, quoting the poet himself, concludes his piece for *The Independent* (the paper cut it). Nevertheless, Arthur continued to send in (or out?) reports from this so remote and yet so close region. It was natural for him to translate from the ancestral tongue and I am convinced that this helped him to further refine his mother but not ancestral language, English. I should like to have quoted lines from many of his poems, but instead I urge readers to buy the book.* Arthur Jacobs's contribution to English literature may not be immediately assimilated, but I share the conviction of his intrepid publishers that it will find its niche.

---

* To order it by post, send your name address and postcode, including payment, £13.99, to: Hearing Eye, Box 1, 99 Torriano Avenue, London, NW5 2RY, or to: The Menard Press, 8 The Oaks, Woodside Avenue, London N12 8AR; Tel: 020 8446 5571.

Some Books Received, with some comments

by Daniel Weissbort

Arc Publications

www.arcpublications.co.uk, Parallel-text translation series 'Visible Poets'. General editor: Jean Boase-Beier.

From The General Editor's statement: 'There is a prevailing view of translated poetry, especially in England, which maintains that it should read as though it had originally been written in English. The books in the Visible Poets series aims to challenge that view . . .' In order to 'render visible the translator's task, each volume in the series is published as a parallel text, with the original language and its English translation on facing pages. Each volume also contains a Preface by the translator(s) and an Introduction by a well-known writer associated with the author or with the language of the original text, both of which serve to illuminate further the strange, the unusual, the new, the foreign.'

As a rule, publishers resist translations which draw attention to and take pride in their status as translations rather than masquerade – this, of course, is putting it negatively – as source texts. Of course, translations that tend towards foreignization, so called, ask more than usual of the reader, who is invited also to consider the impact that one language makes on another. Poetry puts pressure on the language in which it is written; this series aims to transmit some of that pressure, rather than reduce or disguise it. The reader, no longer the more or less passive recipient of a (dubious?) gift, will be enriched by contact with 'the strange, the unusual, the new, the foreign'.

Three titles are published yearly. In 2001, the volumes were: *Recycling* by **Tadeusz Rózewicz**, translated from the Polish by Tony Howard and Barbara Plebanek, introduced by Adam Czerniawski; *Words Have Frozen Over* by **Claude de Burine**, translated from the French by Martin Sorrell, introduced by Susan Wicks; and *Where Are You Susie Petschek?* by **Cevat Capan**, translated from the Turkish by Michael Hulse and the author, introduced by AS Byatt.

I was particularly pleased to see a new collection of Rózewicz in English, especially in a bi-lingual edition, handsomely produced and modestly priced (£8.95). Rózewicz is for me the archetypal poet of post-war Eastern Europe, even among poets of the calibre of his compatriots Zbigniew Herbert and the Nobel laureate Wislawa Szymborska, of Janos Pilinszky, Miroslav Holub, Vasko Popa and others. The cover shows the elderly poet raising the lid of an overflowing dustbin and peering in. One is reminded of his famous remark, in an interview with Adam Czerniawski in 1976: 'I tend to find any old newspaper more absorbing than the finest edition of poems: that a dog is run over or a house got burnt down.' In 1990, alluding to Czeslaw Milosz's acute characterization of Rózewicz as 'a poet of chaos with a nostalgia for order', I complained somewhat presumptuously that 'maybe 'nostalgia' is too dismissive a term to use of a writer who had the courage, hard for us now fully to grasp, to take the first steps in a post-apocalyptical world'. Rózewicz's perhaps most celebrated poem, 'The Survivor', is a depiction, in the starkest terms, of one who has somehow outlived the violence and horrors of the latter part of the first half of the twentieth century. Rózewicz himself has survived war, totalitarian pressures, and – should one add? – post-Communism. He has also survived translation.

As his latest translators tell us: 'In his seventies Tadeusz Rózewicz entered a new period of intense creativity.'

The following short poem about short poems shows him as nimble as ever:

My short poem / sometimes elongates / drags / slips from my grip / / so I trim it / usually at the bottom / rarely the top / because the top is all light / sky / clouds / / they're problems ending / a poem doesn't want / to end / it keeps going / / bores stalls / multiplies words / puts the end off / / what can one do with the end / / drown it in darkness / like Celan / or tie it up in a bow / pretty as a butterfly / / or bring it to a point / and leave it / as bait

In 2000, the three 'Visible Poets' volumes were remarkably grim-voiced: *Anthracite* by **Bartolo Cattafi**, translated from the Italian by Brian Cole, introduced by Peter Dale; *Camp Notebook* by **Miklós Radnóti**, translated from the Hungarian by Francis Jones, introduced by George Szirtes; and *A Virgin From A Chilly Decade* by **Michael Struge**, translated from the Danish by Bente Elsworth, introduced by John Fletcher.

Radnóti was murdered by the Nazis in 1944, his body being exhumed from a ditch after the war and the notebook with poems found in his pocket. *Camp Notebook* reproduces this holy text of twentieth-century poetry in facsimile, together with transliteration of the Hungarian and, of course, the English translation. The versatile translator Francis Jones, whose translations from Dutch and from Serbo-Croatian are well known, has produced formally mimetic versions which yet manage to convey the immediacy of these short poems with, one feels, few semantic compromises. Here is one of them, 'Postcard':

Booming from Bulgaria, wild shell-fire rolls, / beats against the
ridge, hesitates, then falls. / Thronging people jostle with cart
and beast and thought, / the road whinnies and shies, a mare-
tailed sky takes flight. / You are the constant within me amidst
this churning mess, / you shine on deep in my mind, forever
motionless / like the angel in silent wonder at the catastrophe, /
or a beetle burrowed away in the heart of a rotten tree.

Bartolo Cattafi (1922-1979) (*Anthracite* was a Poetry Book Society
Recommended Translation) was born and died in Sicily. He was a
prisoner of war in the Shetlands, lived many years in Milan and travelled
widely in Europe and Africa. Peter Dale draws attention to 'what might
be called the mystery of the ordinary' in Cattafi's poetry. Cattafi is
comparatively unknown outside Italy though he appears, translated by
Rina Ferrarelli, in *MPT* 15 (*Contemporary Italian Poets*). In its concreteness,
its reserve, his work should appeal to English tastes, at least to the
English tastes of my generation. It is not obviously uplifting, but the
focus is intense. Here is an example (admittedly with a somewhat
uncharacteristically dramatic ending), 'One 30th August':

It was immediately clear that things were getting better: / no
macroscopic events, / the sun one step away from September /
gave the first rations / to the islands in front, / the sea sent out
flashes of coolness, / the heat only three hours away, / an
immensity of blue, another day / for the grapes and the other
fruits of the season, / among the quiet sounds of the countryside /
the hissing oxygen said / no more could be done with her heart. /
Early in the morning the death of my mother.

Michael Struge was a Danish writer who published his first collection
in 1978, at the age of twenty. A new collection appeared almost every
year until his death by suicide, at the age of twenty-seven, in 1986. But
before his death he had already stopped writing. In a helpful introduction,
John Fletcher quotes Strunge's farewell to poetry: 'I no longer experience
the tension which I had while writing my early books; the collection [his
last] is different because it is self-critical and has a more positive attitude
to the world I live in.' But he did not long survive the end of his creative
life. This impressive collection of desperate verse, luminously translated
by Bente Elsworth, is not for those seeking consolation. Strunge's voice
is one of absolute authority and with paradoxical exultancy reaches out
to us from the bleakness of existence. One can only marvel at the courage
of a poem like 'Armed with Wings':

I brood in darkness –
hatch myself out
and spread my lashes, fly on visions
into my next life.

I urge readers to subscribe to this very fine Arc series, at a time when few
publishers will even consider translated poetry.

Ars-interpres

http://ars-interpres.narod.ru/contact.html; address, 2080 Wallace Ave.
apt 522, Bronx, NY 100462, USA.

Ars-interpres is a new publishing house with a programme of
translating English-language poets into Russian, published bi-lingually.
The series is recommended in particular to Russianists interested in the
art of translation, or in extending their knowledge of contemporary
English-language poetry. Each collection in the series comprises, of
course, a distinct reading of the source text. It is hoped that the series will
help to stimulate intertraffic between English and Russian at a time
when Russian programmes in universities are struggling for survival.
The rigours of translating from Russian into English are well known to
the present writer, and he looks forward also to perusing the observations
of Russian poets, translating contemporary English-language poetry
into Russian, particularly since the same publishers will also be producing
an annual journal, *Ars-interpres, an International Annual Journal of Poetry
and Translation*. Issued simultaneously in New York, Stockholm and
Moscow, the journal is edited by Vladimir Gandelsman and Grigory
Starikovsky. It will publish primarily English-Russian and Russian-
English translations of modern poetry, as well as articles on poetic
translation and other related matters. It will also include reviews,
review-essays, interviews, photographs and art. *Ars-interpres* can be
ordered by e-mail: ars-interpres@narod.ru

It bodes well for the project that the founder and director is the poet
Vladimir Gandelsman (*see present issue of* MPT *for some poems by him*).
Also on the board of editors, among others, are Billy Collins (the current
US Poet Laureate) and the distinguished senior poet Anthony Hecht.
Three collections have appeared so far: Frederick Smock, translated by
Regina Derieva (see *MPT* 20, *Contemporary Russian Women Poets*, for
translations of Regina Derieva's own poetry into English); Pulitzer Prize
winner Louise Glück, translated by various hands; and Eamon Grennan,
also translated by various hands. The series will include collections by
Billy Collins, Robert Hass, Jorie Graham, Anthony Hecht, Paul Muldoon,
Charles Simic, Mark Strand and many others. The translators include a

number of distinguished Russian poets, both from Russia itself and from the Russian diaspora.

While, on the face of it, this may seem a rather specialised enterprise, I believe it to be potentially of wider appeal, especially if the publishers are able to expand their programme, including in the series English translations of contemporary Russian poetry. It has been a longstanding hope of mine to be instrumental in bringing about a conference, under the title of 'To See Ourselves As Others See Us', that will gather Russian translators of English and English translators of Russian. *Ars-interpres* may more permanently embody such an encounter.

Boris Slutsky

While on the subject of translation from Russian, I would like to draw attention to a landmark volume, published in 1998, which seems to have received little attention in this country, perhaps because it was deemed to be of interest only to Russian specialists, perhaps because it was published by a specialist publisher. This is *Boris Slutsky: Things That Happened*, edited and translated with an introduction and commentaries by GS Smith (Professor of Russian at Oxford University), published by Glas Publishers (Glas, UK, Dept of Russian, the University of Birmingham, B15 2TT. web-site: www.russianwriting.com). The book, however, is best ordered from the following website, which is based in Illinois: www.russianpress.com/glas.

The volume is of interest primarily, of course, because Slutsky (1919-1986) is a major poet, perhaps *the* pre-eminent poet of the Soviet period of Russian literature. As such his creative life is inextricably bound up with the tragic events of that period. He was admired by a host of writers, including the late Joseph Brodsky. Slutsky, however, like Akhmatova before him, remained in Russia (Brodsky, of course, had no choice but to leave). Disillusioned, he continued to write. Since the history of Soviet Russia is inevitably inscribed in his poetry, it is perhaps hard to get the measure of it without to some extent taking into account historical events that should be part of our general consciousness.

While, in this brief notice, I cannot discuss Slutsky's place among the giants of twentieth-century Russian literature, I am convinced that Gerry Smith's volume is a landmark in the presentation of poetry in translation. Besides offering an informed selection in close translations that flout Soviet or Russian conventions, since they do not attempt to mimic the form, Professor Smith embeds these finely precise renderings in a historical and biographical narrative. The book, therefore, in addition to providing readers with a representative selection of Slutsky's poetry, also contextualizes it. We read about and vicariously experience, as it were, the history of the epoch through which Slutsky lived, in which he gloried, and of which he also despaired.

Brodsky insisted that a poet's biography is his or her poetry. This volume goes beyond this. I have not seen it done before and perhaps it would not always be appropriate. But at a time when easy conclusions are frequently jumped to and when so many unhesitatingly claim the high moral ground, here is a book to be pondered.

Pushkin

Still on the Russian theme, it is a pleasure to record one's debt to Antony Wood (Angel Books, 3 Kelross Road, London N5 2QS) whose translations of Alexander Pushkin's verse narratives, his 'Little Tragedies', have been appearing over the last few years. The latest offering is Pushkin's *The Bridegroom*, which contains also the publisher-translator's versions of 'Count Nulin' and 'The Tale of the Golden Cockerel'.

(See MPT *15, Autumn 1999, for an essay by Antony Wood on the translatability of Pushkin and for additional Pushkin translations by Wood; also 'Russia' in* MPT *11 as well as the 'Pushkin Portfolio' for Stanley Mitchell's translation of* Eugene Onegin, *Ch. I and the beginning of Ch. II; and the present issue of* MPT *for Robert Chandler's translation of Pushkin's 'Egyptian Nights'.)*

Where so many English translations of *Eugene Onegin*, for instance, have transformed the eponymous hero into a kind of all-English gent, Antony Wood somehow – without 'foreignizing' – manages to retain the non-Englishness, so to speak, of Onegin, a quality that we may read as quite distant from gentility, though of course Pushkin was an aristocrat, immersed in aristocratic society. His poetry, as Antony Wood points out in a helpful Afterword, 'makes poetry of plain spoken language'; at the same time Pushkin writes lightly. The literary critic Andrei Sinyavsky points out that 'before Pushkin there was almost no light verse . . . and suddenly, out of the blue, there appeared curtsies and turns comparable to nothing and no one, speed, onslaught, bounciness, the ability to prance, to gallop, to take hurdles, to do splits . . .' And Pushkin also writes personally: 'His lyric poems constitute a kind of emotional diary throughout his life . . . ' Any reader of Pushkin soon appreciates the Russian contention that he is 'our everything'.

I am reminded of Ted Hughes's remark in a review of *The Letters of Alexander Pushkin* (*Listener*, 1 October, 1964; see Hughes's *Winter Pollen*, 1994), comparing Pushkin with Byron and Leopardi: 'When these two expose their sufferings, something slightly theatrical struts out. But Pushkin's plight is hopeless, right to the bottom, and his despair radiates more powerfully from these self-concealing letters than from anything in his works.' What strikes me, though, is the extent to which Wood has captured the sense of oppression, menace, in short the horror of Pushkin's predicament, everywhere present in his apparently urbane lines.

Marin Sorescu

Marin Sorescu, *Censored Poems*, translated by John Hartley Williams and Hilde Ottschofski, Bloodaxe, £9.95.

Marin Sorescu's buoyant presence at international festivals and his readings in many country have been much missed, since his uncharacteristic demise in 1996. It was the sometimes hilarious, sometimes absurd comedy in his work – quintessentially Romanian, one was told – that seemed to distinguish him among his fellow poets of the Eastern Bloc, although of course Romania, like Yugoslavia, was always a little to the side of that bloc anyway. There is perhaps a danger now of a brilliant poet like Sorescu being somewhat marginalized, since he arrives on the scene slightly later than the 'great generation' of Herbert, Rózewicz, Popa, Holub and just before the poets of post-Communism. But Sorescu's balancing act, his independence at a time when allegiance of one sort or another was demanded, has more than a little to teach those among us who still believe they know what the future holds.

East and South-East and a Scandinavian

Anthology of Macedonian PEN Poets, edited by Zoran Ančevski. Zoran Ančevski, the Macedonian translator of Ted Hughes, has finely judged this collection of poems by contemporary poets of the Republic of Macedonia.

Liliana Ursu, *Angel Riding a Beast*, translated from the Romanian by the author and Bruce Weigl, Northwestern University Press, $13.95. A volume in the fine 'Writings from an Unbound Europe' series, which Northwestern, alas, has discontinued.

Yannis Ritsos, *Exile and Return*, translated by Edmund Keeley, Anvil Press, £5.95. A substantial and authoritative selection from the work of this major Greek poet.

Yehuda Halevi, *Poems from the Diwan*, translated from the Hebrew by Gabriel Levin, Anvil Press, £9.95. In a review which I wrote for *The Jewish Chronicle* (August 9, 2002) of Yehuda Halevi (c. 1075-1141), the last great poet of the Golden Age of Andalusian Hebrew poetry, I pointed out that

Halevi, 'famous though he be for his *Songs for Zion*, is one of the last flowers of a rich Arabic-Judeo literary culture. Like other devotional poets before him, he combines the secular and religious, the sacred and profane, linking Hebrew and Arabic poetic practice.' Here is a radiant book, the publication of which at this time is particularly apposite.

Oktay Rifat, *Voices of Memory, Selected Poems*, translated by Ruth Christie and Richard McKane, with an introduction by Talat Halman, Rockingham Press, £5.95. This excellent collection was published almost a decade ago, and most recently the same team of translators, Richard McKane and Ruth Christie, with the distinguished Turkish scholar and poet Talat Halman (who also introduces the Rifat volume) has published *Beyond the Walls: Selected Poems of Nazim Hikmet* (Anvil Press), which deservedly attracted a good deal of attention. As far as I can recall, the Rifat volume was virtually ignored. Professor Halman's Introduction offers several approaches, ways of understanding the dynamics of Rifat's poetry. Even so, straightforward though the latter may appear to be, perseverance is called for. What do I mean?

After a while, the apparent ordinariness dissolves and the structure or inner meaning becomes apparent, as in the case of Sufi poetry or of wise sayings. Disparities in literary-historical evolution may lead one to dismiss translated verse that seems to replicate developments we believe to have already been assimilated. But these disparities, it seems to me, are incidental and it behoves us to read *through* them to what attaches itself to a truth or vision, authentic, new, in short unfamiliar.

More or less randomly selected here is a poem, 'Brother', translated by Ruth Christie:

> He enters by door and window together. / He brings me gifts. /
> He's both at the head and the foot of my bed, / and under my bed
> and in it. / / Who is he? Whom does he ask for? / What news does
> he want to give? / How will he tell his trouble? / Where are his
> lips? Where are his hands? / / He sits in every armchair at once,
> / aimless he wanders. / He thinks my room is his. / He drinks my
> water and reads my books. / / But in my dreams, he shows me
> curious pictures from afar, / trees, mountains, houses, more /
> and oh – much more!

6 Vietnamese Poets, edited by Nguyen Ba Chung and Kevin Bowen, translated by various hands, Curbstone Press, www.curbstone.org. This impressive collection provides 'more than just a view of the Vietnamese-American war seen from the inside', but also 'a slice, albeit a living slice, of Vietnam's culture and history enduring one of the most horrific and longest wars of the twentieth century.' Alexander Taylor's

Curbstone Press has persisted, over a long period, in offering us politically radical individual collections and substantial anthologies of work from the less advantaged corners of the suffering world.

Henrik Nordbrandt, *My Life, My Dream*, translated from Danish by Robin Fulton, Daedalus, Poetry Europe Series No. 13, £6.95. Where would we be without the enterprise of publishers like Daedalus Press (24 The Heath, Cypress Downs, Dublin, Ireland)! The Daedalus Press Poetry Europe series has published work from Swedish, German, French, Italian, Finnish, Danish (Inge Christensen, as well as Henrik Nordbrandt), Flemish, Spanish, Norwegian. As one sees, the Nordic countries are unusually well represented. Nordbrandt (b. 1945) is generally regarded as the leading contemporary Danish poet. However, he has spent most of his life abroad. The Scottish poet Robin Fulton has lived in Norway for many years and is our leading translator from the Nordic languages, having translated the work of the major Swedish poet Tomas Transtrømer, among many others.

Foreignized?

Antonia Pozzi, *Breath, Poems and Letters*, edited and translated by Lawrence Venuti, Wesleyan University Press (www.wesleyan.edu/wespress), $16.95. The translator here is, of course, the celebrated translation theorist and historian, author of perhaps the most influential translation theory book of the last two decades: *The Translator's Invisibility* (Routledge), where he makes the case for foreignization as a more appropriate approach than domestication in a post-colonial context. This handsomely produced bilingual edition gives readers a chance to gauge the extent to which Venuti is guided by his own principles.

Vital Process

Exchanging Lives, Poems and Translations, **Susan Bassnett** and **Alejandra Pizarnik**, Peepal Tree Press (17 King's Avenue, Leeds LS6 1QS), 2002, £7.95). This highly innovative book comprises prefatorial matter by Susan Bassnett (Professor of Comparative Literary Studies at the University of Warwick and our leading writer on literary translation, as well as a poet and translator in her own right); translations by her ('Poems from *Tree of Diana*') from the Spanish of the short-lived (1936-1972) Argentinian poet Alejandra Pizarnik, bilingually presented (not en face but with the Spanish text above the English, possible because of the brevity of these poems); and finally poems by the translator, bearing indubitable traces of the encounter with Pizarnik's work.

I quote from Susan Bassnett's brief introduction to her own poems: 'I started to translate her work because it was a way of getting closer to her, of finding out more about her. Then, I came to see that the act of translating was changing my own writing. I became braver, I tried new forms, experimented with different voices. We were and are, utterly different as writers and as women. She succumbed to the lures of silence, I go on killing wolves and making wolf-skin coats for my increasing family. Maybe, if we had met face to face we would have had nothing in common with one another. But I feel a great sense of closeness to her. I know her. She knows me. We have shared something. Through translation.' Here is a remarkably frank exposition of the relationship between two writers and two languages, implicit in any true act of translation. This little collection – along with the very different one, briefly reviewed above (Boris Slutsky) – constitutes something of a landmark in the history of verse translation. And I have not even begun to talk about what is its raison d'être, the poetry of Pizarnik herself!

He dado el salto de mí al alba.
He dejado mi cuerpo junto a la luz
y he cantado la tristeza de lo que nace.

I gave the surge of myself to the dawn.
I left my body joined with the light
while I sang out the sadness of being born.

We receive more books than we can adequately review. The alphabetical list below mentions some publications that we think will be of interest to our readers.

Paul Celan, *Selected Poems and Prose*. Tr. John Felstiner. Norton, 2001. (Bilingual) 0-393-04999-X [*Almost entirely poetry.*]

H M Enzensberger, *Lighter than Air*. Tr. David Constantine. Bloodaxe, 2002. 1-85224-580-8

Horace, *The Odes: New Translations by Contemporary Poets*.
Ed. JD McClatchy. Princeton, 2002. (Bilingual) 0-691-04919-X
[*All 103 odes, with translations commissioned from leading American, English and Irish poets.*]

Philippe Jaccottet, *Landscapes with Absent Figures*. Tr. Mark Traherne. Pref. by Michael Hamburger. Delos/Menard, 1997. 1-874320-20-9 (Menard).
[Readers who admired Jaccottet's poems in Ruth Sharman's versions (MPT 8) may like to experience his prose poétique *in this volume, which has been belatedly drawn to our attention.]*

Max Jacob, *The Dice Cup*. Trs. Christopher Pilling and David Kennedy. (The Printed Head, Vol. IV, no 6.) Atlas Press, 2000. 1-900565-01-3
[Some of these versions of Jacob's profound and pre-Dadaist prose poems appeared in MPT 8.]

Fumiko Miura, *Pages from the Seasons: Selected Tanka*. Tr. with Introduction by James Kirkup. Asahi-Shuppan-sha, Tokyo, 2002. 4-255-00145-6 C0082

Jean-Charles Vegliante, *Will There be Promises/Les Oubliés*. Trs. Peter Broome and Jacqueline Kiang. Pref. by Michael Bishop. Edwin Mellen, 2000. (Bilingual) 0-7734-7595-8
[Interesting afterword by the poet reflects on his response to the translations, which confront him with 'what I didn't think I'd written' and especially 'all that I recognize as mine without ever having written it . . .']

20th-Century French Poems. Ed. Stephen Romer. Faber, 2002. 0-571-19683-7
[54 poets, 200 poems, various translators; Romer's Preface examines the development of French poetry in the 20th century.]

Found in Translation: a Hundred Years of Modern Hebrew Poetry. Tr. Robert Friend. Ed. and introduced by Gabriel Levin. Menard Press, 1999. 1-874320-23-3
[Robert Friend was the Featured Translator in MPT 4.]

Frontier Taiwan: An Anthology of Modern Chinese Poetry. Eds. M Yeh and NGD Malmqvist. Columbia University Press, 2001. 0-231-11847 (paperback ed.) *[Historical introduction; 50 poets; bibliography.]*

Raw Amber: An Anthology of Contemporary Lithuanian Poetry. Eds. Wolfgang Görtschacher and Laima Sruoginis. Tr. Laima Sruoginis. Poetry Salzburg, 2002. 3-901993-12-6
[Lithuania's Official Publication for the Frankfurt Book Fair, 2002. 14 poets.]

Review

Selected Poems
by Adam Czerniawski
Translations and introduction by Iain Higgins.
Harwood Academic Publishers, 2000.
Bilingual and with a CD attached inside the back cover.
Cloth only (approx. £38.00), pp 221.

Adam Czerniawski stands at a distance from, or more likely a tangent to, a lot of recent English poetry and this distance and angularity clearly give his poetry intensities of depth and perception. Czerniawski himself grew up in Poland, born there in December 1934, and his childhood – as is attested by both the title and content of his memoir *A Disturbed Childhood* – was disrupted across its surface, and also at deeper levels, by Nazism and Communism and the ogres of those years. From 1939 he was moving back and forth across Poland with his mother and elder sister, until his father managed to arrange their evacuation via Vienna and Sofia, first to Istanbul and then to Tel Aviv, Jerusalem and finally London. He has made England, and mostly the southern half of England (though he now lives in the Welsh borderlands), his home for many of the years since then, with increasingly frequent visits to Poland from the 1980s on. This childhood opened him to a range of languages, Polish obviously as the lifelong one, but some Arabic and some Hebrew during his early years, and finally a secure and indeed deep foundation in English. *A Disturbed Childhood*, his memoir of his early years, has recently been re-issued in a second, slightly revised edition and it gives not only an immediate insight into the poet's childhood but also a sharp sense of the turmoil, chaos, terror and desperation in Poland at the outbreak of the 1939 war, and a sense of the life and cultures of Polish exile. In an interview he says, 'at a terrible price I have had the chance to see the world', referring specifically to the years and terrors of Stalin and Hitler, and he typically ends two poems 'We happen to live in difficult times' ('Gaunilo's Island') and ' . . . in obsessive memory / to find peace in annihilated childhood' ('Provocation').

In England he took degrees in English literature and in philosophy and spent a number of years lecturing in philosophy. He brings in this manner to his poetry a structured depth of understanding of English traditions and a philosophical grounding. Both are relatively rare among contemporary English poets and it is Czerniawski's philosophical perception of the world and of recent human histories that most noticeably gives to his poetry its unique weight. However, while he is characteristically aware of both political and moral complexity and of the power of irony and disgust, his poetry remains personal, of a deeply worked personal morality, and so also does his language. Iain Higgins, in his perceptive translator's introduction to the *Selected Poems* points us on the one hand to Krzysztof Karasek's comment that 'Adam Czerniawski is one of the most self-conscious lyricists in contemporary Polish poetry' and on the other to Bogdan Czaykowski's suggestion that this is a poetry 'characterised by a deliberate polyphonic dissonance that constantly threatens to dissolve the very principle that holds the artistic composition together'. Holding together lyrical density and philosophical acuity is one of Czerniawski's major achievements; his poetry is at times hearteningly complex; but it can also have an almost nostalgic lyrical simplicity.

The leavening of the political by the personal in his poetry perhaps makes of it a bridge between the moralistic works of the great poets of post-war Poland and the younger generations emerging out of and after the breakdown of Communism in that country. We can go to Wittgenstein's lemma that ethics and aesthetics are one and find in that a concise reflection of Czerniawski's poetic concerns (though he nowhere refers to Wittgenstein that I know of). Perhaps it makes better sense to fasten onto the presence of certain words in the language of his poetry: the regular occurrence, for instance, of the words 'swiat' ('world') and 'gwiazd' ('star') in this *Selected Poems*. Undoubtedly the subject of his poetry, as Krzysztof Karasek has commented, is culture in the widest senses of the word and in the wider senses of the world. Czerniawski is at the same time a very Polish, a very European (he might also want to add 'Western') and yet also a very unascribed poet. Perhaps it is this that has made his work difficult to take into English culture, but it is there with many strengths and much value, if there is in us the generosity so to take it.

Coming to live in England in 1947 when he was twelve, his formative interests in poetry clearly include English, Irish and American examples. And at the point of becoming a poet he chose to write not in English, but in Polish, and he has adhered to that choice throughout his life. This has had various consequences and he himself contrasts, in an interview in the journal *Metre*, the choices and experiences of Michael Hamburger, George Szirtes and Michael Hofman in their decisions to use English at comparable junctures in their lives. Taking the Polish line in an English context brought him early into contact with the Kontynenty group of Polish language poets based in London through the 1950s, and this undoubtedly had important effects on his writing, just as his work influenced the development of Kontynenty during the same period. The history of this group of Polish poets in London and their importance (and uniqueness), particularly in the 1950s and 1960s, has yet to be written in English. Czerniawski is one of the few people who could do this justice and maybe a sympathetic listener should interview him on this subject. Issues of language and politics and indeed the whole raison d'être of writing poetry are implicit in this history. Indeed the whole history and presence of non-English language poetry in England is rich and politically complex and linguistically varied: Czerniawski is clearly a major figure in this history, if he or we choose to see his work in these terms, and his *Selected Poems* allows him to be seen both as a Polish and as an English poet.

Czerniawski's first book in Polish was published in 1956, when he was twenty-one and the first poem in his *Selected Poems* is dated 1953. It is a strong lament for his cousin Jacek S who died in the Warsaw Uprising in 1944 (aged 16 and having falsified his age so as to take part in the Resistance). This poem sets out many of Czerniawski's themes and strategies from the beginning, and indicates just how consistent and honest the language of his poetry is. Lament (though the word nowhere appears in the poem or its title), paradox and dissonance within polyphony and an open and often broken lyric form, concern with and pride in (and of course at times despair of) Polish culture, indeed in culture as such, are constant throughout his poetry. Perhaps his work is best characterised as essentially European and best identified as Polish within a European philosophical tradition, and yet it is also very English in his presence. The language in his *Selected Poems* moves through apparent simplicity and metaphor – 'The world began like this: I opened/my eyes in the morning/.../... I close/my eyes; this is how a cracked skull/sketches the ruin of a conjured world' ('World') or 'and when only its skeleton remains/the white negative of a symmetrical pine/the words will endure forever illegible' ('Fish') both from 1966 and the sequence 'Pentagram' – to a philosophical maturity, already evident early on, that melts lament, concern and desperation with sanguine irony. These qualities show throughout his poetry: 'This is now a late world, a twilight world,/I was born into it and belong there' ('At the End of the Twentieth Century') or a recent lament 'They emerge from hell/ she behind him/unseeing/.../They descend into hell/he behind her/ unseeing' ('Love IV', 1996). A closer analysis of the language of his poetry would show in detail his ability to work lyric in with harsh realities and philosophical lucidity.

Among Polish poets Czerniawski greatly admires and has also been influenced by Tadeusz Różewicz: they are close friends and as Czerniawski aptly says in an interview in the journal *Metre**: 'Some of my poems have that kind of austerity and simplicity which might be attributed to my close reading of Różewicz – and perhaps no reading is closer than that which is demanded of a translator of poetry.' Probably also there is something of Leopold Staff (his late post-war poetry) and

Leon Stroinski, a young partisan and poet who also died in the Warsaw Uprising, both of whom Czerniawski has translated. But surely the strongest influences, even including Różewicz, come from Cyprian Norwid, through his radically complex and uncompromising language, and the late Renaissance poet Jan Kochanowski. Norwid is pivotal to a number of developments in modern Polish poetry and its poetics in general, and Czerniawski, as translator, poet and critic, has been deeply concerned with his work since his early years. With Kochanowski we come back to the nature of lament, the *Treny* of 1583 – surely one of the great threnodies on the sadness of death in all European poetry – where he writes not only and strongly about the death of his daughter Orszula ("a delightful, radiant, extraordinary child", not yet three when she died) but also about a sense of Polishness and how to define and live with this. Czerniawski has translated the *Treny*: the most recent edition was published by Legenda (Oxford) in 2001, where he adheres in his English title to the Polish word. What is clear, both from the translations and Czerniawski's note and introduction, is the central importance of Kochanowski to his translator's own work. Throughout his *Selected Poems* the poet is intimately concerned both with senses of Polish culture (his own and others) and the effects of twentieth-century history on this culture. After four centuries of neglect in English the *Treny* have been published in four different translations over the past seven years. The other editions push the title into English as 'lament' or a variant thereon: Czerniawski leaves it as it is. A comparison of these four translations would be interesting – they include one by Stanisław Barańczak and Seamus Heaney – and Czerniawski's are clearly worth going to both for the quality of the translation and their exact and considered editorial setting.

While Polish sources and influences are immensely important for Czerniawski and give form and particular colour to some of the warmth that undoubtedly exists in his work, his reputation as a translator (and particularly of Różewicz, whom he has regularly published in book length translation since 1968, the second of these being in the popular Penguin Modern European Poets series and thus having a considerable effect on a number of now major contemporary British poets) has undoubtedly diverted our sense of his own poetry in Britain. This is both a paradox and a pity: we are only now (and even this depends on a good distribution of the present, rather expensive book) reading poems that he wrote at various times over the past fifty or so years. Looking at the language that he was using (in England, but in Polish) in the mid-1950s it is clear that poetry in England (in English) could have made use of his moral and aesthetic sense, the natural inclusion of paradox and dissonance at the time. Reading some phrases now (in English) I have a clear sense of his saying things in advance of younger, English poets who are now thought highly of. There is a paradox here, probably typical of English culture of the past fifty years: while Czerniawski's translations of Różewicz (certainly a great poet and at an angle to the Stalinist regime he had to live under) were, quite rightly, taken much note of, the possibility that a Polish poet, living in the south of England over most of the same time span, could have himself been pulled earlier into the English language, for the sake of what he himself had to say and to give to English poetry, has rarely been adequately negotiated. His own sense of Englishness is both simple and paradoxical: and it might be interestingly suggested that he has the closest affinities, among British poets, with a number of poets from the north of Ireland.

This book was the first of a projected series from Harwood in a bilingual format, 'Poet's Voices', with attached CD. The second of this very promising series, whose general editor was Spike Hawkins, is **Árni Ibsen**'s Icelandic selection *A Different Silence,* with translations by the poet and Pétur Knútsson. Sadly the series went no further, the publisher succumbing to commercial trauma, and the poetry being dispensed with in the process. The two published volumes can still be found, with difficulty, and the series, ranging from a completed anthology of contemporary Slovenian poets to the work of twenty or so individual poets from many languages has, very sadly, had to be abandoned, unless another publisher might take it up.

Other titles referred to:

Treny : The Laments of Jan Kochanowski, tr. Adam Czerniawski , Legenda (Oxford), 2001; Adam Czerniawski, *Scenes From A Disturbed Childhood*, A & K Publishers (UK), 2002; *Metre 12**, 'Reports From Central Europe' eds. Justin Quinn & David Wheatley, Autumn 2002 issue (Dublin); Árni Ibsen, *A Different Silence: Selected Poems,* tr. the poet & Pétur Knútsson, Harwood Academic Publishers (Reading, Amsterdam etc.), 2000.

Stephen Watts

---

* This issue of the journal *Metre*, includes in addition to the interview with Czerniawski and an essay by him on Cyprian Norwid, half a dozen translations from Ivan Blatny and Zbynek Hejda's important essay on him, plus essays on Attila József and Gyorgy Petri and other translations and overviews *inter alia* in a long 'Reports From Central Europe' section. Blatny was a Czech poet who lived in increasing obscurity in the south of England from 1947 until his death in 1991. Once again recognised as a major modern poet in his mother tongue, his late work (written in hospitals and nursing homes) intersperses Czech with English words, phrases and lines – not as translation or explanation but as natural shifts of register that reflect the logic of his life – in poems that are exemplary and sobering, comic and tragic. Czerniawski's poetry does not go to these logical extremes of language, but deals with similar issues in parallel, lyrico-philosophical ways. *MPT* 17 included some texts and translations of Blatny's work.

The Corneliu M Popescu Prize for European Poetry Translation

After a gap of six years the Poetry Society is delighted to be relaunching the European Poetry Translation Prize with a new sponsor and a new title.

The **Corneliu M Popescu Prize for European Poetry Translation** is sponsored by the Ratiu Family Charitable Foundation. The prize is open to collections of poetry published between March 2001 and March 2003, which feature poetry translated from a European language into English. The judges for this year are Alan Brownjohn and Fleur Adcock.

Back in 1982 Alan Brownjohn received a letter and a collection of beautifully translated poems by the Romanian poet Mihai Eminescu. The poems had been translated by a 19-year-old translator, Corneliu Popescu, who very sadly had died in the 1977 earthquake in Romania, the worst European earthquake in history. Popescu's father wanted to commemorate his son's achievement with some kind of publication or award.

Now 22 years later the Poetry Society acknowledges this prodigiously talented young man and indeed translators all over Europe with the Corneliu M Popescu Prize for European Poetry Translation. As Alan Brownjohn goes on to explain:

> The translation of poetry is important but sorely neglected by most publishers. There is no shortage of excellent translators. There is simply a lack of will among all except the most courageous of publishers, often, if not always, the smaller presses. This prize, first awarded twenty years ago to commemorate a young Romanian master translator, is intended to encourage translation, translators and all publishers who recognise the value of the art.

For further information
contact **Lisa Roberts**
tel 020 7420 9895
email marketing@poetrysociety.org.uk

From Russian with Love

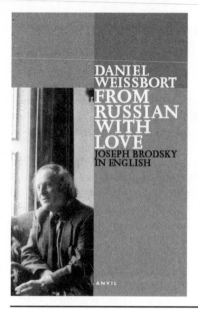

FOR MANY years Daniel Weissbort knew and worked as translator with the late Russian poet, Joseph Brodsky. In addition to being a fascinating biographical – and autobiographical – study, his account of their relations and his detailed discussions of the problems of translating Brodsky's poems make a telling contribution to translation studies, and a deeply considered essay on the nature of language itself.

£12.95   0 85646 342 6

Daniel Weissbort on two major poets: Brodsky in prose and Hughes in verse

FROM ANVIL PRESS POETRY

Letters to Ted

THIS UNIQUE collection of poems commemorates and celebrates the long friendship, both literary and personal, between the author and his fellow Cambridge student of the 1950s, Ted Hughes. Swift-moving, by turns contemplative and dramatic in their narration, the spare, poignant poems conjure up incidents and memories over forty years and create a moving portrait of a great poet.

£8.95   0 85646 341 8